21st Century Jocks

21st Century Jocks

Sporting Men and Contemporary Heterosexuality

Eric Anderson
University of Winchester, UK

First published 2014
Published in paperback 2015 by
PALGRAVE MACMILLAN

Hardback ISBN 978–1–137–37963–4 (2014)
Paperback ISBN 978–1–137–55066–8 (2015)

Palgrave Macmillan in the UK is an imprint of Macmillan Publishers Limited, registered in England, company number 785998, of Houndmills, Basingstoke, Hampshire RG21 6XS.

Palgrave Macmillan in the US is a division of St Martin's Press LLC, 175 Fifth Avenue, New York, NY 10010.

Palgrave Macmillan is the global academic imprint of the above companies and has companies and representatives throughout the world.

Palgrave® and Macmillan® are registered trademarks in the United States, the United Kingdom, Europe and other countries.

ISBN 978–1–137–37963–4   hardback
ISBN 978–1–137–55066–8   paperback

This book is printed on paper suitable for recycling and made from fully managed and sustained forest sources. Logging, pulping and manufacturing processes are expected to conform to the environmental regulations of the country of origin.

A catalogue record for this book is available from the British Library.

A catalog record for this book is available from the Library of Congress.

Typeset by MPS Limited, Chennai, India.

Dedicated to my friend, Matt Ripley

Contents

Introduction

I was born a member of Generation X. The prevailing "values" of the 1980s in America had a vast impact on cultural understandings of masculinity and sexuality, and thus a profound impact on my adolescence. Just as I grew to understand what hippies were, they had lost their cultural resonance; the anti-conformist beatniks were beaten by a fervently conservative Reagan-led social ideology. Although I questioned social conservatism, and looked upon organized religion with extreme suspicion, I was not entirely immune from the prevailing conservative culture. I was partially conditioned by it.

I grew up believing that communism was wicked, the Soviet Union an evil empire determined to annihilate the United States. I had nightmares of nuclear holocaust, a result of practicing nuclear raid drills in elementary school, and therefore supported the expansion of the United States Armed Forces and our nuclear arsenal. I even wanted to be a jet pilot myself. I blush to recall how, aged 16, I put a sticker for Ronald Reagan to win the presidency on the back of my nine mile per gallon Camaro.

By the time I was 17, however, I began to question social conservatism and American hegemony. I began to vocalize my opposition to Christianity's demonization of all those who did not fit its very narrow caste of privileged characters. My liberal empowerment almost came too late, though. I was a closeted gay teenager during the 1980s; damaged, beaten, sent into a suicidal state over the vehemence of conservative ideology. As a closeted gay teenager, I was victimized—forever scarred—by a fanatical revival of fundamentalist Christianity hell-bent on yet another moral panic: this time against the supposed evils of homosexuality.

I maintained strange relationships with my friends at this time, who were also my teammates; liking their companionship but hating

1

their homophobia. I felt like a charlatan in my own body. I was only accepted because they did not know the real me: My body sexually desired theirs.

It would take me until I was 29 before I began to understand that although my friends and teammates espoused homophobia, they were not active agents in their disgust of homosexuality. Rather, they were socialized into it. They took whatever core of homophobic beliefs they had adopted and, in most cases, exaggerated their feelings in order to prevent suspicion of homosexuality from falling upon themselves. Although straight, they too were victimized by this culture. The use of homophobia was thus a matter of self-survival. We all knew that homosexuals existed, and we readily believed that they comprised one in ten of us, but nobody in my adolescent community wanted to be thought of as one of them—not even me.

I look back with sadness over the way in which the 1980s treated and conditioned me and my peers. We were born squarely in the middle of Generation X—too young to profit from the anti-establishmentarianism and free-loving ethos of the 1960s, instead having our formative years smack in the middle of what are now known as "the culture wars." The impact on our masculinity was horrific: we were denied physical touch with our male friends (outside of sporting or other aggressive activities), emotional expressionism, or even the ability to admit loving a same-sex friend.

Our sexualities were also damaged. They were silenced, and we all told lies about them: gay kids desperately hiding theirs, and straight kids wholly exaggerating theirs. We were *all* entirely heterosexual; we were all vehemently homophobic. I even recall my teammates expressing that they would rather take a bullet than kiss another male. None of my heterosexual friends had had sex with a female, but we all said we had. We all masturbated, but none admitted to it—lest we be thought a "fag." We were severely damaged young men, conditioned by monsters of Christian immorality, politicians and preachers alike. In short, we were casualties of Generation X.

Generation X

There are no agreed definitions of what, precisely, it means to be a member of Generation X—we can't even sufficiently say what birthdates serve as catchments for generational tropes—but the notion of generations loosely reflects political events that are thought to influence adolescence. The terms we assign to generations therefore remain loose cultural signifiers designed to show that the experiences of one's formative years are likely to influence one's perspective on the world after one's adolescence. They are useful terms for contextualizing macrolevel cultural and political events. Generational tropes are, for example, helpful in understanding that there is likely to be an attitudinal difference, as a cohort, between those growing up under the Reagan/Bush years compared to those growing up under the Obama administration. Accordingly, a loosely agreed upon understanding of these generational categories is represented below.

Generation X: Approximately those born 1960–1980
Generation Y: Approximately those born 1980–1990
Millennials: Approximately those born after 1990
*i*Generation: Synonymous with Millennials

This book is largely fashioned around the act of contrasting the sexed and gendered perspectives of those of Generation X with the Millennials. I do not, however, call the young men in this book "Millennials"; instead I use my own generational categorizing of them, calling them "*i*Generation." The reasons for this are forthcoming.

Terms and labels almost always overly generalize, but they nonetheless help us to understand a broad concept. The term Christmas, for example, refers to more than December 25th. It taps into a complex set of both shared and uniquely personal meanings. Similarly, the term jock also embodies a rich set of culturally shared meanings. According to the current—and now outmoded—Wikipedia definition, the term is used "primarily in the United States" and "refers to the classic stereotype of a male athlete. It is generally attributed mostly to high school and college athletics participants who form a distinct subculture." Attributes are given as:

- Stuck-up and self-centered
- Aggressive
- Rude and arrogant
- Handsome, muscular, and athletic
- Unintelligent
- Abusing alcohol and drugs
- Generally popular with girls
- Sex—earlier and more casual
- A bully against people who are "uncool" or less popular than they are such as nerds or outsiders

I would add a few stereotypes of my own to the list. The Generation X jock was also:

- Highly homophobic
- Reluctant to cry
- Afraid to hug or hold a friend too long
- Unwilling to show weakness or fear
- Misogynistic
- And yet culturally revered at the same time

In scanning the books on my shelf about sporting men from Generation X, I looked for an existing title that I could update to be more reflective of what teamsport athletes are like in the 21st instead of the 20th century. I came across Donald Sabo and Ross Runfola's (1980) book, *Jock: Sports and Male Identity*. This book detailed the trappings, aggression, and social elitism of jocks.

Sabo and Runfola used this term to title their book because the word jock was, both at the time and still today, loaded with cultural understandings, as Wikipedia attests to. There was a rationale for the cultural creation of "the jock" during the time. While the type of jock that they described was certainly more complex than stereotypes hold, and while not all jocks met the core principles, as a collectivity they were nonetheless misogynistic, abusive, aggressive—and incredibly homophobic. Thus, the title of this book intends to update Sabo and Runfola's work. It is an attempt to mark a watershed moment—a new paradigm—in how we conceptualize what it means to be a jock in the 21st century.

The principal purpose of this book is therefore to challenge and change the popular conception of what it means to be a jock, and provide evidence for how the jocks' heterosexual masculinities have grown softer and more inclusive. I suggest that the increased range of gendered behaviors for all males of *i*Generation have benefited from what teamsport athletes have done with their heterosexual capital. I show that jocks today push boundaries of gender conformity, rather than set them.

This is the case because this book is written *after*, not before or during, the culture wars. The war has been won—or at least the writing is on the wall that the war is ending. Conservative politicians and fundamentalist theists are in the last stages of despotism. In 2013 the United States Supreme Court even determined that the "Defense of Marriage Act" was unconstitutional and that same year the Conservative-led government in the United Kingdom passed equal marriage.

This book uses empirical evidence on teamsport athletes following these culture wars in order to document that there has been a shift of attitudes concerning sexuality and gender among men. I suggest that those born in Generation X were steeped in extreme notions of hetero-sexual masculinity and highly restrictive notions of human sexuality. Male youth of this era largely desired to be like Sylvester Stallone's movie character, Rambo: buff, stoic, desiring their very bodies to resemble a weapon capable of committing violence. They were soldiers in a war of masculinity over femininity; heterosexuality over homosexuality.

But this cultural ethos of homophobia and political conservatism did more than just influence how individuals valued their masculinity; it caused men to align themselves in a social hierarchy, a stratification of men from the top down. At the top of this hierarchy was the jock. He ruled high school and university youth cultures, and the perception of his masculine capital impacted on those around him long after his playing days had ended (Anderson 2005a).

Conversely, this stratification of boys and men demeaned softer, weaker, less athletic, thinner, and more feminized males. They became the prey of the jocks. This was a jock-ocracy or a jock-ocratic system (Anderson 2005a): both denote a school system (like an American high school) in which jocks rule over all others. Here, athleticism and homophobic discourse stratified adolescent men in a king-of-the-hill style competition for the upper rungs of a masculine hierarchy. Much like the game, where the most dominant male occupies the top of the hill and physically pushes weaker boys down it, the contestation for masculine stratification was (ironically) played out on flat sporting fields and courts in the institutions of sport and education. Most boys were not jocks, but instead of banding together to overthrow the jocks, they desired to be like them. Thus, a continuous process of homosocial gender patrolling occurred, by both self and others, as boys who deviated were routinely chastised for their aberrant behaviors, oftentimes turning around to chastise someone else in order to recoup their masculine worth.

However, the 21st century jock, the type I detail in my research, no longer promotes this dynamic of masculinity. Jocks might still be popular (McCormack 2011a), but that does not mean they desire to bully people off the hill. McCormack shows that what it takes to be popular these days is not the extreme masculinity, aggressiveness, and homophobia of the 1980s, but softer and more inclusive behaviors. Popularity is no longer ruled by fear, but through respect for one's charisma, personality, inclusivity, and social fluidity.

Thus, my research into the lives of young sporting men today, along with that of a plethora of other, mostly young, researchers, details that their heterosexuality and masculinity are nothing like that of their fathers. Instead of representing Rambo, they much prefer the feminized charms and homosocial tactility of the members of the boy band One Direction, or the financial success and philanthropy of Bill Gates (JWT 2013). In a sense, male youth today are better dressed digital hippies. They are young men who have grown up with less interest in religion or soldiering. They have gay friends, and value solving problems through talking instead of fighting. They readily express what men of my generation would have considered a highly feminized notion of masculinity, and they have greatly expanded the gendered and sexual behaviors that are not only permissible, but expected of their friends.

Those in the middle, those of Generation Y, are likely torn between these two generations. I suggest that if they were born in the latter half of the decade, or born in the United Kingdom, perhaps Canada, or somewhere in Western Europe, their life-experience is more likely to resemble that of *i*Generation. Conversely, those born in the earlier half of the 1980s, and/or those born in the United States (particularly those in the American South), are more likely to share the experiences and sexual/gender perspectives of those born in Generation X (PEW 2013).

I call the subjects of this book *i*Generation because they are characterized by: (1) inclusive masculinity, where it is homophobia that is unacceptable, not homosexuality; (2) their use of *i*Pads and *i*Phones, and other internet technologies, which they use to show affection for each other, posting their photos and thoughts on Facebook, YouTube, Instagram, and on other social media sites; (3) their use of these same devices to consume large amounts of pornography that simultaneously condition them to be more liberal toward sexual diversity (Wright & Randall 2013), while sometimes permitting them to masturbate alongside a friend, challenging preconceptions about once highly stigmatized sexual activities.

Finally, I call these young men members of *i*Generation because they do what they think feels good, and not what the culture of older men says they should. They are not afraid to enact their brotherly love to one another, not afraid of being homosexualized by their behaviors. Thus, while they are likely the first generation to never attend a protest, they politic through their Facebook and Twitter accounts. They also take political action against the previous generation's masculinity by engaging in public displays of homosocial affection (same-sex behaviors without sexual attraction).

Men of *i*Generation are not the ones who have won the culture wars. Instead, they are the first generation to benefit from the victory won by left-leaning citizens of Generation X, those who were marginalized in the 1980s but, using logic and reason, came to the fore the day after George W. Bush was voted out of office. This book vindicates those members of Generation X who fought for social change; the evidence I provide in it proves that their vision of culture was better than that which conservative politicians and religious leaders imagined.

In this book, I evidence that whether it be the United States, the United Kingdom or other Western nations with similar cultures, young straight men are running toward a more feminized and homosexualized version of gender. I detail the lives of young straight men who are—without social sanction—kissing, loving, and cuddling one another. These behaviors serve both as proof of the war's inevitable termination, and simultaneously the reward for a hard fought battle. It is for this reason I praise today's heterosexual male youth, those of *i*Generation, and I have chosen one specific exemplar of this ethos to dedicate this book to.

Getting to Know *i*Generation

On September 11, 2005 I landed in England to take a sport sociology post at the University of Bath (I have since moved institutions and am currently at the University of Winchester but readers should, in the first instance, consult my website to contact me [www.EricAndersonPhD. com]). One of the students I met during my first year in England was a young man who would eventually become the musical pop star Joe Brooks. At the time I met him, he was an 18-year-old who found his way onto a sport coaching program because he had, like almost every other British male, thought he would be a professional athlete.

I immediately grew fond of Joe. He was (and remains) charismatic, good looking, and most of all, full of moxie. As an American, I related to that. Joe, however, was not interested in his coaching education studies, desiring instead to be a musician. Even though he placed third in our university talent show, it was obvious that he had the talent to back up his ambition. With significant encouragement from family and friends, he dropped out of university to pursue his musical career. He cut his first album, and began developing an internet fan base.

A year later, Joe had begun to reach a modicum of success. His soft lyrics, boyish looks, and stylish attire were then, and remain now, highly sexualized male attributes in British youth culture: skinny jeans, bold colors, ornate neck scarves, perhaps even mismatched socks. Proud of knowing their friend, I loaded four undergraduate heterosexual males into my car and drove two hours to listen to him perform to a sold-out Southampton audience. Afterwards, we went clubbing with Joe and his friends. Here, my male students began drinking and dancing—with Joe and each other.

I had been to heterosexual dance clubs a number of times, in both Southern California and New York, but even in these bastions of liberalness, young men generally went to clubs to dance with women. It is only in American gay clubs that men would freak each other, look at each other, and perform *for* each other on the dance floor. In the UK, however, matters were different.

It was not the first time I had been clubbing with undergraduates. It was a favorite "research" activity of mine. Here, regardless of the venue or level of intoxication, young men enjoyed dancing together. They danced for the sake of each other's company, for entertaining each other, and bonding their friendship. Regardless of whether they attracted women or not, young men were not and are not today afraid to dance with each other—and to do so much more.

Joe brought some of his local friends to the club, including a gay friend, Luke. Luke immediately took a liking to one of my very attractive, yet heterosexual, undergraduate male students, Adrian. Later that evening, in full view of the dance floor, Adrian looked to Luke, pulled his head in close to his and gave him a passionate kiss on the lips. He unlocked his embrace and smiled. "Adrian is a kisser," his friend Harry told me.

Adrian was not alone in this behavior. It is something I have frequently seen in clubs. I had even kissed young straight men in straight clubs a few times myself. On one occasion, I walked up to an attractive stranger and said, "Hey, can I kiss you?" He responded, "What kind of kiss?" "Just a little one," I answered. And with that, I kissed—on the lips—a young man I have never met. When I pulled away he responded, "Thanks. That was nice," before rejoining his friends.

After leaving the club, we spent the night at the house of a friend of one of my students. He let us into his house and showed us that there were four couches and one single bed to sleep on. There were five of us, so we each had our own sleeping space. Harry went upstairs to take the bed. A few minutes later, nestled under a blanket not quite thick enough to keep out the British cold, Harry came back down the stairs. "Anyone wanna cuddle with me?" he asked. "Yeah, I do," Adrian answered.

As a researcher who has devoted his career to studying the intersection of sport, masculinities, and sexualities, I had to inquire the following day as to what went on in the room. It was here that I first learned of the British penchant for young men to cuddle in bed. In this case, two heterosexual men elected to share a bed, not out of necessity, but because they desired each other's physical and emotional company. This is relatively standard for undergraduates in the UK, particularly athletes. But in more recent years the practice has moved away from just athletes in England. Evidencing this, at the final writing of this book in September 2013 I asked an 18-year-old heterosexual male from my gym and a Facebook friend, the week before he headed off to university, if he had ever slept in the same bed as another male friend, cuddling him. "No," he responded. "And I doubt I ever will." Two weeks later, two days into his university life, he sent me a photo of himself cuddling in bed with another male. He told me that there were three of them in bed, but one had to get out of bed to take the photo.

This example highlights the ubiquity of young men sleeping and cuddling together. Yes, sometimes they simply sleep alongside each other, but at other times they sleep holding each other. There is no fear of being thought gay; not because they are so masculine that nobody would suspect them of being such, but because nobody cares all that much if someone were.

By the standards of masculinity that I grew up with, these are highly feminized men. They express emotional love for each other, kiss each other, and cuddle in bed together. In fact, also at the time of writing this introduction in 2013, I have just returned to my office after lecturing, where two heterosexual male students sat adjacent to each other, one leaning over, resting his head on the other's shoulder. His friend periodically caressed his head, showing his love. This is something I have seen hundreds of times in recent years.

Adrian, Harry, the boy I kissed, or the boys cuddling in my class are not ridiculed or looked upon with homosexual suspicion for their behaviors. This is just how young straight men are in this country. The types of gendered behaviors I write about here are commonplace outside undergraduate populations in the UK, too. They are rapidly on the rise among young heterosexual men in the United States and Australia as well. I will provide empirical evidence to support this statement in this book, too.

What is most fascinating about my examples above is that they are not cherry-picked "extreme" examples of a small group of men who brazenly cast-off heteromasculine gender expectations. Instead, the examples I give are normal vignettes of a normal adolescent male undergraduate life in the UK. These behaviors exist mostly among teamsport athletes (likely because of the high degree of social cohesion they maintain) but they also exist among non-athletes, perhaps in near-equally high measure. This is how 16–18-year-old sixth form (senior high school) boys act in the UK as well, and increasingly I show that this is how 16–18-year-olds are beginning to act in the US.

For those wanting a more extreme version of the types of homo-social activities that young, heterosexual men of *i*Generation engage in, I highly encourage you to go to YouTube, look up member name, Siwonjohn, and click on the video entitled "rugby team." This clip follows an amateur men's rugby team on a night out of extreme drink-ing in Britain. It shows a great deal of homosocial (and public) nudity, love for teammates, same-sex kissing, and a good dose of same-sex pseudo-sexual activity, too (including nipple sucking and playing with each other's dicks). It also highlights that just because jocks today enjoy each other's company and bodies, it doesn't mean that they have changed their approach to the sexualization of women.

If you are not already familiar with this type of heterosexual male youth interaction, the video will essentially shock you into understand-ing the openness, the permissiveness of heterosexual masculinity that I detail among the men of *i*Generation. Best yet, the video ends with a discussion of the young men when sober. Here, they are replayed the video, where they take no regret for their homosocial tactility. Instead, they take pride in their affection, even cheering when they are replayed video of one stroking his friend's flopping penis.

While the behaviors of the men in the rugby video are exaggerated, clearly performed for the camera, my research uncovers very similar behaviors among rugby players without the presence of a camera. My in-depth ethnographies, and those in which my undergraduate and graduate students undertake data collection on my behalf, show legiti-mate, intimate, love and physical affection between heterosexual male youth. This is true not only in the UK, but increasingly in America as well. Here, they kiss each other tenderly, love each other thoroughly, and express it publicly, normally posting Facebook photos or statuses to publicly declare their same-sex affection. They also kiss each other brazenly, get naked with each other wildly, and take pride in showing off their making-out with other men as social banter. There are many meanings and purposes to these kisses, yet none are designed to belittle gays or promote homophobia.

Finally, in this book I also show that once these behaviors have ceased to be stigmatized as a sign of homosexuality, they open the door for other forms of physical interaction, including threesomes with two boys and one girl, and occasionally young men masturbating together (generally while webcamming with a woman). I show that there is less concern over one act of homosexuality "making" one gay; and that young men today take a more balanced perspective on sexual orientation, complicating it in their own ways.

This is the purpose of this book; to show that whereas men of previous generations separated their bodies and restricted their emotions from one another with utmost urgency, today's youth perform just the opposite: their bodies linger in each other's proximity. I show that today's heterosexual male youth have rejected the emotionally and physically restrictive practices of their fathers' generation.

Whether it be in the volumes of pornography that young men of *i*Generation masturbate to on their laptops and smartphones, or the oftentimes stronger emotional affection that they show for their best friend compared to their girlfriends; or even in the fact that sexually cheating on one's lover is nearly a standard practice among men of this generation, I highlight these as *progressive* changes. This is not an alarmist account of the emerging generation. I do not clamor for a return to yesteryear. I suggest that these actions and beliefs free men from the once restricted gendered and sexual masculine self. I argue that straight men are beginning to enjoy the same freedoms that gay men do, that straight men are essentially becoming "gayer" all the time.

I suggest that these changes occur largely because of the loss of cultural homophobia and that, perhaps surprisingly, jocks seem to be leading the way in re-visioning a softer, more inclusive, more honest, and yes, more fun, version of heterosexual masculinity. This book is therefore about young, heterosexual men kissing, cuddling, and loving; how they came to this disposition, and the positive implications this has for their own selves, as well as for sexual minorities.

How I Came to Study Masculinities, Sexualities, and Sport

In 1993, as a 25-year-old high school coach, I broke the guiding principle of masculinity of the age: I came out as gay. More so, I came out of the closet at a conservative high school, in what used to be known as a highly conservative location: Orange County, Southern California. Here, I experienced just how much privilege heterosexuals had, not only in sport, but also in the dominant culture. Whereas I was once a privileged white, middle-class, athletic, young, ostensibly heterosexual male, after coming out matters rapidly changed. My public identity transformed from that of being an outstanding coach to being "the faggot coach." The phenomenal success I maintained as a coach, an un-paralleled winning record compared to other sports in our school, failed to buy me immunity from the homophobia. Worse, the athletes on my team were also victimized by the homophobic zeitgeist. Accordingly, my heterosexual athletes and I began to face the discrimination that accompanied the stigma of the time. Athletes ceased to join my team and those remaining found themselves immersed in daily battles with ignorance and violence.

My status as the first publicly recognized gay male coach in the United States went relatively unnoticed until an American football player brutally assaulted one of my heterosexual athletes in 1995, erroneously believing him to be gay. Although the vicious attack was witnessed by other football players, none bothered to intervene. It seems they enjoyed watching a "faggot" being brutally assaulted. Without intervention, the 250 pound American football player knocked my 150 pound runner to the ground, sat atop him, and continuously pummeled his face into the cold concrete. After breaking four facial bones, the assailant next tried to gouge my athlete's eyes out. A woman emerged from her home and pleaded the football player to cease: "Stop it! Stop it!" she yelled. "You're going to kill him." The assailant responded, "It isn't over until the faggot's dead."

Knowing his life depended on it, my runner somehow squirmed from beneath the legs of his assailant. He stumbled to his feet, and although his eyes were clouded with blood, he managed to sprint away and climb over a fence that the football player was too heavy to scale. My athlete was left with four broken facial bones, two permanent screws in his pallet, and a copy of a police report that described the incident as "mutual combat." This, according to the police, was *not* a hate crime: it was not even an assault. This, according to police, was not a crime at all.

I was not a sociologist when I first wrote of these experiences in my autobiography *Trailblazing: The True Story of America's First Openly Gay Track Coach* (Anderson 2000). Nor had I read the works of any sport scholar on the matter, but being gay made me what I call an "organic sociologist."

I always knew that I was gay, and I grew up hearing anti-gay rhetoric from not only preachers, but teachers, coaches and, of course, every young male I knew—particularly my homophobic older brother. But I always knew that there was nothing wrong with being gay; thus, despite what adults said, despite what those with authority preached, and despite what the masses believed, I knew them all to be wrong. I was gay, and this in itself was not an issue; the issue, I knew, was society.

This type of criticality served me well as I entered my adolescent years. My closeted sexual orientation forced me to examine the influence of institutions and culture on people in many other matters. So after my athlete was beaten, the masses tried to explain it away as young men being homophobic through fear of what they don't understand. This, I knew, was not the case. People are instead fascinated by what they don't understand: they are *taught* to feel disgust, hatred, and anger.

I knew that the beating was influenced by a number of events, key individuals, and above all, the young man's American football team's "jock-ocratic" culture. I knew that it was in this environment that he was taught to hate. Although I could not articulate it at the time, I knew that the assailant played within one of the most revered hyper-masculine arenas in society; one which used homophobic discourse to mark certain types of people as sacred and others as profane. What was evident to me was that the assailant's aggression was influenced by indoctrination into an extreme form of masculinity: one predicated almost exclusively on homophobic hate. He was encouraged into homophobia. Indeed, after the beating, the American football player earned hero status among his teammates, and they boasted about how he got away with it.

Today, I understand that this abusive football player, his teammates and coach, were not entirely to blame. Rather, it was the sports-obsessed, homophobic, and hyper-masculine American culture which essentially created him. His conservative-Christian, American upbringing influenced him into a violent, masculine ethos with the promise of masculine glory and praise should he succeed. In American football, he was taught that the most important principle was an othering of a largely invisible group of demonized men—"faggots." Should we then be surprised that this 16-year-old boy would take the opportunity to show that he received the message well? When faced with an actual homosexual, or even the sympathizer of a homosexual, not beating him would be to violate his sanctified beliefs. Had he *not* assaulted this demonized "homosexual," he would have failed his teammates. He would have failed as a man.

It was this valorization of heterosexual masculinity and its associated violence that led to my return to graduate school in 1998, to earn a PhD in sociology in 2004. I desired to understand the cultural mechanisms that influenced a young boy to hate, to better understand the relationship between gay athletes, sport, and compulsory heterosexuality. I hoped that in becoming the expert on the topic, I would maintain cultural power to help undo the association between homophobia and teamsport masculinity.

As a sociologist of some years now, I better understand the operation of hegemony, and the near-seamless manner in which groups of people can maintain power by policing ideologies, both through the threat of force and the willing compliance of those oppressed. I now work with the complex role that sports play in society. I understand how and why the masculinity of the 1980s and part of the 1990s was predicated on a violent, homophobic disposition. I have a better understanding of how the very structure of team sports influenced boys and men to develop a narrow sense of heteromasculinity. However, I now also realize that matters have changed.

In 1999, I began collecting in-depth interviews of openly gay high school and university athletes. Much to my surprise, I found openly gay athletes playing, surviving, and sometimes thriving on their teams (Anderson 2002). Although most of these athletes swam in a sea of heterosexism (and often contributed to it themselves), all played in absence of overt homophobic violence and marginalization. None were overtly called faggots, and none experienced the violence that my athletes and I endured in the early 1990s. These almost exclusively white, openly gay men from various locations, sports, and levels challenged the hegemonic form of masculinity.

In 2005, I published a book concerning the experiences of openly gay and closeted gay male athletes across the country (Anderson 2005a). The take-home message of the book was, as Dan Savage's successful internet campaign lauds, "It gets better." I recognized that while hegemony is enduring, it is not seamless. To me, the antecedents of a more inclusive culture, a softer form of heterosexual masculinity were abundant in the years after the turn of the century. Thus, in that book I wrote:

> If the softening of masculinity continues, the older conservative form of masculinity may be less alluring, and the masculinizing context of sport may have to adjust to the new version of masculinity or risk losing its effect on socializing boys and men in the culture as a whole. In other words, if everything changes around sport, sport will either have to change or it will lose its social significance and be viewed as a vestige of an archaic model of masculinity. (Anderson 2005a: 16)

And now, with the publication of this book in 2014, I stand on firm ground that I was correct. After conducting dozens of investigations into the lived experience of heterosexual and gay male athletes— qualitative and quantitative in nature—in what are ostensibly straight team sports, I show that undergraduate athletes are rapidly running from the hegemonic type of masculinity that scholars have been describing since the mid-1980s.

Heterosexual men in these studies no longer physically assault their gay teammates, and heterosexual men increasingly refuse to symbolically wound gay men with homonegative discourse (see McCormack & Anderson 2010a). Instead, perhaps influenced by the decreasing rates of cultural homophobia of the broader society, many of these men are politically charged to change the landscape of masculinity, while the majority simply adopts an inclusive approach to masculinity because it is what their teammates are doing. Collectively, this book shows that today's sporting youth are essentially no different than their non-sporting counterparts. Youth today are socialized (by the internet, the media, and most important, their peers) into inclusivity, instead of homophobia.

But this book details much more than the acceptance of gay men in sport. I also show that once heterosexual young men cease to be bothered by homosexuality as a construct, they are less concerned with being thought gay in their gendered interactions. Thus, young straight males today are highly feminized compared to their fathers. They bond with each other in ways that the sociological literature used to show only women could (Cancian 1986).

This book details this new, inclusive, form of heterosexual masculinity. It details it for all its glory, showing how heterosexual male youth wear skinny jeans, pink shoes, and designer underwear; lie in bed and cuddle their best friend, kissing them on the cheeks and lips, and sometimes partaking in masturbation or even threesomes with their friends. In this book, I show the rise of the bromance and the symbolic importance of expressing one's dire love for a heterosexual male friend on Facebook; the value they take in being nude together; and the negligible difference that exists between friends if one happens to be gay. Whereas some might examine this as a shocking expose on the abhorrent nature of the loss of masculinity among men, I instead view it as cultural progression—the humanization of heterosexual masculinity.

Underpinning Research Projects

To illustrate the changing relationship between men, masculinity, and homohysteria (Anderson 2011d) I utilize multiple ethnographies, qualitative investigations, and quantitative research on teamsport athletes conducted in both America and Britain. I also examine athletes traditionally marginalized by mainstream, competitive sports (i.e., male cheerleaders and runners) to see if masculinity operates differently throughout this stratification. Also, because the more competitive a team is, the less freedom there is for variable conceptions of athletic masculinity (Anderson 2009), I interview athletes from both low and high quality teams, hoping to better understand the operation of masculinity throughout the institutional progression of sport. Data represented in this research is drawn from multiple research projects listed at the end of this section.

Although not formally coded, I add other data to my conceptualization of the inclusive masculinities of *i*Generation. This comes from the personal relationships that I have maintained with my sport students in the UK, as well as those I coach in the US every summer (when I return home to visit). I believe in decreasing social distance between students and their professor, or athletes and their coach, and thus I often socialize with, run, go clubbing or drinking (in the UK) with them.

It is in these relationships, the countless informal interviews with men of *i*Generation, that I develop my deepest understandings of what it means to be a young man today (Anderson 2013). It is here that I often develop my best social theories to explain their lives. Of course, one might also argue that I am only drawing inclusive students to interview, suggesting that I am only tracking changes amongst an already inclusive group. However, I often have the occasion to meet these men's friends; men who do not know me. They share with me how they think their friends from other groups view things, too. And, because they have learned something about the sociological imagination through my lectures, they make excellent key informants. I also highlight that many other researchers are rapidly coming to the same conclusions that I do regarding *i*Generation (e.g., Adams 2011; Dean 2013; McCormack 2012a; Silva 2013).

Because this research involves sexuality, I reflected upon the influence of disclosing my sexual identity to my participants within my ethnographies. Politically, I align myself with the feminist mantra that the personal is political, and I maintain that remaining closeted constitutes a deeply socio-negative political act (Rofes 2000). To that effect, it is possible that my coming out positively influences the data, but it does not bias it. I have in some ethnographies come out three days into the research and seen no measurable difference in attitudes before or after coming out.

However, my coming out does help me to engage in better, more honest conversation with those I research. This is because it has been shown that disclosure of homosexuality helps to minimize power disparities between researcher and informant. Kong et al. (2002) suggest that when researchers come out as gay, informants reciprocate by divulging more of their lives. Accordingly, I find that the more I disclose about my sexual identity, even my own socio-sexual perspective of enjoying recreational sex despite being married (in an open relationship), the further disclosure it elicits among my informants. It also significantly reduces social distance. This helps facilitate invitations into my informants' worlds that other researchers either do not get, or dare not take.

I am frequently invited to their parties, where I drink and often get drunk with them. I am invited to their homes, and introduced to members of their non-athletic social networks. I become friends with many of these informants, many of which friendships have lasted for years. My willingness to be so open, and my desire to be comfortable in my informants' social worlds, enables me to collect much of the data I show here.

I recognize that it is possible that my openness influences informants to overstate their socio-positive beliefs about gay men and inclusive masculinities in my interview research, too. However, this fits with my political aim of conducting emancipatory research. My research *is* political, and I make no pretense to enter the field as a strictly neutral observer. It is for these reasons that I maintain that a heterosexual researcher, or even a homosexual researcher who is unwilling to engage in lengthy and personal discussions about one's own sexual behaviors, will not elicit the same response or perhaps even come to the same conclusions.

Finally, all ethical procedures of both the British Sociological Association and the American Sociological Association have been followed. Research approval was first obtained prior to conducting all of these research projects, informed consent was given by all participants, and their names and institutional affiliations have been changed in order to protect anonymity.

Australia Interviews

90 short interviews with undergraduate heterosexual men from one university

United States Interviews

26 openly gay male high school and college athletes from a variety of sports (2000–2002)
22 openly gay male high school and college athletes from a variety of sports (2002–2005)

20 closeted gay male high school and college athletes from a variety of sports (2002–2005)
26 openly gay male high school and college athletes (2008 and 2010)
68 heterosexual male high school collegiate cheerleaders from various teams (2001–2002)
32 fraternity members from one fraternity in California (2002–2004)
20 collegiate soccer players from the American South (2009)
20 collegiate soccer players from the American Midwest (2009)
20 collegiate soccer players from the American Northeast (2009)
75 undergraduate men from 11 universities across the United States (2011)

United States Ethnographies

1 team of co-ed collegiate cheerleaders from the American South (2001–2002)
1 team of co-ed collegiate cheerleaders from the American Midwest (2001–2002)
1 team of co-ed collegiate cheerleaders from the American Northeast (2001–2002)
1 team of co-ed collegiate cheerleaders from the American West (2001–2002)
1 fraternity in Southern California (2002–2004)
1 team of men's collegiate soccer players from the American South (2009)
1 team of men's collegiate soccer players from the American Midwest (2009)
1 team of men's collegiate soccer players from the American Northeast (2009)
1 high school boys cross country running team in California (2012–2013)

United States Surveys

698 male athletes from four universities in the Southeastern United States (2004)
442 short interviews with undergraduate men at 11 universities across the US (2011)

England Interviews

19 university men's hockey team members in the Southwest of England (2003–2009)
19 university men's rugby team members in the Southwest of England (2003–2009)

16 university men's soccer players in the Midlands of the UK (2009)
22 male sixth form students (some athletes) in the Southwest of England (2009)
24 university rugby players in the Southwest of England (2009)
39 teamsport athletes in the Southwest of England (2009)
40 heterosexual university athletes in the Southwest of England (2008–2009)
20 gay university students in the Southeast of England (2009)
22 academy level soccer players in the Southeast of England (2013)

England Ethnographies

1 university men's hockey team in the Southwest of England (2003–2009)
1 university men's rugby team in the Southwest of England (2003–2009)
1 university soccer team in the Southwest of England (2007)
1 university British rugby team in the Southwest of England (2009)
1 university soccer team in the Midlands of England (2010)
1 sixth form college in the Southwest of England (2010)
1 group of sixth form students from the Southeast of England (2013)

England Surveys

107 heterosexual male university students in the Southwest of England (2009)
120 heterosexual male university students in the Southeast of England (2013)

My Writing Style

The theories I use, along with my writing style, are designed to be inclusive of most all readers. I eschew dense theoretical writing and post-structural theorizing. If a sociologist can't explain his or her ideas in a relatively straight-forward manner, with language that any undergraduate can understand, then that academic probably is not worth listening to. Oakley (2002) says post-structural writing is "dense, imprecise, long-winded, grammatically complex, hugely inaccessible and hence intrinsically undemocratic" (p. 190). I shorten this to say that it represents a shameful act of academic exclusion. Albert Einstein reportedly said, "If you can't explain it simply, you don't understand it well enough." I have taken the *opposite* approach to the poststructuralist, and done my best to make my writing straight-forward. If readers have questions about what is meant by something, I encourage them to email me: I'll do my best to answer. My email address is on my website www.EricAndersonPhD.com.

Contextualizing Results

The data I present in this book represents males who are 16–23 years of age. There is simply not enough data to make generalizations beyond this age-group, even though other scholars have shown that my notion of inclusive masculinities is either spreading to older men (Bridges 2013; Cashmore & Cleland 2012; Dashper 2012; Gottzén & Kremer-Sadlik 2012), or at least that once men are socialized into softer, more feminine versions of masculinity they do not seem to lose it as they age.

It is also assumed that this research reflects middle-class men. This is largely because this demographic is overrepresented in university attendance. However, when others have looked for inclusive masculinities among lower-class men (McCormack 2014; Roberts 2012) they have found them. McCormack (2014) demonstrates that while social class may have a dampening effect on inclusive attitudes, it certainly does not preclude them.

While my sample of men from my various research projects is not intentionally designed to exclude people of color, they are the minority (although not absent) in this research. This is not necessarily because I desired this as part of my design limitations. For example, I searched (for years) to find openly gay athletes of color to interview, but I could locate very few. I am also limited to a dominance of white men in my British studies. The population of Britain is 93 per cent white, and this demographic is reflected in my research. However, research on an American running team, an American fraternity, and an academy level British soccer team were highly varied in their racial representation— but I found no substantial differences in their attitudes or behaviors regarding masculinity or homosexuality. Thus, I do not provide an account of intersectionality of race with my findings; if substantial differences exist this would be a matter of class, not race. I have elsewhere written about race and homophobia and heterosexuality for those interested. These articles can be found on my personal website www.EricAndersonPhD.com.

This research is strengthened by the multitude of geographical locations in which data is collected. Participant observations and interviews come from men in the American South, North, East, and West, one location in Australia, as well as numerous locations in England. This sample is also strategically positioned to permit me to assess what is occurring amongst men who perhaps have (or will have) significant cultural capital to influence social understandings in the broader culture, thus influencing the construction of masculinity for the next generation. The informants in my research are individuals who are more likely to coach sports, and teach physical education. Perhaps some will even become professional athletes. Equally significant, because they have a university education, those who leave sport are more likely to become leaders of businesses and governments, where they might potentially maintain more power in influencing organizational or institutional culture. So, while my sample is not representative of all university-aged men, it does account for a demographic that is likely to have significant influence in shaping the culture of heterosexual masculinity in the future.

Finally, my thesis, that decreasing homohysteria is leading to more inclusive versions of masculinity among the men of *i*Generation, manifests itself differently in various cultures. I show that America lags behind England, but that young men in the United States are, year-in and year-out, rapidly moving toward the model of masculinity I show in the United Kingdom. Numerically, if pressed to offer a "lag difference" I would suggest it to be about an eight-year difference. So when American readers maintain that this particular result is not occurring in their culture, I would encourage them instead to examine what *is* happening and to recall that further changes are just around the corner. This is one reason I describe these changes as inclusive "masculinities," as opposed to inclusive "masculinity."

Part I
20th Century Jocks

1
Birth of the Jock

The purpose of this chapter is to explain to the reader why we once valued organized, competitive, and combative team sport in Western cultures (i.e., American football, rugby, soccer, etc.) and how that value has changed. I begin by highlighting that organized sport emerged at a particular historical moment in the West. It was a time in which culture was rapidly changing as a result of industrialization. Simultaneously, society was gradually recognizing that homosexuality existed as an immutable, unchangeable characteristic. This led to a turn-of-the-20th-century moral panic; a fear emerged that young men were becoming weak, soft, feminine and thus homosexual. Sports were adopted at this time because they were thought not only to build positive attributes in young men's (and now women's) lives that were useful in an industrial economy (like notions of sacrificing for the family/team or being complicit to authority), but also to be vital in turning young men away from softness, weakness, and homosexuality. Combined with Christian dogma, sport became a vessel for male youth to prove they were heterosexual.

I will then show that, a century later, sport still maintains an underserved esteemed social status. The purposes for which we engage with it have radically changed. We now think sport is necessary, no longer to teach complicity to authority, but instead to teach teamwork. Instead of using sport to heterosexualize male youth, today we use it in an attempt to ward off obesity. Thus, competitive, organized, violent team sports still reserve a mythical place in our cultural perspective—even if this merit is entirely unearned (see Anderson 2010a).

More importantly, this chapter also provides the explanation of how men's masculinity became entangled with men's (supposed) heterosexuality; and how the expression of femininity among men became associated with men's homosexuality. It argues that, because homo-sexuality is not easily identifiable (unlike race, sex, or age), heterosexual men (and gay men who desired to be thought heterosexual) found hyper-masculinity as a mechanism by which to prove their social status as heterosexual—cementing homophobia into masculinity as well. This, then, is a chapter about old-school ways of thinking on masculinity, sexuality, and sport.

The Impact of the Industrial Revolution on Sporting Masculinity

Although the invention of the machinery and transportation necessary for industrialization began early in the 1700s, the antecedents of most of today's sporting culture can be traced to the years of the second Industrial Revolution—the mid-1800s through early 1900s. During this time farmers replaced their farm's rent for that of a city apartment instead. The allure of industry, and the better life it promised, influenced such a migration that the percentage of people living in cities rose from just 25 per cent in 1800 to around 75 per cent in 1900 (Cancian 1986).

However, just as cities attracted people, the increasing difficulty of rural life also compelled them to leave their agrarian ways. This is because the same industrial technologies that brought capitalism also meant that fewer farmers were required to produce the necessary crops to feed a growing population. With production capacity rising, and crop prices falling, families were not only drawn to the cities by the allure of a stable wage and the possibility of class mobility, but were equally repelled by an increasingly difficult agrarian labor market and the inability to own land (Cancian 1986).

For all the manifestations of physical horror that was factory life before labor laws, there were many advantages, too. Families were no longer dependent on the fortune of good weather for sustenance, and industry provided predictable if long working hours. Having a reli-able wage meant that a family could count on how much money they would have at the end of the week, and some could use this financial stability to secure loans and purchase property. Also, the regularity of work meant that between blows of the factory whistle, there was time for men to play. The concept of leisure, once reserved for the wealthy, spread to the working class during this period (Rigauer 1981). It is the impact of this great migration that is central to the production of men's sport in Western cultures.

Sport maintained little cultural value prior to the Industrial Revolution. Social historian Donald Mrozek (1983) wrote:

> To Americans at the beginning of the nineteenth century, there was no obvious merit in sport...certainly no clear social value to it and no sense that it contributed to the improvement of the individual's character or the society's moral or even physical health.

However, by the second decade of the next century these sentiments had been reversed (Miracle & Rees 1994). Sport gave boys something to do after school. It helped socialize them into the values thought necessary in this new economy, and to instill the qualities of discipline and obedience of labor that was necessary in the dangerous occupations of mining and factory work (Rigauer 1981). Accordingly, workers needed to sacrifice both their time and their health, for the sake of making the wage they needed to support their dependent families.

In sport, young boys were socialized into this value of self-sacrifice, asking them to do so for the sake of team victory. As adults, this socialization taught them to sacrifice their health and well-being in the workplace for the sake of family. Most important to the factory owners, however, workers needed to be obedient to authority. This would help prevent them rebelling or unionizing. Sports taught boys this docility to leadership and authority. Accordingly, organized competitive team sports were funded by those who maintained control of the reproduction of material goods.

Spontaneous street-playing activities were banned, and children's play was forced off the streets and into parks and playgrounds where children were supervised and their play structured. In the words of one playground advocate (Bancroft 1909: 21), "We want a play factory; we want it to run at top speed on schedule time, with the best machinery and skilled operatives. We want to turn out the maximum product of happiness." Just as they are today, organized youth sports were financially backed by business, in the form of "sponsors." Today, as part of a compulsory state-run education, they are also backed by the state. This is an economical way of assuring a docile and productive labor force. Sport teaches us to keep to schedule, under production-conscious supervisors (Eitzen 2000).

This shift to industry had other gendered effects, too. Although there was a gendered division of labor in agrarian work, there was less gendering of jobs and tasks compared to industrial life. Here, both men and women toiled in demanding labor. Accordingly, in some aspects, heterosexual relationships were more egalitarian before industrialization. Factory work, however, shifted revenue generation from inside the home to outside. Mom's physical labor no longer directly benefited the family as it once did, and much of women's labor therefore became unpaid and unseen. Conversely, men's working spaces were cold, dangerous, and hard. Men moved rocks, welded iron, swung pick axes, and operated steam giants.

These environments necessitated that men be tough and unemotional. Men grew more instrumental not only in their labor and purpose, but in their personalities, too. As a result of industrialization, men learned that the way they showed their love was through their labor. Being a breadwinner—regardless of the working conditions in which one toiled—was a labor of love (Cancian 1986).

Furthermore, because women were mostly (but not entirely) relegated to a domestic sphere, they were reliant upon their husband's ability to generate income. Thus, mostly robbed of economic agency, women learned to show their contribution through emotional expressiveness and domestic efficiency. Cancian (1986) describes these changes as a separation of gendered spheres, saying that expectations of what it meant to be a man or a woman bifurcated as a result of industrialization. Accordingly, the antecedents of men's stoicism and women's expressionism were born during this period.

But was sport truly necessary to teach young boys and men the values of industrial life? Before labor laws, children were permitted to enter the workforce well before puberty. Would they not just learn these values of toughness, sacrifice, stoicism, and courage in the workplace anyhow? Was sport really necessary to accomplish this? The answer is, no. Not entirely. We learned to value sport for yet another highly influential reason as well.

20th Century Masculine Moral Panic

During the Industrial Revolution, fathers left for work early, often returning home once their sons had gone to bed. Because teaching children was considered "women's work," boys spent much of their days (at school and home) socialized by women. Here, they were thought to be deprived of the masculine vapors supposedly necessary to masculinize them. Rotundo (1993: 31) writes, "Motherhood was advancing, fatherhood was in retreat...women were teaching boys how to be men." A by-product of industrialization, it was assumed, was that it risked creating a culture of soft, weak, and feminine boys. Boys were structurally and increasingly emotionally segregated from their distant and absent fathers. This set the stage for what Filene (1974) termed *a crisis in masculinity.* Adding to men's fears, simultaneous to this was the first wave of women's political independence (Hargreaves 2002). The city provided a density of women that made activism more accessible. Smith-Rosenberg (1985) suggests that men felt threatened by the political and social advancements of women at the time. Men perceived that they were losing their patriarchal power. The antidote to the rise of women's agency largely came through a re-masculinizing of men; and this was facilitated by sport.

These tropes about the birth of 20th century masculinity are well explored in the sport and gender literature. However, a much under-theorized influence on the development and promotion of sport at this time comes through the changing understanding of sexuality during this period, particularly concerning the growing understanding of homosexuality.

Agrarian life was lonely for gay men. One can imagine that finding homosexual sex and love in pastoral regions was difficult. Conversely, cities collected such quantities of people that gay social networks and even a gay identity could form. This coincided with a growing body of scholarly work from Westphal, Ulrichs, and Krafft-Ebing, early pioneers of the gay liberationist movement. These scholars sought to classify homosexual acts as belonging to a *type* of person; a third sex, an invert, or homosexual (Spencer 1995). From this, they could campaign for legal and social equality.

Previously, there were less entrenched heterosexual or homosexual social identities. In other words, a man performed a sexual act, but his sexual identity was not tied into that act. Under this new theorizing, homosexuality was no longer a collection of particular acts, but instead, as Michel Foucault (1984: 43) famously wrote, "The homosexual was now a species." This, of course, meant that heterosexuals were now a separate species, too.

Sigmund Freud helped explain the creation of this "immoral" species (the homosexual). Fears emerged that an absent father (who was working in the factory) and an over-domineering mother (who was domesticated) could make kids homosexual. This created a moral panic among Victorian-thinking British and American cultures. It seemed that because industrialization pulled fathers away from their families for long periods of occupational labor, it had structurally created a social system designed to make boys gay.

Accordingly, in this zeitgeist, what it meant to be a man began to be predicated in the idea of not being like one of those sodomites/inverts/homosexuals. Being masculine entailed being the opposite of the softness attributed to homosexual men. Kimmel (1994) shows us that heterosexuality therefore grew further predicated in aversion to anything coded as feminine. Accordingly, what it meant to be a heterosexual man in the 20th century was to be unlike a woman. What it meant to be heterosexual was not to be homosexual. In this gender-panicked culture, competitive, organized, and violent team sports were thrust upon boys both as a wrongheaded way to sculpt them into heterosexuality, and to prove to others that they were not one of those reviled homosexuals. Essentially, sport became the cure for the feminizing and homosexualizing effects of industrial modernity.

Sport as a Masculine Cure-All to the Feminization of Men

It was in this atmosphere that sport became associated with the political project to reverse the feminizing and homosexualizing trends of boys growing up without father figures. Sports, and those who coached them, were charged with shaping boys into heterosexual, masculine men. Accordingly, a rapid rise and expansion of organized sport was utilized as a homosocial institution principally aimed to counter men's fears of feminism and homosexuality.

Part of this political project was elevating the male body as superior to that of women. Men accomplished this through displays of strength and violence so that sports embedded elements of competition and hierarchy among men. Connell (1995: 54) suggests, "men's greater sporting prowess [over women] has become...symbolic proof of superiority and right to rule." But sport could only work in this capacity if women were formally excluded from participation. If women were bashing into each other and thumping their chests like men, men wouldn't be able to lay sole claim to this privilege. Without women's presence in sport, men's greater sporting prowess became *uncontested* proof of their superiority and right to masculine domination. Thus, sport not only reproduced the gendered nature of the social world, but sporting competitions became principal sites where masculine behaviors were learned and reinforced (Hargreaves 2002).

Social programs and sporting teams were created to give (mostly white) boys contact with male role models. The Young Men's Christian Association (YMCA) came to America in 1851, hockey was invented in 1885, basketball was invented in 1891; the first Rose Bowl was played in 1902; and the first World Series was played in 1903. By the 1920s track, boxing, and swimming also grew in popularity, and with much of the nation living in urban areas, America entered "the Golden Age of Sport"; the country was bustling with professional, semi-professional, and youth leagues.

Unfortunately, when we think of sport today few consider its origins and intent. Few recall that Pierre de Coubertin's reinvention of the ancient Olympic Games was because he saw French men becoming soft, not because he wanted to unite the world's nations.

Christianity also concerned itself with the project of masculinizing and heterosexualizing men during this period. Muscular Christianity concerned itself with instilling sexual morality, chastity, heterosexuality, religiosity, and nationalism in men through competitive and violent sports (Mathisen 1990).

This muscular movement aimed to force a rebirth of Western notions of manliness, to shield boys and men from immoral influences by hardening them with stoic coaches and violent games. Ironically, some of those pushing hardest for masculine morality began the YMCA, which almost immediately served as a gay pickup joint (something reflected in the Village People's song "YMCA").

This period of history also saw playful, less organized youth sporting practices co-opted by adults (Miracle & Rees 1994). Prior to the 1890s, sporting matches were controlled by students—they were coached by students, and organized and played by and for students. However, with new reasons for valuing sport, coaches were paid to manage sport. It was also during this time that recreational sport became enveloped by school systems, a relationship that exists today, most strongly in America. This mirrors, and therefore trains youth to cooperate with, the bureaucratic structures that define contemporary modernity. So while British youth enjoy a bit more flexibility in self-run sporting programs, American youth maintain no control over their organized school sports. This reflects how a once unimportant social institution suddenly found merit/purpose, by those in power.

Few people, outside a select group of sport sociologists, think of sport as a social mechanism to demonstrate support for masculine and heterosexual dominance. Most are misled into believing that all is equal in sport because women now have more segregated sporting opportunities. Furthermore, we scarcely think about what types of sports we culturally esteem—those that highlight the differences between the male and female body, such as American football and rugby. We value sports where bodies clash, jump, and sprint, and not those where finesse, extreme endurance, or balance determine success. In other words, we value sports that favor whatever biological advantage men as a whole maintain. This is because these sports are thought to imbue their participants with masculinity, and heterosexuality.

Modern sport was therefore born out of the turn-of-the-20th-century notion that it could help prevent male youth from possessing characteristics associated with femininity. It was designed to compel boys to reject all but a narrow definition of masculinity: one that created good industrial workers, soldiers, Christians, and consumers. The construction of sport as a masculine and homophobic enterprise was both deliberate and political.

Homophobia and Sporting Social Exclusion

Sport, it would seem, has served well the principle for which it was designed. It has created a social space in which boys are taught to value and perform a violent, stoic and risky form of masculinity for over a hundred years: one based in antifemininity, patriarchy, misogyny and homophobia.

Indeed, organized sport in the 20th century was a highly homophobic institution. Hekma (1998: 2) stated that, "Gay men who are seen as queer and effeminate are granted no space whatsoever in what is generally considered to be a masculine preserve and a macho enterprise." Pronger (1990: 26) concurred, writing: "Many of the (gay) men I interviewed said they were uncomfortable with team sports...orthodox masculinity is usually an important subtext if not *the* leitmotif [in team sports]."

Even today, when most think of sports (particularly contact sports) they think of them as a place in which a dominant form of masculinity is reproduced and defined, as an athlete represented the ideal of what it meant to be a masculine man. This is a definition which contrasts with what it means to be feminine and/or gay. And as women increasingly gained access to once masculine-dominated institutions in the last decades of the 20th century, sports became contested terrain in which men tried to validate masculine privilege through their ability to physically outperform them, thus symbolically dominating women (Nelson & Rowe 1994).

But homophobia hurts more than just gay men. It also negatively impacts upon the lives of straight men. This is because, if boys and men desire to be perceived as heterosexual and masculine (heteromasculine) among peers—and they do (see Anderson 2005a; Pollack 1999)—they must avoid the homosexual stigma of feminized terrains both at work

(Williams 1995) and during play or leisure; requiring them to avoid acting in effeminate ways (Kimmel 1994). Accordingly, heterosexual boys and men, or those wishing to be thought heterosexual, traditionally position themselves away from femininity to show they are not feminine and therefore should not be perceived as gay. Epstein et al. (2001: 165) note, "Even little boys are required to prove that they are 'real boys' in ways that mark them as masculine, even macho, and therefore (by definition) heterosexual." This is accomplished through the repeated association with cultural codes of heterosexuality and disassociation from codes for homosexuality. It can be found in:

• A willingness to commit violence to self and others
• Emotional stoicism
• Always being willing to fight
• Separation from anything coded as feminine
• A sequestering into certain sports, arts, and entertainment choices
• Limiting physical contact with other men
• Positioning oneself as being 100 per cent straight

But if gay male athletes, who are stigmatized as being feminine, can be as strong and competitive as heterosexual male athletes, they could threaten the perceived distinctions between gay men and straight men, and thus the perceived differences between men and women as a whole. Bourdieu (2001) argued that the gay male is uniquely situated to undermine masculine orthodoxy because of his unique ability to invisibly gain access to masculine privilege before coming out as gay. Because of this ability, the gay male may be uniquely positioned to align with feminists in a terrain of progressive coalition politics to symbolically attack male dominance. Thus, gay male athletes—who are seen as a paradox because they comply with the gendered script of being a man through the physicality involved in sports, but violate another masculine script through the existence of same-sex desires—may threaten sport as a prime site of hegemonic masculinity and masculine privilege.

Homophobia, therefore, was thought to present itself in the form of resistance against the intrusion of a gay subculture within sports; to serve as a way of maintaining the rigidity of orthodox masculinity and patriarchy (Pronger 1990). Sports not only rejected homosexuality, but also venerated hyper-heterosexuality. Gay males were therefore perceived "largely as deviant and dangerous participants on the sporting turf" in that they defy culturally defined structures of hegemonic masculinity (Clarke 1998: 145).

Although parents may not consciously suggest that they desire to put their sons into American football, or soccer in Britain, in order to assure that they grow up heterosexual, glimpses of this thinking often emerge when fathers learn that their kids are gay, where it is common to hear, "I should have put you in football." While this might sound absurd to most young men of *i*Generation today, a great number of fundamentalist Christians still believe this. Even after the "ex-gay" conversion therapy group Exodus International abandoned their organization in June 2013 saying that one could not be turned straight, many Christian churches still employ sport as a way to supposedly turn gay men straight.

Extremely masculine sports are still valued in our culture for a reason, and this is because they are used to help boys publicly prove to their peers, families, and society that they too are a proper, masculine, heterosexual guy/lad/man. There are other reasons we value these types of barbaric sports too; but most of those rationales fall flat under empirical scrutiny.

The Myth and Realities of Contemporary Youth Sport

If you ask my first year university students why sports are "good," they will not say "because they make boys heterosexual." This is a "background" belief which, in more recent decades, has been trumped by the lore of other mythical attributes. For example, my students will maintain, without critically evaluating their beliefs, that sports promote teamwork, cooperation, fitness, and self-esteem. American students in particular suggest that sports help minorities out of poverty; that they promote school attendance, decrease drug use, crime, and other forms of mischief; and that sport helps certain athletes earn scholarships to pay for the rising costs of university attendance. Almost everybody erroneously believes that sport builds fitness, often overlooking the trail of their own broken bodies and concussed minds in the process.

These myths of positive attributes, the lore we maintain for sport, encourages parents to sign their kids into organized programs, rather than permitting children to invent, play, and bend the rules of physical games that they determine for themselves. The lore for sport, and all its socio-positive myths, is so strong that governments encourage, and even pass legislation forcing, youth to play sport in public education. Accordingly, academic investigations of parents with kids involved in organized, competitive team sports show that they believe that sport will teach their kids moral character, self-restraint, and a sense of fair play. This is a longstanding finding (Miracle & Rees 1994). For example, compared to the 6 per cent of American parents that discouraged athletic participation in the 1980s (an important time for my analysis of heterosexual masculinity), 75 per cent encouraged it (Miller Lite 1983).

In the United States, where sport is intertwined with public education (Gerdy 2002), matters are worse. American high schools report participation rates as high as 72 per cent (Carlson et al. 2005). The fact that sports are run from within schools exerts cultural and institutional pressure for youth to participate in them. The ubiquity of teamsport participation also means that there is a great deal of peer pressure, even if not direct, for other youths to play these "games." As a result, if there is any institution outside of education that should be described as being *all-encompassing* in the lives of Western male youths, it must be that of competitive sport.

There is some, very limited, evidence for sporting participation having positive effects on these youths. For example, researchers find that the most salient benefits of organized sport participation is better school attendance and increased educational aspiration (Eccles & Barber 1999). Researchers even show higher rates of university attendance and even possibly better post-schooling employment for jocks (Carlson et al. 2005). However, these quantitative investigations are somewhat misleading because they fail to examine whether the benefits associated with sporting participation are the result of something intrinsic to teamsport participation, or whether they reflect the physical, symbolic, and emotional dominance that a socially elite group of youth (jocks) exhibit over marginalized lesser-than-athletes in jock-ocratic school cultures. In other words, do athletes have higher self-esteem because they score goals, or is this a statistical reflection of the lowering of non-athletes' self-esteem in response to being subordinated by athletes who are culturally and institutionally glorified?

Conversely, when many studies purport to examine the socio-negative attributes of teamsport participation (Miller et al. 2005), they often examine variables that lend themselves to quantifiable analysis, like disciplinary referrals. In doing so, they fail to examine the more important socio-negative variables, like the volitional and unintentional damage inflicted upon those who do not fit the athletic mold, or the emotional and physical damage that sport often brings to the body or brain when used as a weapon in search of temporary glory (all readers should Google "chronic traumatic encephalopathy"). Nor do they examine the way sport is used to shape youth into a working-class ethic of hard work, sacrifice, and stoicism that benefits corporations, religion, and the military (Anderson 2010a). These studies fail to examine how sport operates to break down an individual's sense of self and restructures them as complicit to the orders of one (usually male) leader; namely, the coach.

One of the most fanciful beliefs is that sport serves as a social vessel for the acceptance of young kids into peer groups, and that it provides them with a system of adult-support in growing up. Michener (1976: 19), for example, wrote: "Young people need that experience of acceptance; it can come in a variety of ways...but in the United States it is sports that have been elected primarily to fill this need." While it is certainly true that most of us need to feel that we belong to something, and while sport certainly can and does fill that necessity for some, it is a far-stretch to suggest that sport *is* that place, without problem. To me, all of this fluff about the virtues of sport is mere hyperbole. Sport is a terrain where kids are evaluated according to their physical worth, where those who do not make the grade are cut, socially excluded, and/ or marginalized. While there are other institutions that cut kids, and while there are other institutions in which children and young adults fail, none are as visible, as public as sport.

Thus, I conclude this chapter in writing that sport was valued for the first time in Western cultures because it had an important purpose, not because it was fun to play. Sport was no longer, as Thomas Jefferson said, "a waste of God's time." As a result of industrialization, and in the hands of religious fundamentalists, it became a key ingredient of proper heterosexual adjustment for boys. To be a jock was not to be gay, soft, or feminine. But what happens when jocks cease to care about being thought such?

2
Homohysteria

This chapter examines the evolution of social theory explaining men and their masculinities, illustrating how social theories are a product of their time. I first explain how the leading theory for men of Generation X and some of those of Generation Y organized their masculinities in the 1980s and 1990s, before highlighting the inadequacies of this theory in contemporary times. The chapter then examines a theory of masculinity which takes the significant impact of declining homophobia into account. I do this by advancing the concept of homohysteria.

I show that it is the fear of being homosexualized through the wrongdoing of gendered behaviors which leads men to align themselves with extreme notions of masculinity. However, as cultural homophobia diminishes, fewer social sanctions against being thought gay exist, and thus there is less reason to police one's gendered behaviors. Homohysteria contextualizes a culture's matrix of awareness of the existence of homosexuality, and a degree of cultural homophobia. Differing degrees of each are shown to impact a culture differently. Thus, this chapter explains why it is that straight men were able to sleep in the same beds, hold hands, sit in each other's laps, and profess their love for one another in 1884, but not in 1984. I then explain why, in 2014, heterosexual men are again able to engage in these behaviors without being thought gay.

Masculinity Theory of Generation X

The most prominent tool for understanding the social stratification of masculinities has been Connell's (1995) concept of hegemonic masculinity. From a social constructionist perspective, hegemonic masculinity theory articulates two social processes (Demetriou 2001). The first concerns how all men benefit from patriarchy and the second concerns how men arrange themselves into hierarchies of diminishing power. Collectively, Connell describes hegemonic masculinity as "the configuration of gender practice which embodies the currently accepted answer to the problem of the legitimacy of patriarchy" (Connell 1995: 77). The masculine stratification component of her theorizing (how men create social hierarchies) concerns the mechanisms by which a hierarchy is created and legitimized. Connell argues that these two processes work interactively and simultaneously to produce a gender order—one where certain men are privileged over other men and all men maintain power over all women.

However, Demetriou (2001) critiques Connell's work for a lack of focus on the interaction of these two processes, arguing that scholars tend to focus on just one of them (usually intra-masculine processes), and that research does not demonstrate how the marginalization of groups of men affects patriarchy (and vice versa). While some use it to theorize about patriarchy, none have been able to show empirical proof of the theory's utility. Connell's notion of the reproduction of patriarchy is also quite fundamentalist. Her theory necessitates that patriarchy can never be unseated. This is because Connell says that a hegemonic form of masculinity is the source of patriarchy, simultaneously postulating that there will always be one form of hegemonic masculinity—thus, patriarchy will always exist.

Still, the intra-masculine component of Connell's theorizing, what Demetriou calls "internal hegemony," has been extremely useful for gender scholars, particularly those studying masculinities in the 1990s. It is here that Connell's theorizing has greatly benefited the field of masculinities.

In conceptualizing intra-masculine domination, Connell argues that one archetype of masculinity, which she calls hegemonic masculinity, is esteemed above all others, so that boys and men who most closely embody this standard are accorded the most social capital. Gay men are at the bottom of the hierarchy, and straight men who behave in ways that conflict with this valorized masculinity are marginalized. Thus, according to this model, homophobia is a particularly effective weapon to stratify men in deference to a hegemonic mode of heteromasculine dominance (Connell 1995).

While this has been a model with great utility for two decades, hegemonic masculinity theory today now not only fails to describe why patriarchy exists, but it no longer accounts for how men organize themselves socially either. It does not accurately account for what occurs in a societal, institutional, or organizational culture of *decreased* homophobia: cultures that did not exist when Connell conceptualized her ideas in the early 1980s. This is to say that the theory is incapable of capturing the social organization of masculinities among youth today. This is for several reasons, including that the model only permits one form of "hegemonic" masculinity to reside atop a social hierarchy; it does not explain the social processes in an environment in which more than one version of masculinity maintain equal appeal (Anderson 2005b). Even in their reformulation of the concept of hegemonic masculinity, Connell & Messerschmidt (2005) reaffirm that hegemonic masculinity presupposes the subordination of non-hegemonic masculinities, and that it is predicated upon *one* dominating (hegemonic) archetype of masculinity. While they continue to note that attributes of this archetype can change, they maintain that an essential component is that other masculinities will be hierarchically stratified in relation to it. Accordingly, hegemonic masculinity as a concept (which I call a theory because it has predictive power) is incapable of explaining empirical research that documents multiple masculinities of equal cultural value (Anderson 2005a; McCormack 2011a, 2014).

This was not an issue in the early 1980s when Connell developed her work, or the 1990s when it was widely taken up in the literature—all of which occurred during a highly homophobic zeitgeist, where gay men faced extreme social marginalization. However, the inability of Connell's theory to explain the social organization of masculinities became increasingly problematic as homophobia began to decrease (McCormack & Anderson 2010a, 2010b; Savin-Williams 2005; Weeks 2007); it simply could not account for the varying masculinities that researchers found flourishing without hierarchy or hegemony (Anderson 2009; Dean 2013; McCormack 2011a). It is for this reason that I developed inclusive masculinity theory (2005a, 2009) to provide a theoretical explanation of these changes, one that better takes into account the power of stigma.

Masculinity Theory for *i*Generation

Inclusive masculinity theory (Anderson 2009) situates hegemonic masculinity theory in its historical context. I argue that Connell's theory only works in periods of high homophobia, like the 20th century. In these times, boys and men are compelled to express homophobic and sexist attitudes, to raise their masculine capital through sport and muscularity, and to raise their heterosexual capital through sexually objectifying women. They also avoid emotional intimacy or homosocial touch

(Field 1999). All of this is to escape the stigma of being considered gay (Anderson 2008a). It is within this cultural context that Kimmel (1994) suggests homophobia *is* masculinity.

However, inclusive masculinity theory maintains that as homophobia declines, multiple masculinities can be *equally* esteemed. This is an important theoretical difference: inclusive masculinity theory situates hegemonic masculinity as the product of homophobic cultures and enables the understanding of a horizontal alignment of masculinities in settings where men do not fear being labeled as homosexual. Thus inclusive masculinity theory uses a more sophisticated operation of gender power. Conversely, hegemonic masculinity theory is always hierarchical stratification of masculinities; archetypes of masculinity cannot exist without struggle between them. In a culture of inclusive masculinity, however, not only will multiple masculinities co-exist harmoniously, but fewer behaviors will be associated with homosexuality.

Inclusive masculinity theory supersedes hegemonic masculinity in explaining the stratification of men because it is a more adaptable heuristic tool and it is able to explain the social dynamics of masculinities in times of lower homohysteria (see the following section). In inclusive settings with low homohysteria, heterosexual boys and men are permitted to engage in an increasing range of behaviors that once led to homosexual suspicion, all without threat to their publicly perceived heterosexual identities. Proof of my concept lies in the chapters that follow: men today engage in behaviors that defy a strict social hierarchy with just one dominating archetype.

In my explication of inclusive masculinity theory (Anderson 2009), I theorize that this cultural shift, from homophobia to a stigmatization of homophobia, was due to multiple influences: the internet, the media, decreasing cultural religiosity, the success of feminism, the success of gay and lesbian social politics, and the influence of the increased number of gay and lesbians coming out of the closet. Interestingly, these changes have frequently occurred against the desires of their coaches or other influential males who represent members of Generation X (A. Adams et al. 2010; Anderson & McGuire 2010; McCormack & Anderson 2010b).

Homohysteria

Homohysteria is different from homophobia. Homophobia is a culturally produced fear of, or prejudice toward, homosexuals that sometimes manifests itself in legal restrictions or, in extreme cases, bullying or even violence against homosexuals (sometimes called "gay bashing"). The term *homophobia* was coined in the late 1960s and was used prominently by George Weinberg (1972), an American clinical psychologist, in his book *Society and the Healthy Homosexual*. Although the suffix *phobia* generally designates an irrational fear, in the case of homophobia the word instead refers to an attitudinal disposition ranging from mild dislike to abhorrence of people who are sexually or romantically attracted to individuals of the same sex. Homophobia is a culturally conditioned response to homosexuality, and as such, attitudes toward homosexuals vary widely across cultures and over time.

However, homophobia is not in-and-of-itself an appropriate term to capture many of the dynamics I see at play concerning sexuality and masculinity today. It is for this reason that I created the term homo-hysteria. The term refers to one's fear of being thought homosexual through the "wrongdoing" of cultural gender norms. I will detail the concept with an example.

In 1999, playwright and AIDS activist Larry Kramer told *Salon* magazine: "There's no question in my mind [President Abraham Lincoln] was a gay man and a totally gay man. It wasn't just a period, but something that went on his whole life."

I had little trouble believing this when I read it. A few years earlier I had read a biography about the 16th president, revealing that Lincoln maintained a deep emotional relationship with a same-sex friend, Joshua Speed. In the 1999 article (available at www.salon.com/1999/04/30/lincoln), author Carol Lloyd writes:

> The 28-year-old traveler was tall, with rough hands, a chiseled jaw and unforgettable, deep-set, melancholy eyes. He arrived in town, his worldly possessions in two battered suitcases, and inquired at a general store about buying some bedding. But the price was far beyond his budget. The strikingly handsome 23-year-old merchant took pity on the man and invited him into his own bed, free of charge, which happened to be just upstairs. The traveler inspected the bed and, looking into the merchant's sparkling blue eyes, agreed on the spot. For the next four years the two men shared that bed along with their most private fears and desires.

I frequently used Lincoln as an example of a gay man when lecturing on historically influential sexual minorities. When my students inevitably protested, I simply pointed out to them his four-year bed sharing. I added that Lincoln continued to share a bed with multiple other boys and men well into his years as a statesman. None of my students contested this evidence.

To my male students of the mid-1990s, sharing a bed with another man as a permanent feature of one's living arrangement served as indisputable evidence that one was gay. Supporting this, when I began coaching in the late 1980s (Anderson 2000), my high school students did not want to share a bed when the team traveled, not even for one night. Because bed sharing was nonetheless an economic necessity, they frequently heterosexualized themselves to their bed-sharing peer: "You better not make a move on me." From this perspective, Abraham Lincoln's willingness to sleep in the same bed with another man for years on end clearly identified him as gay.

Although I did not know it at the time, Larry Kramer, my students, and myself, were all making judgments concerning the past based on our current, socially constructed, understandings of sexuality. I made my Lincoln-as-gay analysis based on my own experiences, something historians call *presentism*. I only started to undo my biased opinion when I started to understand the behaviors of young male athletes who share beds today.

The fact that Lincoln was able to share a bed in the 1840s without being thought gay, but boys were not able to share beds in the 1980s without being thought gay, raises an important question. Were men not equally as homophobic in Lincoln's era? The answer to this is, in short, yes, but they also did not readily believe that one could be gay. This is where homohysteria comes into play.

I argue that in order for a culture of homohysteria to exist, three social factors must coincide: (1) the mass cultural awareness that homosexuality exists as a static sexual orientation within a significant portion of the population; (2) a cultural zeitgeist of disapproval toward homosexuality; and (3) disapproval of men's femininity or women's masculinity, as they are associated with homosexuality.

I suggest that in times of high homohysteria, heterosexual men are compelled to align their identities and behaviors with orthodox (hypermasculine) notions of men's masculinity, the way I described the 1980s jock in the previous chapter. The manifestation of this form of masculinity was principally designed in order to avoid cultural suspicion of being thought gay, something I call homosexualization. Conversely, heterosexual men retain considerably more gendered freedom in times of low or no homohysteria. I describe this as a cultural process related to homophobia, and define the term homohysteria as men's fear of being homosexualized, through association with feminized behavior.

Homohysteria can work the other way, too. Heterosexual women who play sport will recognize that they are socially perceived as lesbian for doing such (Anderson & Bullingham 2013). In the sections below, I describe three conditions that a culture might move through concerning homohysteria: from the erasure of homosexuality, which negates the possibility of homohysteria occurring; to the mass recognition and dislike of homosexuality, which permits a culture of extreme homohysteria to exist; to the recognition of homosexuality without cultural homophobia, which extinguishes homohysteria.

Men's Gendered Behaviors in a Culture of Erasure

Professor of American Studies, John Ibson (2002), thought he had hit the jackpot. Ibson found for sale photos taken at the dawn of professional photography; photos of men posed together. Although clothed, the men in the photos were positioned intimately. Recognizing them as gay ancestors, Ibson was delighted to learn that the vendor he purchased them from had many others to sell—all capturing a similar level of tactile intimacy between men. The outright visibility of gay men a hundred years earlier fascinated Ibson. Had sexuality historians missed something about turn-of-the-20th-century America? Were, contrary to historical accounts, gay men actually out of the closet and visible during this time? Ibson embarked on a quest to find more photographs, so that he could perhaps re-write gay history.

However, somewhere between collecting his first few photographs and his current collection of over 5,000, Ibson figured out that these were not necessarily gay men pictured. Instead, they were heterosexual men doing what heterosexual men did at that moment in American culture: expressing affection for a friend.

After years of careful analysis—and in what must be the most significant yet underappreciated gender studies book ever written—Ibson (2002) uses his collection of 5,000 photos to describe the history of men's relationships from the 1880s until the 1980s. Ibson is very clear not to explain what the photographs mean to us today (that would be presentism), but rather what they meant to the subjects at the time the photos were taken. Specifically, Ibson uses the photos to illustrate the changing nature of physical intimacy between men in response to the cultural contextualization of homosexuality in modern society.

For example, his book contains images of athletes before the 1920s, as well as friends, servicemen, brothers, collegiate, and prep school boys in many settings. In different pictures, the boys and men are lavishly dressed, provocatively undressed, arms wrapped around each other, embracing, lying in piles, sleeping in the same beds, holding hands, and sitting on each other's laps—all to show their affection for one another.

It was these photos (and Ibson's astute analysis) that heavily influenced my thinking about the role of homophobia in producing gendered behaviors and men's masculinities (Anderson 2009). The photographs he collected suggested that the gradual awareness of homosexuality as a static identity (not just an abhorrent behavior) resulted in an equal growth in cultural homophobia.

This was displayed in his photographs which, when organized by passing decades, clearly suggest that as American culture grew increasingly aware of homosexuality, men began to pry intimacy away from fraternal bonding. This mass awareness of homosexuality, combined with social homophobia, increased men's fear of being falsely homosexualized by their behaviors, attitudes, emotions, or associations. Accordingly, as the awareness of homosexuality grew (in the presence of homophobia), so did the space between men.

This growing distance between men is clearly illustrated through multiple subsets of Ibson's photographs. Thus, Ibson shows that cultural space has been added between men in many walks of public and private life. However, none is more germane to this book than Ibson's photographs of men's sport teams.

Here, Ibson uses images of teams to illustrate the evolution of the team portrait, and consequential growing rigidity that athletes displayed through the passing years. For example, prior to the 1920s, his photographs show athletes hugging, laying their heads in each other's laps, holding hands, or draping their arms around each other. Soon after, however, teams appeared in straight rows. Men first stand with their hands at their side, and years later their arms are folded across their chests. Men ceased to touch each other when being photographed.

Ibson's photographs provide visual evidence regarding the relationship between homohysteria and male intimacy. They help one understand that homohysteria has greatly limited the expression of gender and intimacy among all men. His photographs represented men before modern understandings of a gay identity, and the effect that this identity had on heterosexual men's gendered behaviors.

Establishing a Gay Identity: The Beginning of Homohysteria

Although little is known about pre-modern women's sexualities, it is largely believed that the sexual desire of one man for another was an acceptable, often venerated, form of love in ancient cultures (Spencer 1995). However, intolerance toward homosexual behavior grew in the Middle Ages, especially among the adherents of Christianity and Islam—with each being near-compulsory in many cultures. During these times there were less entrenched heterosexual or homosexual social identities: a man performed an *act* of sodomy, without necessarily being constructed as a "sodomite" or particular sexual category. Under the new theorizing that I spoke of during the turn of the 20th century, however, homosexuality was no longer a collection of particular acts, but instead, an identity. As Foucault (1984: 43) wrote:

> We must not forget that the psychological, psychiatric, medical category of homosexuality was constituted from the moment it was characterized—Westphal's famous article of 1870 on "contrary sexual sensations" can stand as its date of birth—less by a type of sexual relations than by a certain quality of sexual sensibility, a certain way of inverting the masculine and the feminine in oneself. Homosexuality appeared as one of the forms of sexuality when it was transposed from the practice of sodomy on to a kind of interior androgyny, a hermaphrodism of the soul. The sodomite had been a temporary aberration; the homosexual was now a species.

The 1895 conviction of Oscar Wilde for "gross indecency" animated this newly created deviant identity. So extensive was the media coverage and public discussion around the trial of Britain's celebrated author and playwright that it breathed public awareness into homosexuality, and consequently engendered elevated social homophobia. In Wilde, homosexuality found a spokesperson.

All of this is to suggest that Western cultural awareness that some men existed as a different type of sexual person, a homosexual, came into existence during this period. But it takes more than the knowledge that homosexuality exists among a few, to create a homosexuality-panicked culture like that of the 1980s. It also takes awareness that homosexuality exists as a significant, static, and immutable percent of the population.

In the Western world, particularly the United States, the first inclines that homosexuality met the above conditions came from the work of the first sexologist, Alfred Kinsey, and the publication of his book *Sexual Behavior in the Human Male* (Kinsey et al. 1948). Here, Kinsey reported that 10 per cent of the American population was either homosexual or had such tendencies. It is possible that Kinsey got higher response rates to homosexuality than any research following because he took a more aggressive approach. In a face-to-face memorized interview script, Kinsey and his associates privately asked of the men they studied, "How many times have you had sex with a man?" and not "Have you had sex with a man?" When the participant said that they had not, Kinsey refused to believe it. This is a more aggressive approach than sex researchers use today (Laumann 1994). Others suggest that he found higher rates of homosexuality because he interviewed a significant number of prisoners, too. But what is important about Kinsey's research for my theory of homohysteria is not whether his 10 per cent figure is correct—but instead, whether people *believe* it to be correct.

Thus, with Wilde we had a visible example of what it meant to be a homosexual male (i.e., feminine); with Freud (1975) we had an understanding of what made one gay (absence of the father); and with Kinsey, we learned that 10 per cent of men were gay. In short, Wilde gave us an image of the pervert; Freud explained the disease; and Kinsey promoted its prevalence. It is this last stage that initiated the processes of men looking to their homosocial groups, knowing that one in ten are gay, and speculating who it was. This homospeculation, however, remained just speculation. This is because, apart from "acting feminine," nobody could (or can) accurately determine who is gay. There is no litmus test for homoseuxality.

I thus argue that the awareness of homosexuality existing as a static trait, an unchanging sexual orientation, was first thrust into Anglo-American culture through the visibility of the Wilde trials. However, the unusual aesthetic appearance that Wilde represented, and his penchant for aesthetic art and beauty, helped formulate homosexual suspicion only for men who resembled Wilde. This stabilized the stereotype of the homosexual for decades, excusing all others of homosexual suspicion unless they acted in Wildeian ways. Under this model, James Dean or Rock Hudson are not suspected of maintaining sexual desire for men, while Harvey Fierstein and Stephen Fry are.

Thus, while Kinsey made us aware of the ubiquity of homosexuality, it was only abstractly. If a male was living with his best male friend for 15 years, they were still considered bachelor roommates, and not homosexual; as long as they were not effeminate (the Oscar Wilde archetype). But this changed in the 1980s. Here, with "normal" (i.e., gender typical) men dying in normal families from AIDS, the veneer of heterosexuality that average masculinity brought was no longer enough. Now, anybody could be gay. Accordingly, men tried to prove to their peers that they were not one of the 10 per cent by adopting and valuing extreme masculine behaviors.

Homohysteria of the 1980s

It would be difficult to call the 1950s, 1960s, and 1970s gay friendly. But compared to the 1980s they seemed so. Men were permitted to be a bit softer, less muscular, and less violent during these times. The hippies of the late 1960s and 1970s showed progressive attitudes toward homosexuality, too. However, Western cultures hit an apex in both homophobia and homohysteria in the 1980s. The stereotype of the flamboyant gay man certainly remained, but the public understood that this was just one form of homosexuality; the public understood that men could be gender-typical and gay as well.

This was because the gay community was hit by two substantial sociopolitical events that raised the general public's exposure to homosexuality (McCormack & Anderson, forthcoming). These events changed not only gay masculinities (Levine 1998) but men's gendered understanding as a whole.

The 1980s ushered in a revival of homophobic and patriarchal religious fundamentalism. At a time when church attendance began to decline, the advent of cable television brought various ministries into millions of living rooms. Christianity used the hysteria about homosexuality to milk money from callers who could donate with their credit cards over their new push-button phones. Unfortunately, this further helped inspire Christianity to move from the pulpits and into the political arena.

The true propellant for homohysteria, however, came in the form of a virus. In the early 1980s AIDS brought such visibility that it solidified in every citizen's mind that homosexuals existed in great numbers. It secured a public awareness that homosexuals lived and worked alongside "the normals" in every social institution. The ubiquitous presence of gay men could no longer be denied as they were dying in great numbers. Homosexuality was now not only pathologized as a lack of masculinity, but it was associated with viral genocide (Halkitis 2001; Peterson & Anderson 2012). Gay men were now stigmatized as being both effeminate and diseased. This, combined with the religious right's crusade to stigmatize homosexuality, meant that Americans were hellbent on having yet another crisis in men's masculinity (Kimmel 1996). Heterosexual male gender roles were to be recalibrated through organizations like the "Promise Keepers," films like *Rocky*, and a homophobic cowboy president in Ronald Reagan, or a homophobic Prime Minister, Margaret Thatcher, who said, "Children who need to be taught to respect traditional moral values are being taught that they have an inalienable right to be gay" (www.margaretthatcher.org/document/106941).

These concerns heralded the introduction of Section 28 of the Local Government Act 1988 in the United Kingdom, which stated that local government "shall not intentionally promote homosexuality or publish material with the intention of promoting homosexuality" or "promote the teaching in state schools of the acceptability of homosexuality as a pretended family relationship."

This scapegoating of homosexuality revitalized Freud's explanation of men's homosexuality as the product of an absent father figure, finding renewed emphasis in the 1980s. The "men's movement" of the AIDS era was a way for men to distance themselves from what one was not to be. It was as if muscular Christianity were revived. This time, however, Americans (in particular) had more than just a religious reason to "prevent" homosexuality—it was now epidemiological.

General Social Survey (GSS) data shows that throughout the 1970s, an average of 70 per cent of Americans said that homosexuality was always wrong, but those numbers increased to 77.4 per cent in 1988 (Loftus 2001). When one adds in from that year those who thought it was (mostly or sometimes wrong) 84.2 per cent of Americans had negative perspectives on homosexuality! Other polls show a more dramatic shift in rising homophobia of the mid-1980s. For example, a Gallup poll (Gallup.com) shows that in 1985, 44 per cent of Americans thought homosexuality should be legal, but that number dropped to 33 per cent in 1987.

Attitudes toward homosexuality were slightly less extreme, but overall only slightly better, in Britain than in the United States during the 1980s. Still, the trend of rising homophobia throughout the 1980s was paralleled in the UK. The British Social Attitude Survey shows that in 1983 (the first year the question was asked) 49.5 per cent of the population said that homosexuality was always wrong. However, that number climbed to 63.6 per cent in 1987, and when one adds in those who thought it was only sometimes or mostly wrong, we have 83 per cent of the British population maintaining negativity toward homosexuality. In other words, 1987 or 1988 seems to be the apex of homophobia in both countries. Today, Britain has progressed much more rapidly than the US: in 2010 in the UK only 20 per cent of British citizens thought that homosexuality was always wrong, while in the US it was 43.5 per cent. Yet when one looks at Americans aged 18–29, that figure falls to 26 per cent. Finally, when discussing this data, we should be clear to remember that we don't really know what people are thinking when they answer these questions. They may, for example, be interpreting the question as "Is it always wrong for me?" If one is heterosexual, the answer to this might be "yes" without intending to imply homophobia.

The point is that the growth in homohysteria in Western societies occurred simultaneous to the awareness of homosexuality. AIDS severely elevated homohysteria because scores of dying gay men proved how ubiquitous gay men were. And, as almost everyone knew that homosexuality now existed, heterosexual men felt compelled to distance themselves from the highly stigmatized homosexual identity. Homohysteria therefore remained at its all-time-high during this period, and gender signs coded as "feminine" consequently edged toward extinction among men. Thus, the 1980s created a social culture in which men were socially compelled to publicly align their social identities with heterosexuality in order to avoid homosexual suspicion. Much of this included males participating in competitive, aggressive team sports.

Accordingly, it is between the years 1983 and 1993, I argue, that boys in Western cultures needed to, more than ever, use masculine sports in order to prove their heteromasculinity. It is for this reason that the research from this period (i.e., Pronger 1990) shows that American football players were heavily esteemed; it is the jock-ocracy I earlier spoke of.

Finally, homohysteria cannot exist in a culture that is not homophobic. This is because it is homophobia that stigmatizes gay identities and motivates people to distance themselves from it. Without homophobia, boys and men have nothing to fear from being socially perceived as gay.

Inclusive Masculinities of the New Millennium

If AIDS did anything positive for gay men, it is that it started us talking about homosexuality from a "rights" perspective in far greater numbers than gay liberationist campaigns had been successful with before. Then, as the virus later took hold in the heterosexual community, the stigma it brought to those infected slowly began to wane, bringing a further emancipatory call for gays and lesbians. This is not to say that what was now known as HIV/AIDS was not (and is still not) overly-associated with homosexuality, or that it is not still stigmatized, but today we are at least more nuanced in our understanding that it is not caused by homosexuality. As this occurred, social attitudes began to change.

The late 1990s and first decade of the new millennium have seen the political labor of feminist and gay, lesbian, bisexual, and transgender identity politics come to fruition. Sexual and gender minorities have come together under an umbrella of coalition politics not only to promote equality in legislation (i.e., the overturning of sodomy laws and the advancement of gay marriage) but also to erode cultural homophobia.

Attitudes toward homosexuality have significantly improved in recent years. For example, a survey of over 200,000 undergraduates finds that 65 per cent of American freshman support same-sex marriage (Pryor et al. 2011). Most recently, an ABC News/Washington Post opinion poll (Langer 2013) shows support for gay marriage across America is now at 58 per cent, with a net approval rating of 22 per cent. They highlight a shift of 26 percentage points since 2004, and that the number of people who think homosexuality is a choice has decreased from 40 per cent to 24 per cent, while those who think it is "just the way they are" (p. 3) has increased from 49 per cent to 62 per cent. Significant to my research, recent PEW (2013) research also finds that 70 per cent of Millennials (those born after 1990) support same-sex marriage in the US, and 74 per cent of these Americans believe that "homosexuality should be accepted by society."

While more progressive attitudes toward homosexuality are partly due to demographic changes, such as generational replacement and better educational status, the greater change is the result of attitudinal improvement among individuals across the US (Baunach 2012). In a statistical analysis of the General Social Survey data, Keleher & Smith (2012) demonstrate that all demographic groups became more tolerant and, importantly, that they became more tolerant at the same rate. While it is possible that survey research reflects social desirability, this would be evidence of a public perception that homophobic attitudes are stigmatized and would support the argument that a macro-level shift has occurred in relation to attitudes toward homosexuality.

I have advanced my career by examining the changing nature of men's gendered behaviors as homohysteria and homophobia diminish. In studying young men in both the United States and the United Kingdom, I show that today's white, undergraduate men (particularly athletes) are eschewing the homophobic orthodox masculinity of the 1980s. Instead men are establishing homosocial relationships based on (1) increased emotional intimacy, (2) increased physical tactility, and (3) decreased violence and sexism.

In this book, I show that inclusive masculinities are gaining cultural, institutional, and organizational power among middle-class, university-attending heterosexual men but also among lower-class men and men apart from just those who are white. Most of the youth I study are distancing themselves from the corporeal pissing contest of muscularity, hyper-heterosexuality, and masculinity of the1980s, something evidenced through the sexualization of young, thin boys in mainstream culture. One no longer needs to be muscular and violent; one no longer needs to be a teamsport athlete to be popular (McCormack 2011a).

Supporting my thesis, 2013 data from one of the world's largest advertising agencies, JWT (formerly known as J. Walter Thompson Company), of 500 American and 500 British men aged 18 and over shows that men are rapidly losing orthodox notions of masculinity, in multiple arenas (JWT 2013). The report summarizes:

> Conventional ideals about male and female domains, activities, behaviors and styles are evolving: we are moving toward a more nuanced concept of gender that questions some stereotypes and revises old assumptions. Millennials are leading the way, less confined to traditional gender roles and more willing to break long-standing norms to express their individuality. And…[this generation]…is poised to hold the least rigidly defined views of gender as they reach adulthood.

Among their results they find that 75 per cent of men agree with the statement "Men and women don't need to conform to traditional roles and behaviors anymore"; 72 per cent agreed that it was okay for boys to wear pink and for girls to play with trucks; and 78 per cent thought there was as much pressure on guys to take care of their bodies as women. The report suggests that men today are as interested in cooking as cars. Most striking, however, are the differences between men among various ages. For example, when comparing those aged 18–34 with those aged 48–67 the following is found:

	18–34	48–67
Approval of using skin care products	60%	50%
Approval of body hair removal	45%	22%
Wearing foundation	18%	4%
Wearing eyeliner	12%	1%
Wearing pink	39%	26%
Wearing a "man bag"	51%	28%

So what do these 1,000 men suggest makes a man in contemporary society? The most frequent response at 70 per cent is being a "gentle-man" with good manners, and the second and third most frequent are keeping his word, at 65 per cent, and his personal values, at 64 per cent. Indicative of changing masculinity requirements, the next most frequent was intelligence, at 57 per cent. A man's ability to "bond over sports," at 21 per cent, was ranked lower than 15 other variables! Men ranked emotional support for family, parenting, and attractiveness higher. At the bottom of the list was number of sexual conquests, at just 8 per cent.

Data from my dozens of ethnographic studies of heterosexual men in both feminized and masculinized spaces supports this research. After spending the previous decade researching openly gay athletes (Anderson 2011a, 2011b), fraternity men (Anderson 2008b), soccer (A. Adams et al. 2010) and soccer players (Adams & Anderson 2012; Anderson & Adams 2011; Magrath et al. 2013), cheerleaders (Anderson 2005b, 2008b, 2008c), rugby men (Anderson & McGuire 2010; McCormack & Anderson 2010b), and a host of other groups of university-aged men (Anderson et al. 2012a, 2012b), on both sides of the Atlantic, the evidence suggests that inclusive masculinities are increasingly dominant among adolescent youth (McCormack 2012a), and that the homophobia, misogyny, violence, and homosocial separation associated with orthodox masculinity is increasingly unfashionable (McCormack 2012a; McCormack & Anderson 2010a).

Collectively, this research suggests that we at least need to be measured in our claims when we generalize about the orthodox nature of undergraduates and university athletes in Anglo-American cultures. To portray them as old-school jocks is not only stereotyping, but likely prejudice.

I do not however claim that inclusive masculinities, of which one characteristic is being free of homohysteria, are completely free of oppression and subordination. A diminished state of homohysteria is not to be mistaken as a gender-utopia. Men categorized as belonging to one archetype of a set of inclusive masculinities might still be heterosexist (Ripley et al. 2012); they might still sexually objectify women (Anderson 2008b); and they might still value excessive risk-taking (A. Adams et al. 2010).

My data indicates that in the process of inclusive masculinities proliferating, gender itself, as a constructed binary of opposites, may be somewhat eroding. I argue that the efforts of the first, second, and now third wave of feminism—combined with the gay liberationists and gay assimilationist efforts of the past four decades—slowly withered it. Increasingly, gender is the business of decreasing polarization, at least for white undergraduate men.

This has socio-positive implications for the tolerance of gay men as well. Many of the long-held codes, behaviors, and other symbols of what separates masculine men from feminized men (who were therefore homosexualized) are blurring, making behaviors and attitudes increasingly problematic to describe as masculine, feminine, and thus gay or straight. Yesterday's rules no longer seem to apply. The codes of gay are increasingly adopted by heterosexuals, and therefore become meaningless as symbols of sexuality.

Part II
21st Century Jocks
and Inclusivity

3

Including Gay Teammates

I purposefully chose to lead into the results of this book with a chapter on gay male athletes. This is intentional, as it highlights that there are now a great number of openly gay male teamsport and individual sport athletes playing in our high school, university, and community leagues. Their mere presence beckons a fundamental question: does one need to be heterosexual to be a jock today? No, I suggest, one does not. Whereas being a jock used to be predicated upon extreme homophobia, the existence of openly gay jocks must therefore highlight that they feel comfortable enough with their straight-jock teammates to come out.

This chapter reports on the findings from interviews with 26 openly gay male athletes who came out between 2008 and 2010. I then compare their experiences to those of 26 gay male athletes who came out between 2000 and 2002, showing that the athletes in the 2010 cohort have better experiences after coming out, experiencing less heterosexism and maintaining better support among their teammates. I place these results in the context of inclusive masculinity theory, suggesting that local cultures of decreased homophobia created more positive experiences for the 2010 group.

I add to this data my experience of having been in the field conducting ethnography on three separate teams when an athlete came out of the closet. This gave me the opportunity to study coming out on teams "in the moment" instead of relying on recall. Here, I highlight how an athlete's coming out bonds the team closer together; that either the gay athletes I studied are jocks on equal standing, or nobody is a jock.

Collectively, the results of this chapter suggest that young gay male athletes are coming out and having successful experiences in sport. In fact, not one of the over 120 gay male athletes I have interviewed in the previous decade has had what can be considered a troubling experience. Quite the opposite, most are thriving on their teams. This is because their fellow heterosexual jocks are un-bothered, and oftentimes quite delighted, to include gay men as teammates.

Gay Men in Old-School Competitive Sport

Competitive sport is traditionally a social institution which has been principally organized around the political project of defining certain forms of masculinity as acceptable, while denigrating other forms of masculinity (Anderson & McCormack 2010a, 2010b). Sports traditionally associated boys and men with masculine dominance by constructing their identities and sculpting their bodies to align with hegemonic perspectives of masculinist embodiment and expression. Boys in competitive team sports were therefore constructed to exhibit, value, and reproduce traditional notions of masculinity.

Men's homophobia played the central role in an intra-masculine stratification traditionally found among males (Plummer 1999). Accordingly, research in the 20th century has shown that organized, competitive team sports were highly homophobic in Western cultures (Hekma 1998; Pronger 1990). This is because sports, particularly contact sports, maintained an institutional culture in which conservative notions of masculinity were traditionally reproduced and defined: an athlete was thought to represent the ideal of what it means to be a man—a definition predicated in opposition to what it meant to be feminine and/or gay.

However, in 2002, I published the first ever study of openly gay male American athletes in mainstream, educationally-based sports (Anderson 2002). These openly gay athletes were not verbally or physically harassed about their sexuality. However, because I could only find openly gay athletes who were exceptional athletes among their peers—the best on their teams—it appeared that the ability to come out was dependent on maintaining high sporting, and therefore high masculine, capital.

Furthermore, I found very few contact sport athletes to research; most were swimmers, runners, or tennis players. Because I looked extensively for athletes, both on the internet and by sending letters to tens of dozens of college athletic directors, I determined that the atmosphere of individual sports was more conducive for coming out than competitive contact sports. I found that about half of my participants played on a team with a culture of heterosexism: a *don't ask, don't tell* culture in which both the gay athlete and teammates colluded in silencing the voices of gay men.

I had not yet devised inclusive masculinity theory at the time, and thus theorized these results through Connell's (1995) hegemonic masculinity theory (see Chapter 2), while suggesting that the athletes represented a "challenge" to hegemonic masculinity in the sport setting. This is because openly gay athletes were thought to disprove the myth that one had to be straight to excel at competitive sport. I then suggested that openly gay athletes had the potential to aid the erosion of hegemonic masculinity in the sport setting through their success, particularly in team sports.

In the next section, however, I draw upon on interviews conducted almost a decade later, and with a more diverse group of athletes. I explore whether the climate for gay men in sport has changed, and whether these earlier findings still hold.

Updating the Experiences of Gay Men in Sport

In order to understand how things have changed for gay male athletes, I designed research (Anderson 2011b) to involve interviews with a group of openly gay male high school and university athletes that enabled me to compare the findings to those of my original sample of gay athletes collected between 2000 and 2002 (Anderson 2002). By using the same semi-structured interview schedule used in my 2002 study and the same number of interviews, my newer sample should illuminate any differences in experience.

This is a very specific group of gay athletes that I study. They are primarily white; they are known to be openly gay by the other members of their teams; and they were all able to be located—or they located me—through the internet. I collected data from these 26 men between 2008 and 2010. They represent the same racial/class/age demographic of the men I studied in my 2000–2002 research (Anderson 2002).

There are, however, two important differences between these groups. The first is that it took considerably more effort for me to locate the participants of the 2002 group than the 2010 group. With both groups, athletes sometimes contacted me. However, with the second group I found stories of athletes on Outsports.com and used snowball sampling from there. I did not contact athletic directors as I did with the first. It is important to note that, as with the 2002 research, the athletes I interviewed for the 2010 research were either comfortable enough to be on Outsports.com or comfortable enough to contact me. It is therefore probable that this group of participants represent elevated levels of confidence over the average openly gay athlete.

As with my previous research I did not include athletes from recreational or club-level sporting teams, athletes who identified as heterosexual or bisexual, or athletes who identified as being heterosexual but have sex with men. Also, because this research is on the experience of openly gay male athletes, I excluded closeted gay male athletes from this sample. Athletes self-identified as gay, and I judged them to be out of the closet on their teams if they had explicitly told most of the members of their team, or if team members had knowledge about their sexuality from some other source. This too is consistent with the previous research. I only included interviews of athletes if they were actively playing, or if they had played within the previous year. Finally, as with my original study on gay athletes, I limited the sample of high school athletes to those over the age of 18.

Coming Out in Sport

Neil is an openly gay soccer player at a small, Catholic college in a rural Midwestern state. "My teammates are very supportive," he said:

> I think it's good that we played together for a long time. So they got to know me before I came out. But they have been amazing. Absolutely nothing has changed since I came out...I should have come out earlier.

Like Neil, none of the other athletes I interviewed had any substantial difficulties on their teams after coming out as gay. Just as with my first study of openly gay male teamsports athletes, no gay athlete I interviewed was physically assaulted, bullied, or harassed by teammates or coaches.

Much of the internal turmoil and anxiety that I found with the 2002 athletes is absent from the 2010 men's narratives. Athletes in the 2010 group came out without the same struggle over whether they thought it would be appropriate or disadvantageous for them. For example Tom, a high school runner, had no real fear in coming out to his teammates. "I knew it wouldn't be a problem. Why would it be?" When I expressed to him that athletes did not always think that way, he replied:

> There are at least a dozen openly gay kids at my school. None of them have problems, and so I knew I wouldn't either. It just doesn't

make sense to be homophobic today, everybody has gay friends. You might as well be racist if you're going to be homophobic.

Charlie, a college soccer player in California, came out through a different mechanism: he was never in the closet. "It's hard to say how they found out I was gay," Charlie said, referring to his teammates:

> It said that I like men and women on my Facebook profile, but I think it was the first week [of college] when I was making out with a guy at a party. I've never bothered to be anything other than out. And nobody, I mean nobody, has cared.

Like these men, most of the athletes I interviewed did not expect that there would be homophobia from their teammates. Neil said that his teammates were "an excellent group of guys" and that he did not expect that any of them would have a problem with his coming out. "None. No. I knew they would be fine with it."

These narratives reflect a different experience than the narratives of the men in my 2002 research, where I found athletes sometimes viewed their sports as being highly homophobic social spaces. In my 2002 research, most (but not all) of the athletes I interviewed feared violence, bullying, discrimination, and/or harassment from their teammates. Some of this was because they had heard their teammates discussing homosexuality negatively. With the 2010 group, however, none expected bullying, harassment, discrimination, or violence. This, they suggested, was because their peers were not overtly homophobic, both inside and outside of sport. When I asked Neil if he ever heard his teammates speaking negatively of gay men, he answered, "No. Never. Not before or after I came out." However, this result might also partially reflect the bias of a more confident group of men. Unlike in my previous research, these are young men who found me, as opposed to me finding them.

In the 2002 research all athletes heard frequent use of the word "fag" and phrases such as "that's so gay." However, athletes in the 2010 study heard these less often and many athletes reported that these words and phrases were not used at all. Furthermore, athletes in the 2010 research who did hear such language interpreted it differently. In 2002, I determined that half of the athletes judged levels of homophobia on their teams through the amount of homophobic language their teammates used. This half of the 2002 sample suggested that the term "that's gay" and the use of the word "fag" were indicative of homophobic attitudes among those who used them; the other half argued that this was not the case. In the 2010 sample, however, athletes did not judge the level of their teammates' homophobia through the use of this language. Neil explained:

> Gay doesn't mean gay anymore. And fag doesn't mean fag. You can't say that because someone said "that's so gay" or "he's a fag" that they are homophobic. I guess they could be, but you know when someone is using those words as a homophobic insult and when someone's not.

Like Neil, all the players in the 2010 sample who heard use of the words "gay" and "fag" argued that these phrases were not homophobic. Scholars have traditionally argued that athletes view this language as homophobic (Hekma 1998). However, Pascoe (2005) uses the notion of "fag discourse" to understand the use of the word "fag" as a gendered form of homophobia that did not necessarily intend to stigmatize same-sex desire. For example, Pascoe (2005) highlighted that "some boys took pains to say that 'fag' is not about sexuality" (p. 336). Fag discourse conceptualized the use of anti-gay epithets that come from antipathy toward gender non-conformity, not homosexuality. More recently, however, scholars have argued that the reason athletes and others dismiss these terms as homophobic insults is that the social context of this language use has changed (Lalor & Rendle-Short 2007; McCormack 2011c; McCormack & Anderson 2010b). More specifically, the word "gay" has become a homonym; it is a word with two discrete meanings. "That's so gay" describes something disliked, where "gay" means "rubbish" and is independent from usage of "gay" when it refers to sexuality (Lalor & Rendle-Short 2007). It is this conceptualization of language—that I call "gay discourse"—that is supported by athletes in the 2010 cohort. For example, Tom said:

> You hear ["fag"] now and then, but what everybody said is "that's so gay" now…and it has nothing to do with sexuality either. You can't judge homophobia that way. If you do, you'll think everyone is being homophobic, including me…I say "that's so gay" all the time, too. The word has different meanings, and most of the time it's not got anything to do with gay.

What is important here is that the athletes in the 2010 study talk about this use of language qualitatively differently than those from 2002.

Whatever the implicit and insidious effects of this language, the athletes in the 2010 sample are markedly less affected by it. You can read more about the changing nature of discourse related to homosexuality in the next chapter.

Nullifying Athletic Capital

Compared to the 2002 sample, the athletes in the 2010 cohort are more accepted by their teammates, who discussed their sexuality openly. Further, whereas most of the athletes in my 2002 sample had high sporting capital—they were stellar athletes who used their athletic ability to buy resistance against homophobia—the athletes in the 2010 sample did not match this characteristic. Of the 26 men I interviewed, only six reported being among the top athletes on their teams; most described their athletic performances as average.

"I wouldn't say I was the best," Joey said. "I'm a good wrestler, but certainly not the best." John, a university swimmer, maintained that his ability had nothing to do with his positive experience being out: "Maybe being better would be good, but not because I think my teammates would be any cooler with it. I think it would just be more fun." Unlike Joey and John, Mark is one of the top players on his high school ice-hockey team:

> Yeah, I'm good. But that's not why my teammates accept me. They accept me because I'm Mark. I don't think my skills have much to do with it. They liked me before I came out, why wouldn't they like me now?

These attitudes are remarkably different than those I previously documented with the 2002 group. In the previous study, I found athletes only came out once they had achieved a particular standard of ability, and thus importance to the team. While it may be the case that athletic capital matters in homophobic settings, for the men in this particular group it was not a variable of importance. Their positive experiences appear to be largely independent of their athletic abilities.

Cohort Differences in Social Support Networks

The homosocial bond between members of sports teams bridges many arenas of their social lives. Teammates often spend large parts of their days together practicing, attending school, and (in the case of most collegiate and professional athletes) living together, in what I describe as a near-total institution (Anderson 2005a). This has traditionally created a rigid and tightly policed bond between team members in accordance with the mandates of hegemonic masculinity. Accordingly, in my 2002 research, I stressed that, in this narrow social world of hyper-heterosexuality and hyper-masculinity, the presence of an openly gay male athlete creates dissonance where there was once masculine homogeneity. Gay athletes reminded their teams that athleticism did not necessarily imply heterosexuality.

However, the athletes in the 2010 group maintained that being out to one's peers was the same as being out to one's teammates. These athletes suggested that the delineation between friends and teammates was not a factor in their experience of being out; that it was their perception that their teammates were not more homophobic than non-athletes, and that there was not a clique or cluster of homophobic athletes at their school. Thus compared to the earlier group, whose identities were segmented, gay athletes today maintain holistic identities.

Neil found that when he came out, it actually drew him closer to his teammates. However, he did have difficulties with staff (members of Generation X). One of the athletic directors asked him, "Why don't you just choose to be straight?" It was, Neil said, "only adults" who had a hard time with his sexuality.

Grant had support from his friends, too. Yet, like many others, Grant feared coming out to his parents: "My dad is a major homophobe." He added:

> He's always bitching about my gay uncle. He said things like, "Bob is making an issue out of things." He won't say it in person, but after he leaves he does. It's really awkward and uncomfortable...I have to be careful that when my friends come over they don't say anything.

Joey attributed his teammates' silence to their parents. "I don't think they have a problem with it, actually. I think they don't want their parents to know [that Joey is gay] because *they* will have a problem with it!" Referring to the generational divide that I discussed in the opening chapter, there is often a real disconnect between many of these young men and (at least some of) the adults in their lives. John said, "It's a whole different thing coming out to old people. Some will be fine with it I'm sure, but like is it really worth it? They are from a generation who just doesn't get it." Thus, from the perspective of the athletes interviewed in this research, decreasing homophobia is an uneven social phenomenon.

The Influence of Coming Out

Although decreased homohysteria comes via many media, political, and other influential cultural factors, McCann et al. (2009) suggest that among the numerous ways social attitudes toward homosexuality are enhanced is social contact with sexual minorities. They show that when the homosexuality of a friend is revealed, homophobic men are forced to quickly re-evaluate their impressions of someone they had previously viewed positively. In other words, once they understand that a friend is gay, they experience an "awakening of new ideas" which challenges their preconceptions of homosexuality (McCann et al. 2009: 211). This finding is something that I have retrospectively accounted for concerning gay athletes (Anderson 2005a).

Pettigrew (1998) further identifies the importance of contact in reducing prejudice between heterosexuals and homosexuals. He shows that knowing a gay male helps reduce heterosexual prejudice, but that maintaining the ability to speak to him about sex provides a further reduction in personal homophobia. Thus, in my research I show that discussing homosexuality with teammates is useful in reducing sexual stigma about homosexuality. This is something that was greatly improved in the 2011 study on gay male athletes on ostensibly heterosexual male teams.

The improved experience of those in the 2010 cohort compared to those in the 2002 cohort is further evidenced by the manner in which gay athletes discuss homosexuality with their teammates. All but two evaded the culture of *don't ask, don't tell* that I found in half of the athletes I interviewed in my first study. In 2002, athletes reported that teammates simply did not discuss their sexuality; it was as if they did not know that their teammate was gay. Gay athletes often upheld this heteronormative standard through self-silencing—permitting heterosexism to dominate team culture and nullifying a gay identity.

Conversely, men in the 2010 sample told me that their heterosexual teammates discussed their homosexuality openly. Gay athletes were asked about the types of guys they liked, and even asked about which teammates they thought were attractive. "Of course we talk about my sexuality," Mark said. "We talk about it all the time." He added:

I think it's fair to say that I'm known as "the gay hockey player'" at my high school. I'm the only gay athlete who is out, even though I suspect a few more... It's funny, I'll be at a party, and meet someone new and they will be like, "hey, I heard of you. You're the gay hockey player, huh?"

I asked Mark what type of reception he received after having these start-up conversations. "Oh, it's always something positive. Like, 'that's cool, man' or whatever... No. I never have a problem... In fact my teammates will sometimes introduce me as their gay friend."

However, Joey, who is an openly gay wrestler at his high school in a state known for its Mormon religious conservatism, said that while he has no difficulties, even with his fundamentalist teammates, they do not all talk about his sexuality. "Yeah, they all know. It's just not a big deal." But Joey added:

> I try not to make a big deal about it...there are a lot of [religious guys] on my team, and they never say anything about it, but at the same time I try not to put it in their faces... Other guys on the team talk about it, but I just think that it's an interesting mix of people on the team. So yeah, some of the guys talk about it with me, and like sometimes we make jokes when practicing, but the [religious] guys don't so much.

I asked Joey if there are ever difficulties when the more conservative boys have to wrestle with him in practice. "No," he said. "They just wrestle me. It's not an issue, really. They are still my friends, we still hang out together after practice, but we don't really discuss my sexuality much." Joey's statement reflects the type of *don't ask, don't tell* narratives that existed among half of the men in my 2002 research.

However, among these men Joey's statement is an outlier; the rest *did* talk about their sexualities to their teammates. Tim, for example, said that his swimming teammates often joke about his sexuality:

> They love it. I mean do you have any idea how much shit I get for it? Not like bad stuff, I mean, it's always guys pretending to be interested in fucking me, or guys bending over in front of me. That sort of thing. They laugh, I laugh. Everybody just has fun with it. It's like, we joke about it, daily.

I wondered whether this repartee might also be a method for venting internalized homophobia. I therefore asked Tim if they had more serious conversations about his sexuality. "Not serious," he said. "Not like, 'oh man, you're gay, wow, that's serious.' But yes, we talk about it." I asked him for an example:

> We were driving to an away meet once, and the entire time we were talking about what makes people gay and stuff like that...the guys

thought it was cool that I was so open with it and we just talked about it for like an hour... We talked like that at other times, too. Like we have talked about it so much that when others ask [non-teammates], like my teammates can just carry on answering for me. They got it down; like little gay ambassadors or something.

At the time of interview, Chris was an NCAA Division I American football player at a university in the American South, which highly esteems American football culture. He told me that he is out to his teammates, his coach, and friends in college. Not only is he accepted by the players, and not only do they discuss his sexuality with him, but they symbolically show their acceptance through touch as well, hugging him and giving him high-fives as they do other players:

One time I told one of my teammates [about being gay], and I was sort of on the fence about whether he'd accept it or not...anyhow, so I told him in [restaurant] and there are like students everywhere. I said, "I'm gay," and he paused just a second and then got up, came to my side of the table, gave me a big hug and said, "you're my boy. End of story." Like ever since then he gives me longer hugs than others. It's just his way of showing love I guess.

Today, a few years after writing about "Chris" he can be recognized by his true name, Alan Gendreau. He is trying to become the National Football League's first openly gay player by trying out as a placekicker and a Google search will reveal some good stories about him.

First-Hand Experiences of Athletes Coming Out

As an ethnographer of sport, I have now been fortunate enough three times for an athlete to come out during the period that I was conducting research on a team. This is a novel situation, and it permits me to measure a team's attitude toward homosexuality before and after one of their players comes out. In this section I discuss the outing of Brent, a university soccer player.

During this ethnography of a Catholic college's soccer team in the American Midwest, Adi Adams and I had interviewed six men before Brent came out to his team. When discussing homosexuality (among other topics), three of the men thought all of their teammates would accept a gay athlete, while the other three suggested a gay athlete might not be accepted by *all* members of the team. They could not, though, name any particular player they thought might have difficulty with a gay teammate. Furthermore, they all maintained that they would have no difficulty with a gay teammate themselves. This is known as the "third-person effect." Everybody on a team is gay friendly but suspects someone else will not be.

Although two of the members of this team said that showering situations might be awkward, they did not consider this particularly troubling. Tom said, "It might be strange in the locker room, but I think you'd get used to it pretty quick." Jason added, "Like anything new, it would definitely throw you off a little. Maybe some people would struggle with it more than others. But we all adapt, that's part of being a team." Howie agreed, "It might be a little awkward at first, but I'd get over it."

None of these six players said they would blame a gay teammate for *making* them feel awkward. Instead, they suggested that they would need to overcome their personal discomfort. Tom said, "Besides if he's been closeted, he may have been checking us out already." Mark added:

> I can say to you as much as I want that it wouldn't bother me one bit, and it wouldn't in the sense that I'm not at all homophobic, but I've never had that situation...so I know it would be on my mind. But it would just be something that I, personally, had to get over.

Finally, these six athletes also argued that an openly gay player would not negatively impact upon the team's level of cohesion. "No," Tom speculated. "Why would it lower morale? A friend is a friend, regardless of his sexuality."

However, none of this inclusivity stemmed from suspicion that there was a gay player on the team. During the first two days of observations, none asked me if Brent was gay. In fact, on the second night, while sitting around a board game with eight players, Max, a freshman, was asking Brent about his trip to Amsterdam. "Did you pay for pussy?" he asked, referencing the legal trade of heterosexual prostitution in Amsterdam. Brent simply answered, "No."

Brent said that this is how he normally manages his sexuality; by offering short, direct answers that do not reveal his sexuality. It is a tactic which permits him to be heterosexualized by the heterosexist standards of his teammates. Brent's strategy seemed to work, as players were surprised to learn that he was gay.

Brent determined that he would prefer to out himself to several of the seniors first, and that I should out him to the others. Thus, Brent outed himself to a number of close teammates on the third day of our research. He received favorable responses from all. For the younger players, I determined that it would be best for one of my research colleagues (who is heterosexual) to out Brent (to reduce researcher effect).

While talking about homosexuality with Ben, the heterosexual researcher (Adi Adams) asked, "How do you feel about the fact that Brent is gay?" Ben responded, "Brent is gay? You serious?" After receiving confirmation, Ben said, "That's cool. I just had no idea, that's all." And when talking in Tom's room that same night, the same question evoked, "What? Brent's gay?... That's fucking awesome."

In the evening, I outed Brent to Max. Referring to the discussion about Amsterdam, I said, "I thought it was funny you asked a gay guy if he paid for pussy." He responded, "Wait, you're saying Brent is gay?" "Yeah," I answered. "Oh. I didn't know that. Well, shit, I feel bad now." Max clarified, "It's no big deal. I just didn't know."

It therefore appears that the acceptance of homosexuality documented on this team is less attributable to researcher effect and more accurately reflects a majority position of positive attitudes toward gay men before we came to the team. In order to examine for this, my research assistant and I inquired about exposure and attitudes toward homosexuality in the interviews of remaining players.

All but three of the men knew a gay male before the start of this research. Most maintained informal relationships with gay men, but some had strong friendships, too. The common narrative was that most had a friend or family member who is gay, and they used this association to learn and then express a degree of social inclusion. Men talked about gay uncles, friends, neighbors, etc. While most reported never being homophobic, a few expressed that they learned to work through homophobia after meeting a gay man. What these men had not known, however, was a gay male teammate.

The Influence of Open Communication

As mentioned above, teammates often live within what I call a near-total institution. This is to say that they train together, live together, travel together, and party together. Accordingly, they grow emotionally close to each other. Thus, men on teams generally feel free to discuss homosexuality (in-depth) with openly gay male athletes. When discussing Brent, John said:

> I've known gay guys, yeah; but Brent is the first one that's part of my core of friends...we spend lots of time talking about all types of deep or personal things...and now I can ask him stuff I've never been able to ask other gay guys.

Steve states matters more bluntly:

> I've always wondered whether it feels good to be fucked. I asked, and now I know. I asked Brent all kinds of stuff about gay sex. It's cool, it's totally different than what you'd talk to your straight friends about; but then again it's really not different.

While most of the 22 heterosexual men on Brent's team had some previous contact with gay men (and while their coach is a pro-gay Catholic priest), most players have not had the opportunity to ask detailed questions about homosexuality. Tim said, "My uncle is gay, yes. But you can't just talk to your uncle about what anal sex feels like, can you?" Similarly, participants found talking to us about matters of sex to be of value. For example, Howie said to my graduate student, Adi, "When Eric said he was gay, we were like, alright, whatever, that's cool. I think we talked about it [homosexuality] more those few days because Eric was around. And then Brent came out, so now it's here on our doorstep." Howie added, "And now we've had even more chances to talk about homosexuality with gay men, so I think people are just even more comfortable with it." Ed said, "I wasn't homophobic before I knew Brent was gay. But knowing him has made me pretty positive about gay stuff." And when Ed is asked how knowing Brent is gay has specifically facilitated this, he answered:

> We've spent the last few nights just lying on the couch talking about sex and about what it was like being closeted...I've grown to understand things from his perspective... Hell, I can even tell you what kind of guys he's attracted to now. I think the more you understand something, the more you accept it.

Also reflecting on his new-found sensitivity to Brent's homosexuality, Scott said, "We were walking between classes yesterday and I just knew Brent was checking out a guy, and I just said, 'Yep, I saw him, too.'"

David is another player that is close to Brent. When asked about how his friendship with Brent has been influenced by his coming out, he said, "Yeah, Brent is great. I mean, you can talk to him about anything, and I learned a lot about homosexuality from him already. I think his coming out has really bonded us. We're great friends." Mike added:

> We've both been here for four years, and I've always considered him a good friend. Things are the same as they were before I found

out that he was gay, but now he can be more honest. I think that's real cool.

Mike also suggested that his perspectives on sexuality had evolved during the research period. "Talking with you [Eric] about this stuff has been awesome. I never really had anyone to talk to about that kind of stuff before." And when asked if talking about homosexuality has made him feel more endeared to Brent, he said, "Absolutely, it's like he's told us this, and he didn't have to. I just love him even more now."

Similarly, Jason recognized the potential influence that social contact with both homosexual men and pro-gay men can have, not only in reducing prejudice, but in further facilitating their existing tolerance and acceptance of homosexuality:

I think people would be more open to homosexuality if they were around it more. It would open their eyes; make people a little more open to the possibilities...I mean, most of the guys here [on the team] knew gay people before they came here [to college], so we are pretty cool with it...but now Brent is gay, I mean now we *know* he's gay and we know him personally and stuff, and this whole thing [the research] has brought that to our attention. I think it's opened up our eyes to new levels of openness beyond how open we thought we were.

Danny added:

I wanted to know what he [Brent] thought, being gay and all. Maybe I'm ignorant, but I asked him if it was a choice, not that that was what I believed. I just wanted to hear it from him, so I spoke to him about it a little bit. He said he knew from a young age and that he didn't just *turn* gay. It's not conclusive, but when you hear it from a gay guy directly it's gotta tell you something.

It is also significant that these men often ended discussions about the origins of homosexuality with a statement of indifference. We often heard them remark that it makes no difference what made one gay. One said, "I wouldn't treat him differently," and another asked, "Does it matter?" Trent said:

It didn't matter to me if someone was gay before I met you guys; people are what they are. But I guess Brent is the first gay guy who

I would call a true friend, and talking with you guys about this stuff has really been cool. I understand things so much better now. I feel like I can tell you guys anything.

Thus, the combination of Brent coming out publicly alongside an openly gay researcher in the field provided these players with the opportunity to partake in sexualized conversations: the type of conversations they had not been able to have in an ostensibly heterosexual, homosocial environment. The event of Brent's coming out to the team encouraged teammates to talk about their own sexual and gendered experiences, and their social experiences of other gay men they had previously met. It is also evidence of the problems of a culture where homosexuality is not discussed.

Challenging *Don't Ask, Don't Tell*

In addition to finding that these participants maintained pro-gay attitudes prior to our arrival, and that discussing homosexuality with gay men further enlightened their views on homosexuality, once Brent came out to his teammates there was an immediate change to the once heteronormative discourse used by the team. As noted earlier, my 2002 research found that about half of gay athletes existed within a *don't ask, don't tell* culture, where gay athletes and their teammates silently agreed upon a culture in which none spoke of the gay player's sexuality. Inclusive language was therefore not part of the team's communication style under *don't ask, don't tell*. However, coming out publicly, and discussing homosexuality openly, seems to have warded off a *don't ask, don't tell* policy with Brent's team.

Exemplifying the efforts of these players to discursively integrate Brent's sexuality into their conversations, while driving home from a match Drew talked about how he thought a few of the female soccer players, who played on the field adjacent to them, were attractive. He immediately followed this statement by asking Brent, "Did you find any of the guys hot?" Brent answered, "Yeah, a few...I thought number nine was hot."

Another time the men determined they should not go to the normal dance club they frequent, because there was no gay club in the same area for Brent. Instead, we drove to a different venue, so that Brent, myself, and a few of the players could visit the gay club. Furthermore, when players were asked if they would support Brent's (hypothetically) bringing a boyfriend to a match, none voiced concern. Conversely, at one of the three games we observed, players introduced their parents to a gay researcher with positive language, thus inculcating homosexuality in an inclusive manner: "This is Eric, and he's doing a study on Brent's coming out."

Coming Out on a Team with a Highly Homophobic Coach

It is fair to say that most gay male athletes do not come out of the closet, publicly, if they exist on teams that have highly homophobic coaches. In all of my research on the topic, I show that the athletes take into consideration the attitudes of their coach before making their decisions about coming out. Sometimes they value their sport more than their freedom of sexuality expression, and choose to remain closeted, and other times they quit. Michael (2013) shows us a case of a high school wrestling team in which all of the players were gay friendly, as were two assistant coaches, but the head coaches was highly homophobic.

The solution to their difference in perspective on homosexuality was complicated by the fact that high school wrestlers are often homosexualized, because their sport involves a great deal of intimate personal contact with other males. Thus, the players had two driving forces for reasons to espouse homophobia: (1) to prove to their peers that they were not gay; and (2) to align their perspectives with the head coach, who has destiny over their playing careers. Yet, they did not. Instead, they framed wrestling as an aggressive sport of "war," a hyper-masculine venture that only the brave partake in, regardless of sexual orientation. They included their gay teammate and friend, and only asked of him not to sexualize the sport—i.e., to make comments about the attractiveness of his teammates that he was in close physical contact with. Apart from this, there was no isolation of the teammate. This rich ethnography thus highlights the power of the inclusive culture toward homosexuality that these youths inhabit.

Decreasing Need for Open Communication in Reducing Homophobia

During the summer of 2012 and again in 2013, I conducted a three-month long ethnography on a high school running team in Southern California. I had run with this team twice before, once in the fall and again in the spring. It was during my first of the three bouts of ethnography that I met Jordan, a top-notch varsity runner. Having helped coach his team, I grew to know Jordan, an aspiring model, quite well. I did not know it at the time, but Jordan was closeted.

Before I returned to Southern California in the spring of 2012 to run with the team for another few weeks, Jordan came out to me on Facebook. While I doubted this at first, I soon realized that he was being honest. I began mentoring Jordan in the coming out process, and because he was 18, promised to introduce him to the gay world of clubbing when I returned.

A week into my return to Southern California, Jordan determined that he was ready to come out to his team. I asked to be present, directly in some cases, and within vicinity to hear but without my presence necessarily noticed, for others. This was exciting: unlike Brent, Jordan wanted to do the outing himself, and this gave me the opportunity to observe.

I observed as Jordan told his coach, "Coach, there is something I want to tell you. I'm gay." The coach responded, "That's cool," and then began to talk to Jordan about the day's workout. A few days later I watched Jordan come out, individually, to the rest of his varsity team as they arrived for dinner the night before a race. Here, Jordan said, "Hey, Max, I just want to tell you I'm gay." His teammates' responses ranged from, "Oh, I didn't know that," to, "Wait. What?"

What was fascinating to me as a researcher however is that none of the athletes needed or wanted to talk about his sexuality. This was seemingly not because they wanted to deny, suppress, or hide it. This is because they had known so many other gay male friends, including me, that they had already asked all the questions about it.

The following summer, I returned to run with the team again. One day while stretching, Jordan and I were engaging in banter in front of the rest of the team. The night before we had been out to a gay club, and I was making fun of the way he danced. I then remarked to the other 40 athletes on the team that together Jordan and I would give gay dance lessons to the rest of the team. To this, one of the 15-year-old freshman quipped, "I think Kenneth would do a better job." I took this as banter, a "burn" to insinuate that Kenneth was gay, when he was not. It was only in running with Kenneth later that I asked him if he was bothered by the insinuation that he was gay, to which he responded, "Well, I am gay."

This was a striking revelation for me. Kenneth had been out of the closet to his teammates, but there was such division between the freshmen and sophomores (years one and two), compared to the juniors and seniors (years three and four), the first group did not know that Jordan was gay and the second did not know that Kenneth was gay. In my previous research, the outing of a gay male was so novel it became gossip—spreading rapidly across teams and schools. Today, however, openly gay males are increasingly common in school settings. This means that having an openly gay male on a school-based sport team (as most sport teams in the US are) is also less novel. Increasingly, when athletes come out to their teams, they are met with some version of "so what?" This is not a begrudging form of acceptance; instead, it might suggest total acceptance (see also McCormack 2012b; Riley 2010). Evidencing this, when I asked Kenneth why he didn't tell me before he answered, "I don't know. It's not really a big deal I guess."

Apparently it is not that big a deal. When I returned to run with this same team in 2013, another bisexual male joined the team, another gay male came out who ran on the team a year prior, and when I said to another student, in front of a few teammates on a run, "You've never declared a sexual orientation to me, so I don't want to assume, but do you have a girlfriend?" He replied, "No. I don't. I am not bothered by that though, I'm only a sophomore. And I don't care who comes along, a girl or boy."

Openly Gay Men in Professional Sport

Thus far, this chapter has identified the social and historical contexts of how sexualities and masculinities have been traditionally perceived and their cultural shift in contemporary society. Highlighting the shift of increasingly positive and inclusive attitudes of sporting teams, it can be argued that sport is no longer overtly, and perhaps even covertly, a homophobic culture. At the professional level, this is perhaps best exemplified by the different reactions faced by openly gay English soccer player Justin Fashanu and openly gay players Anton Hysen (who came out in 2011) and Robbie Rogers (who came out in 2013).

In 1990, Fashanu came out as a premiership player in the UK, and was harassed and bullied by his family, teammates, and fans. His mistreatment was so awful that it is generally accepted it was a contributing factor to his suicide a few years later. However, when one compares that with Anton Hysen (Europe) and Robbie Rogers (who plays for the LA Galaxy) the improvement to soccer culture is evident. Both of these players were celebrated and supported: by their teammates, the media, and fans. Add to this the accepting attitudes of both contemporary British soccer fans (Cashmore & Cleland 2012), and young professional soccer players telling me that they would have no issues with an openly gay male athlete coming out on their team (Roberts et al. 2014), and the variance in culture over those 20 years is evident.

Nevertheless, one of the continuing issues in Europe is the lack of openly gay professional soccer players. This is a similar issue in the top four American sport leagues (American football, baseball, basketball, and ice hockey). At the writing of this book, using game-day rosters as the criteria, there are 3,496 men in the four major North American sporting leagues: National Football League (NFL, 32 teams, 53 players in each team); Major League Baseball (MLB, 30, 25); National Basketball Association (NBA, 30, 12); and National Hockey League (NHL, 30, 23). Assuming the proportion of gay athletes is similar to the proportion in the general population, and using a conservative measure of 2.8 per cent (Laumann 1994), we should observe approximately 100 gay men at this level of sport. Yet in 2013 there is only Jason Collins—who came out at the end of the previous basketball season as an old, failing NBA player—and as of the final writing of this book has played for ten days with the Brooklyn Nets. Furthermore, openly gay American Football player Michael Sam looks posed to be drafted into next season's NFL.

Over the previous 40 years, these leagues have had another nine men who are publicly known to be gay: six in American football (Jerry Smith, David Kopay, Roy Simmons, Esura Tuaolo, Wade Davis, and Kwame Harris); two in baseball (Glenn Burke and Billie Bean); and one in basketball (John Amaechi) (Kian & Anderson 2009). There have been none in hockey. Burke appears to have been out of the closet during his career in the late 1970s. Smith died of AIDS without ever publicly declaring his sexuality, though it was confirmed by Kopay. Harris was recently revealed to be gay by public court documents stemming from a domestic assault trial. The remaining players came out voluntarily after retirement. Matters are only slightly better in the UK: Gareth Thomas came out in rugby before retiring, as did Stephen Davies in cricket.

These (American) figures indicate that only about 0.03 per cent of professional contracts have been signed by men known to be gay. Similar patterns hold for major European soccer leagues and, perhaps surprisingly, even other individual sports such as tennis and boxing. In all cases, we know of exceptionally few gay athletes. This value, 0.03 per cent, is significantly lower than homosexuality estimates in the general population, which average about 2.8 per cent. No statistical techniques are needed to confidently assert that this is more than sampling error. An explanation is warranted.

I have previously (Anderson 2005a) highlighted multiple rationales for the lack of openly gay athletes in professional sport: (1) gay men in these leagues remain silent about their sexuality—the "silence" hypothesis; (2) gay men choose not to play sports—the "non-participation" hypothesis; (3) gay men are less likely than straight men to achieve professional status—the "selection" hypothesis. Ogawa (2014) combines the second and third hypotheses as the "non-existence" hypothesis, as both imply a non-existence of gay male athletes.

Due to a small number of gay athletes coming out previously, the silence hypothesis is often the most assumed explanation for more openly gay athletes not coming out. In soccer, Cashmore & Cleland (2011) describe this as "a culture of secrecy" (p. 421). Ogawa (2014), however, maintains that the aforementioned silence hypothesis is "an untenable way of understanding the silence among *all* athletes." He suggests that gay men might just not be physically demonstrative enough to play sport at the professional level of combative sports. He doesn't discount that some gay men are capable of playing at the elite level, but he suggests that at the tail end of a muscular/athletic distribution, a small biological difference can exaggerate the effect.

I, however, take a more balanced perspective (Anderson 2005a). I suggest that the absence of the openly gay athlete at the professional levels of most all team sports exists because of a variety of reasons. Evidencing this, I suggest that many gay men are not interested in these types of macho sports. And once gay men come out in sport (at younger ages) they tend to drop out (Anderson 2005a; Hekma 1998). I suggested that this is because they find a life of gay friends, clubbing, and sex more appealing than sport.

While it is possible that there is "some" truth to the fact that gay men are morphologically differentiated from straight men (Bailey 2003), this effect should represent itself mostly in sports like American football, which requires extreme strength; but soccer players are required to be athletic: they must possess sprinting speed, but also endurance; they must be strong, but not too muscular. It is for this reason that I suggest the absence of the gay male athlete in soccer comes down to self-deselection and the silence hypothesis.

First, athletes predicate their master identities as that of sportsmen. Athletes live together, go to school together, train, travel, and compete together. Coming out to even gay-friendly teammates is difficult when one is different than the others. Athletes fear that their difference will interrupt the homosocial camaraderie, that they will be treated differently. Also, athletes know that while their teammates might be "true friends" they are also competition for selection to the next level of play in a rapidly decreasing opportunity structure. Athletes therefore perceive any difference, or distraction, as possibly impeding their progress.

Athletes are also afraid to come out of the closet because of the age of the gatekeepers of their sport. Older men, those whose adolescence was in the 1980s or earlier, serve as their managers: when stakes are high, one over-conforms to norms in order to be selected. In other words, one must not only play well, but must exhibit all of the other emotional and personal characteristics that the coaches desire if one is to be selected for the next level of play: Athletes fear that coming out will result in deselection.

Finally, gay men do come out at the professional level of sport. They oftentimes are out to their close teammates without choosing to come out publicly to the media (Anderson 2005a). Just because the media is not aware of one's sexuality does not mean that one is not gay, very much like Alan Gendreau was out to his entire NCAA Division I American football team in the deep American South, but did not come out to the media about it until after graduating. Another example of this comes from American football player Kwame Harris, who was recently outed after he was arrested for physically assaulting his boyfriend.

Collectively, however, before we begin to see more athletes coming out of the closet, we need to see a generation of young men who have grown up with inclusive attitudes toward homosexuality take to the seats of power within sport. Exemplifying a generational divide on this issue, following the award of the 2022 World Cup to Qatar, FIFA President Sepp Blatter claimed that due to the illegality of homosexuality in Arabic states, gay athletes and fans should abstain from any sexual activity. His sentiment seems reasonable to him, yet unthinkable to today's emerging players.

Chapter Conclusion

In this chapter I showed that the basic qualifying definition of what it meant to be a jock in the 1980s, homophobia, is no longer the case today. I showed that openly gay male athletes are, at the high school and collegiate level, playing sport; and that there is a slow opening up of professional athletes coming out of the closet as well. I compared the findings from my 2002 research on gay male athletes with the experiences of gay male athletes I interviewed in 2008–2010 to show that the latter (who represent the same class and racial demographic) did not fear coming out in the same way or to the same degree as the 2002 athletes. Unlike the men from the 2002 study, they did not fear that their coming out would result in physical hostility, marginalization, or social exclusion (either on or off the field).

Athletes in the 2010 cohort were also a more diverse group; they play American football, rugby, hockey, lacrosse, and wrestling. This is perhaps a result of my sampling procedures, but it might also indicate decreasing homophobia among teamsports athletes in the local cultures where these particular athletes reside. This latter proposition is supported by recent quantitative research showing no difference in attitudes between individual sports athletes and teamsports players on quantitative measures of homophobia in one university setting in the United Kingdom (Bush et al. 2012).

Another significant finding from my research is that openly gay athletes today evade cultures of *don't ask, don't tell* that characterized the experiences of athletes in the 2002 cohort. For example, in 2002 (p. 874) I argued:

> In the absence of the ability to ban openly gay athletes from sport, heterosexual athletes within team sports, both contact and non-contact, resisted the intrusion of openly gay athletes through the creation of a culture of silence around gay identities. Although publicly out, the informants in this study were victimized by heterosexual hegemony and largely maintained a heteronormative framework by self-silencing their speech, and frequently engaged in heterosexual dialogue with their heterosexual teammates.

Conversely, athletes in the 2010 group found their sexualities accepted among their teammates. Men talked about their sexualities frequently, and none reported that their teammates tried to publicly or privately heterosexualize them.

However, it is important to note that these findings do not suggest that all athletes, in all sports, at all levels or locations, would have equally as supportive coming out experiences as the men in this study. As with my previous study, it is possible that these men evaluated their social situations well enough before coming out, helping insure a positive experience. There is a complex web of variables that most athletes use to make such decisions: team climate, social networks, the attitudes of their coach, as well as a host of other identifiable and unidentifiable factors (Anderson 2005a). Thus, these results speak only to these athletes: men who have made informed choices. It might also reflect that there are more gay-friendly local cultures in the United States and United Kingdom now than previously (e.g., McCormack 2012b). However, not all local cultures are supportive. It is also important to remember that this research reflects a bias toward white, middle-class athletes. There exists no empirical work concerning the influence of class on the experience of openly gay athletes in sport.

Even with these limitations stated, there are important implications of this work for assessing the changing relationship between homosexuality and sport. My research clearly indicates that when gay men come out to their teams, they are not only treated well by their teammates, but they also report—and my ethnographic research examining openly gay athletes before and after they come out to their teammates confirms—that the process of sexual orientation disclosure draws members of a team closer together.

Despite these positive findings, however, openly gay men are not equally represented in sport as they are in the broader culture. This is particularly true of gay male athletes at the professional level of sport. Why this is the case is a matter of conjecture. Nobody can be certain. However, it seems likely that as this generation of inclusive men take positions as gatekeepers (Southall et al. 2009, 2011) more gay athletes will come out.

4
Changing Homophobic Language

This chapter draws on two ethnographic studies to explore the relation-ship between sport and language related to masculinity and homosexu-ality. First, it examines how coaches and players construct and regulate masculinity in organized sport through the use of language. I then examine how homosexually-themed language is reproduced in sport settings. Finally, I examine how these two types of language—about gender and about sexuality—are related in these changing times.

My data for understanding language and masculinity comes from a study of a British soccer team, where my colleagues and I (Adams et al. 2010) examined the role of discourses in the construction and regulation of sporting masculinity. Two predominant discourses were present: masculinity establishing discourse and masculinity challenging discourse. I describe these as tools for understanding the use of toxic language in the construction and maintenance of masculinity. I show that coaches frequently use discourses that draw on narratives of war, gender, and homosexuality in order to facilitate aggressive and violent responses for enhancing athletic performance. However, my colleagues and I also found that these discourses now have limited influence beyond the playing field, highlighting the segmentation of the sporting and social identities of these players, and a loosening of the traditional and empirically-evidenced ability of sports to socialize men into narrow forms of masculinity.

I then add to this chapter a discussion of other ethnographic research conducted by me and my colleague, Dr Mark McCormack (McCormack & Anderson 2010b). Here, we use one year of participant observation and 12 in-depth interviews with men on a highly-ranked university rugby team in England in order to nuance the theoretical understandings of the re-production of homosexually-themed language in organized sport. Data collected through this ethnographic investigation is used to complicate our understandings of language with a "gay theme," in order to think beyond sometimes simplistic debates about whether language is homophobic or not. Drawing on further research by McCormack (2011c) into this language use, I seek to understand how masculinity establishing and challenging discourses are related to homosexually-themed language.

Masculinity Establishing Discourse

Sport has traditionally served as a vessel for the transmission of homophobic, misogynistic, and femiphobic attitudes across generations, where boys and men are socialized to exhibit toughness, violence, and aggression (Dunning 2002). I suggest that the coaches (members of Generation X) on the British soccer team we investigated perpetuated this orthodox ethos of sport through the use of what my colleagues and I call *masculinity establishing discourse*. Employing this discourse functions to (re) establish soccer as a masculine sport and, through a process of regulating, disciplining, and policing, it (re)defines the perimeters of the toxic behaviors and attitudes that constitute traditional, orthodox notions of masculinity—the traditional jock masculinity.

There are numerous, often overlapping, forms of masculinity establishing discourse. One form is to situate soccer as a sport specifically for men, despite the fact that women play the same game, by the same rules. Highlighting this usage, in the locker room at half-time, one of the coaches shouted to his athletes, "This is a man's game!" He added, "If you haven't got the balls for it, there's a women's team you can play on." The athletes listened to this tirade submissively, with their heads hung low.

While this "man's game" narrative is frequently employed by coaches to chastise athletes, it is also used in less intense emotional moments. For example, the coaches often watched a Premier League football (soccer) match (the elite professional league in England) with their players on the TV in the team's club-house before their own game. One time, a patron who was not a member of the team commented that the referee missed a dangerous and "obvious foul." The coach challenged him, saying, "It's a man's game, mate. There's going to be some contact." Thus, even in informal moments, soccer was presented as a physical and aggressive masculine endeavor.

Not only did the coaches establish soccer as a "man's game," they also suggested the men who play it have to be so masculine that they are "warriors." Ostensibly, this is done to motivate players to be successful on the field. The coaches, for example, frequently asserted that soccer players must maintain what the head coach called "a warrior attitude." This warrior narrative, noted by Jansen & Sabo (1994), established a guideline of on-field masculinity within which orthodox behaviors are framed as desirable. Highlighting the deployment of this discourse, in the initial team meeting, the head coach said:

> There are two things we judge players by. The first is your playing ability, and the second is whether you're a warrior or not. We need players who are willing to spill blood and die for this team. If we go into battle and you are not willing to die, then we'll get you off [the field] quickly.

The establishing of players as warriors was not, however, a one-time opening diatribe of team expectations. Both the head and the two assistant coaches regularly shouted instructions to players that were heavily saturated with references to bodily sacrifice and violent physical acts.

Homophobia, misogyny, and extreme sexual violence pervaded the language that these Generation X coaches used in an attempt to instill the warrior attitude in their players. For example, a coach said, "If this was a war, you'd put a bullet in the cunt's head. But it's not, it's football [soccer], so stick a boot in on him next time." Another coach yelled to his players, "Go out there and dominate them. Bend them over and fuckin' rape them!" In frustration, a coach shouted, "When you get the opportunity you've got to take your chances. Don't fuck it up. Don't be a fucking poof! [an English euphemism for fag]" Another yelled, "You go out there and finish them off! You've got to cut their balls off!"

Thus, my research colleagues and I describe masculinity establishing discourse as the set of practices that constitute soccer as a man's game, and delimit the behaviors that make a player suitable for the game. For these coaches, the warrior attitude included homophobia, misogyny, and violence, positions which (as they communicated from the sidelines) they apparently deemed fundamental to becoming and being a worthy soccer player.

Masculinity Challenging Discourse

The coaches in this ethnographic fieldwork of a soccer team mapped out soccer as a game played by "real men" through masculinity establishing discourse. However, the coaches also regulated players when they failed to live up to these standards. My colleagues and I conceptualize this systematic set of practices as *masculinity challenging discourse*.

Masculinity challenging discourse served as a mechanism for gender and player performance regulation, when coaches felt that their players had not attained the appropriate form of masculinity established for them. For example, during one game's half-time—and with his team trailing by two goals—the head coach focused on one of his players to reprove his "weak" performance:

> You! No bollocks. If you get kicked, you get up and get on with it. You don't go in a sulk and start whining like a little girl. Stand up for yourself, get stuck in and start showing you're a man. Now you've really got to grow some balls because otherwise they'll walk all over you.

As evidenced in this example, the coaches also combined anti-femininity with male genitalia in their masculinity challenging rebukes. Highlighting this, in times of heightened emotion and frustration, it was extremely common to hear coaches say, "Grow some balls," or "What are you, a pussy?" But an even more effective admonition was to question the players' heterosexuality. "What are you, a poof?" the coach screamed, "Cos you're acting like one!"

Observations evidenced that these messages were less frequent than the "man's game" or warrior narratives, as this specific expression of masculinity challenging discourse was not used on a day-to-day basis. However, the players were cognizant of this discourse, even when it was not in immediate use, and there was some predictability in its deployment. Indeed, there was an elevated use of all examples of gendered discourses in competitive games.

Masculinity challenging discourse is also characterized through homophobic, misogynistic, and other insults that question the heteromasculinity of men who stray from the strictures of orthodox masculinity. The coaches deployed it against men whom they felt did not sufficiently embody the orthodox warrior attitude that they considered integral to soccer masculinity. Although the hyper-masculine hyperbole of masculinity establishing discourse seemed ineffectual on its own, the orthodox framework of esteemed masculinity that it constructs allowed the coaches to individually question the masculinity of their players. We do not know, of course, the number of people put off sport because of these discourses circulating more generally.

Two other examples of this discourse deployed by the coaches served to represent the opposition as either hyper-masculine or as feminine.

For example, one coach said, "If you give these fuckers a chance they'll steal your wallet, your car and the next thing you know they'll have your girlfriend, too. Don't let that bunch of cunts take this away from you." However, coaches also (and sometimes simultaneously) questioned the masculinity of their opponents. For example, one coach referred to members of the opposing team as "a bunch of fucking girls."

In these examples, the coaches were challenging their own players' masculinity, and the intent of this strategy was the same: to position players as needing to manage their (orthodox) masculinity. However, the way in which the coaches addressed the gendered position of their opponents functioned to construct the threat from the opposition in different ways. First, to be beaten by girls is to construct masculinity in relation to the feminized action of others, where the risk is a loss of masculinity. Similarly, the threat of having one's girlfriend "stolen" constructs the opposition as alpha-male types. In this example, the action of the opposition is masculinized by the coach's discourse, rendering his own team at risk of losing the trappings of masculinity. Both tactics invoked the players to position themselves on a hegemonic ladder of sorts, where their constant struggle to (re)prove themselves masculine required them to either fend off challenges from below (feminine girls) or to strive to compete with those above (hegemonic alpha-male types).

These examples highlight how the coaches desired that the players constantly prove that they can maintain a hyper-masculine image, since even the most traditionally masculine players were not safe from having their masculinity challenged. Regardless of the level of aggression or violence they had previously shown, a coach could temporarily void a player's masculinity with this type of discourse. The masculinity challenging discourse therefore led to the normalizing of aggressive behaviors, which individuals employed to "defend" themselves in response to challenges to their masculinity, and subsequently reinforced orthodox attitudes and behaviors as group norms established by masculinity establishing discourse.

Athletes' Use of Masculinity Challenging Discourse

Although predominantly used by the coaches, most of the players also employed masculinity challenging discourse. The players used masculinity challenging discourse to question each other's dedication or effort; particularly when their behaviors were deemed detrimental to performance. For example, after a dispute between Max and one of the coaches, Jamie (another player) interrupted the conversation, saying to

Max, "Just be quiet. Be a man. Shut up and stop whining." For many of the players, "being a man" was predicated on accepting the word of the coach without question, and proving one's worth physically on the field. Not conforming to this hyper-masculine gender norm is considered to be letting the team down (Hughes et al. 2001). This is consistent with research which suggests that loyalty to other men (Russell 1999), aggression (Harris & Clayton 2007), and obeying authority (Cushion & Jones 2006) are celebrated by men as characteristics of masculinity in wider soccer culture.

A good example of the utility of masculinity challenging discourse between players occurred during a small-sided game (where members of the same team were divided into two numerically-smaller teams to play against each other). Steve, who was a recipient of a particularly aggressive tackle from Mike, complained to the supervising coach, asking for a free kick to be given in his favor for what he believed to be a foul. Feeling his tackle was legitimate, Mike said, "Fuck off, you poof. I hardly touched you. Get on with it and stop being such a shit-house [an English euphemism for sissy or coward]." Steve responded by shoving Mike and beckoning him to fight. The coach, referring to the day of their next league match, stopped the escalating violence: "Lads, save it for Saturday!"

This example highlights the mechanisms of masculinity challenging discourse, because in order to legitimize his aggressive tactics (and avoid losing a free kick for what he likely knew was an unskilled and inappropriate challenge), Mike relied on the image of the aggressive and violent man; the way his coaches desired. This reframed the argument from one which might address the notion that Mike made a poor challenge, to one which instead cast doubt onto the masculinity and heterosexuality of Steve, who complained about the challenge. Accordingly, the onus was on Steve to prove that his call was legitimate, and was not a sign of masculine weakness. This influenced him to respond with equal (or greater) masculinity challenging discourse and/or threat of physical violence. Accordingly, in this soccer culture, where aggression and violence are often esteemed, failing to react aggressively to this accusation of homosexuality or femininity means that one is more likely to be subordinated in the masculine hierarchy.

Masculinity challenging discourse was also used between players of opposing teams. Standing over an injured opposition player (who was knocked to the ground), Jonathan snarled to his opponent, "You're not so fuckin' tough now are you?" The phrase "Get up you pussy" was also frequently used between opposing players, and use of homonegative language was also common. In one example, after a free kick was awarded to the opposition, and with a player lying on the ground, injured, an opposing player stood over him, once again reframing the argument (in a self-defensive fashion) from one which might address the legality of the challenge to one which both questions the masculinity and integrity of his opponent, saying, "Get up you fuckin' bender [an English euphemism for fag], I didn't even touch you." The referee did not penalize the player for homophobic language.

These examples demonstrate how, by attempting to dominate other men (and challenging their established masculinity) these players built their masculine credit at the expense of opposing players. This highlights that this soccer setting is much more than just an arena in which these men learn masculinity, it is also an arena in which their masculinity is stratified through success and failure, violence and subordination. Those who prevail are not those who work the hardest or maintain the best camaraderie. Instead, they are those who *win*. Conversely, losing (not just losing a game, but losing an individual tackle, "challenge," or "battle") is associated with "softness" and "weakness"; traits thought to be typically synonymous with femininity.

Resistance to Coaches' Discourse

Although warrior narratives maintained some credence with these players, neither masculinity establishing discourse nor masculinity challenging discourse maintained total influence. First, and significantly, athletes frequently ignored their coaches. But the players also actively resisted the masculinity establishing discourses of the coaches, making fun of their hyper-masculine warrior narratives. For example, after a coach screamed, "Knock his fucking head off," one of the men on the sidelines, almost in disbelief, turned to his teammate and sarcastically said, "Fuck me, is he sure? Why don't we just hunt them down or set fire to their [team] bus while we're at it?" Both this exchange and the dialogue of Nick and his teammates (below) can be interpreted as examples of resistance, in the form of jocular banter. Rather than simply inducing a cheap laugh from teammates, this resistance provided a counter-point to those practices that are simply acts of participation and reproduction.

On one occasion, the coach was increasingly unhappy with the team's performance. He told Liam to prepare for substitution, saying, "We need a real man out there. Someone who's not afraid to smash some people around and get hurt." The assistant coach nodded agreeably. But, as

Liam prepared, Nick, a remaining sub, provided resistance, joking to his fellow benchwarmers, "If it's 'real men' he wants, then that counts me out!" The other men on the bench stifled their smiles, nodding in agreement; acknowledging the irony of a "real man" being selected from among those men already deemed not "man enough" to play (as they all were on the bench).

It could be argued that, in contrast to the "heroic position" of masculinity that the coach called for, these men separated themselves from the conventions of orthodox masculinity in favor of a more ordinary position of masculinity (Wetherell & Edley 1999). It can be argued that the assertiveness and determination required to reject a discourse of people in power is, in and of itself, a demonstration of masculine characteristics. But the fact that players do not overtly contest the coaches suggests this is not a satisfactory answer.

Indeed, while the players sometimes challenged each other's masculinity on the field, it is highly significant that this hyper-masculine posturing was left within the white-lined boundaries of the playing field. This was true even when the men performed traditionally feminine tasks. These players did not aggressively challenge each other's masculinity when applying what would be traditionally considered feminine skin and hair products (such as tanning lotions and conditioners), donning pastel-colored cardigan sweaters, skinny jeans, and other feminized fashion accessories (such as colorful bead-bracelets, Arabic-style scarves, or one-strap satchels), or when emoting or being physically tactile with one another. Players talked about clothes, moisturizers, and music, as much as they talked about soccer and sex; thus their actual use of masculinity challenging discourse, or questioning of each other's sexuality when doing so, was marginal. In other words, once the game was over, they exhibited more inclusive, metrosexual gendered behaviors.

While athletes occasionally used the phrase "that's so gay," they did not call each other "poofs," or challenge each other to be "real men" in other social contexts. When such phrases were used, ironically and humorously, the phrase "that's so gay" appeared to disparage gayness and have homonegative connotations—something I discuss later in this chapter.

The lack of intellectualized homophobia outside of sport is a further indicator of how these men left orthodox notions of masculinity on the field. They did not intellectualize homophobia in any way. Many of the men had gay friends and several of the players had attended local gay bars and clubs. Accordingly, while the masculinity that these athletes exhibited outside of sport is notably lacking the homophobia, sexism, and violence found in the sporting setting, their lack of agency in organizing sport highlights their docility to authority and continues to position them as complicit toward orthodox masculinity in the sport setting.

The relative absence of homophobia, misogyny, and violence outside of sport, as opposed to its relative saturation in the locker room and on the field, suggests that the deployment of masculinity challenging discourse among these men (players and coaches) has shifted toward being primarily a sporting *technique*, or, at least a form that has narrower relevance outside of the structure of sport. In this respect, players' violent behaviors and discourses are predominantly situated in the realm of *sport*, rather than gender *per se*. It is the systematic practices and the cultural and organizational restraints of organized soccer which establishes this as appropriate sporting masculinity, thus making it possible for these coaches to challenge their players to exhibit such toxic practices on the field. With regard to the detachment of their on-field and off-field masculinities, there is increasing truth to the commonplace notion that the use of such violent, homophobic, and sexist language really is "just part of the game."

Homosexually-Themed Language in Sport

Still, one cannot easily situate the homophobic and sexist language of violence we discovered on this team (and it should be noted that this type of language was not used in virtually all other ethnographies I have done on sport). This type of language supports a commonly held argument against the notion of changing masculinities in sport: that the homophobic language used highlights the continued prevalence of homophobic attitudes. One of the pieces of evidence for this is the continued use of the phrase "that's so gay." In this section, I draw on my own research and that of McCormack (2011c) to argue that such a perspective is simplistic and does not account for social context, implicit meanings, and changing relations of power. In order to explicate this fully, I first turn to my earlier research on the importance of homophobic language.

Interviewing 32 openly gay athletes in 2002, I showed that homophobic language was present in all types of men's sports (Anderson 2002). Back then, I suggested that because gay athletes do not fit dominant notions of masculinity, intolerance was exacted in both explicit and covert ways. Here, homophobic discourse acted as a resistance toward the intrusion of gay subculture, serving to maintain orthodox masculinity and patriarchy of sport.

Highlighting the operational aspects of homophobic discourse in discrimination, a number of scholars find that the primary way to subordinate a young male is to call him a "fag," or accuse him of being gay—even if one does not believe he is. Accusing someone of homosexuality demonstrates one's heteromasculinity at the expense of another—something Pascoe (2005) calls "fag discourse." Concurring with prior work on the gendered nature of homophobia (Plummer 1999), Pascoe argues that homophobia is a form of gender regulation rather than demonstrating anti-gay animus. She also maintains that many of those who use fag discourse do not intellectualize homophobia, demonstrating that it is possible for fag discourse to lose its sexualized meaning.

Seeking to understand the shifting meanings of gay language, I used the data of an ethnography of an elite rugby team (McCormack & Anderson 2010b) in order to develop a grounded theory approach to the variability of homosexual discourse, as it relates to intent, sexual content, and effect. We highlight that, as power and definitions shift, prejudice becomes covert, implicit, and complex—but, significantly, that it may also be eroded. Indeed, as the acceptability of cultural homophobia decreases (an uneven social process) we suggest that it is homophobia and not homosexuality that is increasingly stigmatized (Anderson 2009; McCormack 2012a; Weeks 2007). This means that the effect of homophobic language must also change, and new forms of homosexually-themed language will emerge.

Homophobic Discourse and Pro-Gay Perspectives

Grundlingh (1994: 428) describes rugby as the "ultimate man-maker," inculcating characteristics of courage, self-control, and stamina, alongside a deeply engrained culture of homophobia. However, we found no overt or intellectualized homophobia whatsoever among the athletes of the rugby team. A graduate student, Rhidian McGuire (who is heterosexual), conducted ethnography with the team (see also Anderson & McGuire 2010), and similar to my research with the soccer coaches, we found these coaches (again, men of Generation X) using homophobic discourse. Observations found the coaches used the terms poof and queer with regular frequency, to challenge masculinity.

"Don't be a fucking poof," a coach screamed after Graham failed to properly complete a play. And when John told his coach that he should not practice because of an injury, the coach yelled, "For God's sake, what are you, gay?" Here, homophobia was used to maliciously stigmatize and subordinate the players.

In a greater contrast than with the soccer players, however, the athletes despised their coaches' approach to masculinity building. Graham ardently complained about his coach: "He calls players poofs when they are injured all the time, and he frequently said, 'You're fucking gay,' just to put a player down. I don't like it...I hate my coaches." Tom agreed, "It's their old-school way of doing it. It's not right, and I don't like it."

Ben saw his coaches' language as an archaic symbol of the attitudes of Generation X. "That's their generation. But it doesn't work... It doesn't make me think, 'Oh, no. I'm not a real man. I need to play harder.' It just makes me think he's a fucking idiot." Seth, too, was offended by his coach's homophobia: "It's nasty. He should be fired. Period."

Furthermore, the players did not use the same type of homophobic discourse they condemned their coaches for using; nor did any of the players on this elite British rugby team intellectualize homophobia. Conversely, the players valued gay men, highlighting the positive association they have with homosexuality. When asked if he would mind having an openly gay player on the team, Graham said, "Maybe my coach would, but I wouldn't." John agreed, "I wouldn't give a shit. Not in the slightest." Tim added, "Seriously, what kind of people do you think we are?"

These answers reflect the myriad of pro-gay responses to questions that we designed to probe for homophobia. When asked if he thought homosexuality was wrong, Alex said, "No man. Of course not. I have gay friends." Ian said, "I'm for gay rights. I think most people are nowadays." Observations also support these statements. For example, Seth has a gay roommate, Charlie, who occasionally attends nights out with the team. Charlie is always welcome, and players dance with and freak him. Several players have gone to a gay pub with Charlie.

Flirting with Gayness

Although these rugby players intellectually distanced themselves from homophobia, they nonetheless managed to ironically proclaim their heterosexuality through acting gay. McCormack and I (2010a) call this *ironic heterosexual recuperation*. Here, heterosexual men joke about maintaining sexual desire for each other; parody stereotypes of gay men; and act out mock homosexual behaviors. For example, several of the players frequently greet each other with, "Hey, gay boy."

Interviews with these rugby players showed that these greetings were, without exception, interpreted as a sign of endearment. For example, when Graham was greeted this way, he smiled and pointed suggestively to his butt, playing-up to the suggestion that he is gay. Similarly, Mike greeted Colin with, "Hey homo" and Colin replied, "Yeah, sister. Good weekend?" By proclaiming homosexuality, these players ironically assert their own heterosexuality. The participants perceive their greeting as innocuous, maintaining that there is no homophobic intent.

When asked about the "gay" content of this banter, participants said it is decidedly not homophobic. They argued that their pro-gay attitudes prevented this gay banter from being interpreted as such. Mike said, "It's simply banter. We don't mean anything by it." Colin added:

> We do it as a laugh. I don't mean anything nasty. I say "You're gay" all the time to my friends, but I don't mean it that way. Anyway, I normally give them a hug or something so they *know* I love them.

Alex clarified that this type of gay banter is understood as indicative of close friendship. When asked if he would banter with someone on the team he disliked, he responds, "No. Of course not! You only banter with those you like." Accordingly, participants asserted that gay banter is used only among friends, a finding supported through multiple interviews and observations with this team.

Simultaneously, however, this use of language is also part of a larger project of masculine bantering. It served as a form of homosocial bonding between friends. It is not used as an expression of displeasure. However, the nature of power, its invisibility, and its re/production, means that the issue of whether there is an element of homophobia in the "text" remains important.

The Contested Meanings of "Gay"

Although the players intellectualized their support for gay rights, they nonetheless used homosexually-themed language alongside ironic heterosexual recuperation. The most frequent use came with the phrase "that's so gay." For example, Graham failed a technical maneuver in practice and, out of frustration, shouted, "That's so gay!"

This phrase was heard, on average, twice a day in this research. And while this is a regular occurrence, compared to the dozens of times a day it was reported being heard in Anderson's (2005a) research on openly gay athletes, we highlight its declining frequency. Plays are frequently missed, but this language is only *occasionally* used. Players are more prone to swear "fuck" or "shit" to vent their displeasure, than to use homosexually-themed language. It should also be noted that the use of the phrase "that's so gay" is somewhat sporadic—observations document that three practices might go by without our researcher hearing the phrase, but at other times it might occur several times in just one practice.

During interview, all players argued that they did not intend to be homophobic when they said "that's so gay." Dan said, "It doesn't mean gay in that sense. That would be wrong." Colin agreed, "I don't think of sexuality when I say it. Look, when I miss a shot, I don't think that my aim is actually gay. That just doesn't make sense."

When participants were asked about how they thought gay people might interpret their use of "that's so gay" there was mixed response. Some did not use it in front of gay friends for fear of being misunderstood; others said that they used it nonetheless. "I don't mean anything by it," Jack said, "So I don't see why anyone would be offended." Seth defended his usage, arguing that both he and his gay roommate use it to describe things displeasing. "Hey, if gay guys use it, you can't tell me that it's bad." These differing perspectives highlighted participants' attempts to mediate the complex terrain of sexual and gender discourse.

Apart from "that's so gay," "don't be gay" was also used (although less frequently) in this ethnography. This phrase, heard once a week, was normally used between friends, normally as a way of debating the merits of a standpoint. For example, Mike tried to persuade Colin about the quality of a television show. Colin responded, "Don't be gay, man. That program's shit." But when interviewed, Colin insisted that he did not mean this to insult about anyone's sexuality, but instead it was about Mike's standpoint. He did not desire to stigmatize gay men in the process. "I was just expressing my dislike of the program. It has nothing to do with sexuality at all." In order to understand this use of language as distinct from both homophobic language and fag discourse, I call this "gay discourse."

Failed Banter as Homophobic Discourse

In addition to using homophobic language against players, the coaches also tried to relate to their players through gay banter with them. Their attempts, however, failed. Graham explained, "Occasionally he uses it in what he thinks is good humor; to try to be one of the boys and banter with us about being gay. But it is just bad most of the time." Alex agreed, 'No. They don't banter like we do. It's like they try to use our way of relating to each other, but then they twist it to insult." He added, "It's really derogatory. It's more bullying than bantering."

The players rejected their coaches' "banter" for several reasons. Foremost, they perceived that their coaches intend to stigmatize by using this banter—making it a form of homophobic discourse. Seth said, "Yeah, like I'll say to a mate, 'you're gay,' and that will bring us closer. But he does it differently. He said, 'That guy's gay,' and it's a totally different thing." Graham added, 'I hate it how they use homophobia to insult people." Alex agreed, "He [the head coach] talks about gay people in ugly and disparaging ways. You can't say you hate gay people and then say, 'don't be gay' and have us take it in a joking manner. We know how he really thinks, and we don't like it."

Highlighting their homophobia, when discussing the fact that Seth has a gay roommate, the coach remarked how "fucking gross" it must be for Seth to see his roommate bring a guy home. While the players failed to confront their coach, they complained about him to each other. John said, "What an idiot." Seth agreed, "Who cares who he [the gay roommate] brings back." From the players' perspective, Graham said, the coaches' homophobia poisons their attempt at banter:

> Look, if you're cool with gays, people know you like gays, and you make that clear, then you have some freedom to joke around about who is gay, or to joke with friends that are gay. But if you're not cool with it, then you really should just shut the fuck up.

From the players' perspective, gay banter is seen as a way of expressing comfort with homosexuality, and distancing oneself from explicit forms of homophobia, not reproducing homophobia. "One can only banter about homosexuality if a person also espouses pro-gay attitudes," Graham said. This is also found by Lalor & Rendle-Short (2007), who argue that "the new use of *gay* functions as an in-group marker, when talking to peers or when 'having fun', as opposed to being used when talking to adults, parents, or non-familiar acquaintances" (p. 164). These distinctions from the players demand similar classifications from academics, and the utility of gay discourse as a form of language distinct from homophobic and fag discourse is evident.

Reproducing Heterosexism through Gay Discourse

There are several important points to consider when theorizing the use of gay discourse. First, it is important to recognize that the use of the word gay (as an expression of displeasure), without intent to reflect or transmit homophobia, is well documented in youth settings

(Lalor & Rendle-Short 2007; McCormack 2011b; Rasmussen 2004). However, these men are not cognitive of the complexity of discourse and its effects. They fail to recognize the heteronormativity of "that's so gay." From their perspective it "simply" serves as a cathartic expression of dissatisfaction, but it also reproduces privilege. This phenomenon can be understood through Ogburn's (1957) lens of cultural lag. Cultural lag occurs when two interlinked social variables become dissociated because their meanings change at different rates. In this case, youth employ this discourse without knowledge or consideration of what it once conveyed. That is, their use of homosexually-themed language lags behind their attitudinal positioning on homosexuality.

For these young men, the word "gay" is a placeholder for their negative emotions—but it is not intended as an expression of homophobia. We therefore argue that it is unjustifiable to see "that's so gay" as part of homophobic discourse. It might continue to privilege heterosexuality depending on how it is said, but it does not have the pernicious, deleterious effect that homophobic discourse has been shown to have (Rasmussen 2004).

Without being immersed in the data, or indeed in contemporary youth culture, it might be difficult to interpret this discourse according to this suggested framework. I have found that it is older academics, who experienced the homophobia of "that's so gay," who have the greatest problem accepting this framework, whereas younger scholars and undergraduate students reject the argument that it is homophobic and find utility in my argument.

One example of the argument against the framework uses the analogy of racial discourse to analyze gay discourse, concluding that it is pernicious and homophobic (Parker 2009). This position articulates that because the term "that's so black" is not used because it would be considered racist and unacceptable, it is therefore equally homophobic to say "that's so gay." Certainly there is credence to this argument, but this analogy is also faulty.

This race analogy fails because scholars do not allow for multiple meanings of the term "that's so gay." However, there is growing evidence that "gay" in the equivalent phrase does not connote sexuality. This is true for young people in particular. Indeed, Lalor & Rendle-Short (2007), McCormack (2011b), and Rasmussen (2004) all document that gay has multiple meanings—referring to being happy, a sexual identity, and being passé—and that young people are particularly skilled at differentiating the second and third meaning.

Cultural lag theory contributes to our understanding of the use of this type of language because it is overly-simplistic to conceive of the broad range of homosexually-themed discourse as all (equally) homo-phobic. In order to explicate the effect of cultural lag on discourse, I call homosexually-themed discourse (where there is no intent to wound) *gay discourse* instead of homophobic discourse. It is my central thesis that because the effects of homosexually-themed discourse vary in their intensity and damage, it is necessary to distinguish them (McCormack & Anderson 2010).

In order to do this, it is necessary to have clear definitions of the terms in play. Homophobic discourse is the form of homosexually-themed language that is well established in the literature (Plummer 1999), the kind the coaches on this team use. This type of discourse will dominate in cultures of high homophobia. Gay discourse, however, conceptualizes homosexually-themed language where there is no intent to subordinate or marginalize another person; an effect brought about by a culture of decreased homophobia (see also McCormack 2011c).

While I present two discrete categories of language, I highlight that the complexity and contextual specificity of discourse means that rather than being distinct classes, this language use is a continuum. Homosexually-themed language is far more complex than "being homophobic," or not. When determining how to categorize a particular phrase, it is necessary to consider *how* it is said, as well as what is said. That is, the social context in which it is said, and the relationship between speaker and listener, are also important. Accordingly, there is much slipperiness in how discourse is used, and the intent with which it is spoken.

In this classification, intent is the determining factor in which type of discourse is employed. That is, we identify language as part of homophobic discourse if *intended to wound*, regardless of whether it stigmatizes sexuality or gender (Pascoe 2005); whether it is meant to "make the man" (Plummer 1999), or just improve performance (Anderson 2005a); what counts is that there is a desire to subordinate another person with its usage.

This intent to wound is important, because it affects both the manner in which discourse is used, and how it is received. However, the perception of prejudice in interaction is as important as the intent of the speaker. As Brontsema (2004: 11) writes, "Intent alone cannot control the fate of a word." In other words, discourse can still have negative impact even if this is not the intent. However, since scholars document that harmful intent exacerbates the negative effect of pernicious discourse (Plummer 1999; Thurlow 2001), it is logical to argue that the intent to wound is a determining factor in the effect discourse has.

There is yet a further reason for a more nuanced perspective of homosexually-themed discourse. Consider, for example, the espousal of pro-gay attitudes. It would be erroneous to suggest that a proclamation of gay support is convincing evidence of equality for homosexuality, because the claim alone does not substantiate annulment from re/producing homophobic discourses. Similarly, to argue that this new form of discourse is universally homophobic is equally unconvincing; such an argument diminishes the progress that has been achieved concerning homophobia. Instead, it needs to be recognized that, in a culture that stigmatizes overt homophobia, the impact of homosexually-themed discourse is different—because of the way it is *perceived*.

It is fundamental to distinguish homophobic discourse from the use of gay epithets when there is no intention to stigmatize any individual or group (Thurlow 2001). Again, it is for this reason that I call this use of language *gay discourse*, highlighting that it is widely used to express displeasure not homophobia (Lalor & Rendle-Short 2007; Savin-Williams 2005). I am not alone in examining homosexually-themed language from a more complex standpoint. Rasmussen (2004: 304) comments, "it does not *always* have to be read as homophobic. It can also be ironic, self-referential, habitual, or even deployed without a 'knowing' relation to gayness as a sexual signifier."

Understanding the Changing Meanings of Language

The complexities of homosexually-themed language, and how its meanings and effects change in different contexts, have been developed by my colleague, Mark McCormack (2011c). He develops a model to understand transition from homophobic language through fag discourse and gay discourse to pro-gay language. Importantly, he relates it to the levels of homohysteria in a culture—arguing that when the social context changes, so does the intent, the shared implicit meanings between groups, and also the effect this has on the language (see Figure 1).

In his research, McCormack (2011c, 2012a) also documented heterosexual men using gay banter to bond with their gay peers—and that these gay men reciprocated with similar banter. He found no evidence that this language use was problematic, and instead found both gay and straight participants arguing that it had helped consolidate their friendships. Accordingly, McCormack labeled such discursive interaction as "pro-gay language."

Another fundamental point in understanding the changing nature of homosexually-themed language is that how people understand particular words is dependent on their lived experiences. Plummer (2010) develops the notion of *generational sexualities* to understand the

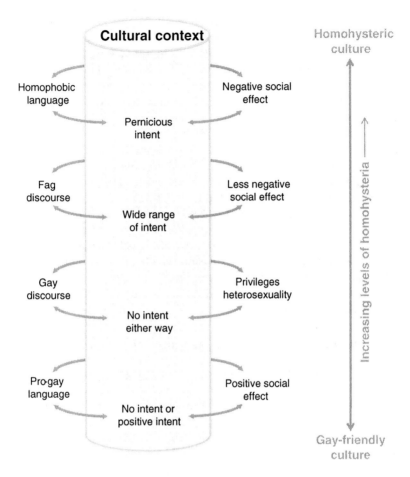

Figure 1   A model of homosexually-themed language

importance of the age in which we are born—that how we understand our sexual identities and mediate the social world will be dependent on the age and cohort into which we were born. This helps explain why academics aged 40 and above hear "that's so gay" as an example of terrible homophobia, while young heterosexual and sexual minority youth use it as a way to express frustration with no homophobic context.

McCormack (2011c) argues that context—situational, social, generational, etc.—is fundamental in understanding the meanings of homosexually-themed language. Particularly important, the word "gay" cites markedly different cultural norms in settings where homophobic discourse is absent or stigmatized (Anderson 2009; McCormack 2011c). It may be easy to read homophobia in today's gay discourse. Yet these discourses do not invoke images of gay subordination and homophobia for younger men (Lalor & Rendle-Short 2007). It is poor sociology to apply one's academic framework to those one studies, without hearing their voices, meanings, and narratives. Accordingly, McCormack and I argue that scholars need to give central consideration to context when discussing the impact and effects of discourses of sexuality and gender.

McCormack (2011c) argues that it is fundamentally the level of *homohysteria* that affects the meanings of gay language. In a homohysteric setting, "that's so gay" will be intended to be homophobic, will be experienced in that way, and will serve to reproduce gay stigma. Yet in a setting where homohysteria is absent, the same phrase will be more likely to bond gay and straight peers in friendship, or have no relation to sexuality for the people at all.

This linking with homohysteria is vital, and it also enables us to understand the links between homosexually-themed language and masculinity challenging discourse. In homohysteric settings, masculinity challenging discourse will be subsumed within homosexually-themed language. This is because the best way to challenge masculinity in a setting is to use homophobia to stigmatize a man. However, as homohysteria decreases, the utility of such homosexually-themed masculinity challenging discourse decreases—until it gets to the stage for the rugby players where such language use is detrimental to the coaches' relationship with the players. In a setting of low homohysteria, masculinity challenging discourse would likely exist by questioning a man's strength or his sexual prowess (most often with women).

Chapter Conclusion

In examining the construction and regulation of masculinity on a semi-professional British soccer team and a high-ranked university British rugby team, my research colleagues and I found that the coaches of Generation X and athletes of *i*Generation deploy two types of discourse to (re)construct themselves and other men according to systematic sets of gendered practices. We collectively refer to these as *gendered discourses*, and delineate two mutually enforcing forms: (1) *masculinity establishing discourse*, and (2) *masculinity challenging discourse*. We then found separate uses for *gay discourse*.

Our notions of masculinity establishing discourse and masculinity challenging discourse contribute to the literature on sport and masculinities because they conceptualize, as a systematic set of processes, a broad range of factors that construct and regulate gendered behaviors in sport. In this specific setting, the coaches' combined use of these gendered discourses established an appropriate framework of masculine behavior, and a mechanism for its regulation.

The findings from the soccer research also demonstrate that the athletes on this team model some aspects of hegemonic (orthodox) masculinity when in sport, but distance themselves from it outside of sport. The athletes likely use the language on the field because they live with the ever-present threat of being deselected. They adhere to the language usage of their coaches' generation because they understand that, from their coaches' generational perspective, the good soccer player is one who compliantly "does" orthodox masculinity.

Concerning gay themed discourse, in categorizing the use of homosexually-themed discourse according to intent, we nuance the theory that underpins how sexual language in social settings might be understood. We documented that these men bonded through ironically proclaiming their homosexuality—something we call ironic heterosexual recuperation. Here, the intention was to ironically draw heterosexualizing attention by demonstrating comfort with homosexuality, while also maintaining one's heterosexual identity. In this setting, homosocial bonding has appropriated homosexually-themed greetings, and mock gestures of homosexuality, as a way of demonstrating friendship and proving heterosexuality, without overt homophobia.

However, this local meaning is likely to derive its codes through the exceptional degree of heterosexuality and heteromasculine capital that these men are accorded because of their teamsport affiliation (Anderson 2005a). Indeed, the masculine capital accorded to rugby players means that it is possible for them to conditionally transgress some of these heteromasculine norms in ways that might not be permissible for non-athletes (Harris & Clayton 2007). The heterosexualization of rugby players that was developed through generations of homophobia and femiphobia means that today's participants have their masculine capital raised simply by being associated with rugby (Nauright & Chandler 1996). We argue that, in examining the use of gay banter, it is important to recognize that the intent and meaning of homosexually-themed discourse will be, in part, determined by the culture in which it is used.

Another central issue with regards to context is the difference in levels of homophobia of coaches and players. While we recognize that attitudes toward homosexuality are never homogenous (it is possible to find pro-gay coaches, for example), we emphasized that there were clear and substantive differences between players' language and banter and its interpretation, compared with the language and interpretation of their coaches' failed banter.

However, because gay discourse does not serve as a traditional, pernicious form of heterosexual weaponry (that intentionally inscribes a subjugated framework around gay identities), it should be considered differently to the old form of homophobic discourse. It is for these reasons that we postulate the need for a continuum of homosexually-themed language—a notion that recognizes the historical situatedness of the subject and audience. Taking cultural lag into consideration, we highlight that the same phrase can be interpreted differently. Thus, intent, cultural context, and affect are all important in judging the relationship between homosexually-themed language and effect. McCormack's (2011c) model of homosexually-themed language powerfully demonstrates this, and questions the frequently held assumption that *any* form of homosexually-themed language is necessarily damaging in some way.

5

Recognizing Bisexuality

In March of 2013, British Royal, Prince Harry, was reported by PinkNews. co.uk as having graciously accepted the phone number of a gay man in a nightclub. While details of the actual exchange are unknown, the gay man tweeted, "I gave Prince Harry my number tonight, he promised he'll call me if he changes his mind about women. Or men. #epicwin." If reported properly the exchange is indicative of the fact that this young, laddish, helicopter-flying, war-veteran Prince is not offended by being sexually propositioned by other men. This means that when he is politely propositioned by a gay or bisexual male, it is incumbent upon him to reject the offer graciously. In this case, the Prince has found a way to do this.

More important is that the young Prince does not appear to be defensive about his heterosexuality. His expressed attitude, even if in jest, is one of acceptance for the legitimacy of same-sex intimacy. Backed by his support of gay charities, the Prince exemplifies the inclusivity of young men of his generation.

Yet it is more than just acceptance of gay men that characterizes this generation, it is their assuredness that bisexuality exists. When Harry Styles of the hugely successful boy band One Direction was rumored to be gay because he stayed the night at his gay friend's house, swapped some clothing items with him, and showed physical tactility with him, instead of telling the press that no, he was not gay, he said he's "pretty sure" he's not bisexual. With those words he managed to say he was attracted to women, while recognizing that one can be dual attracted.

But it is not just that *i*Generation recognizes that bisexuality exists, it is their willingness to engage with it, to understand that sexuality is complicated, and that in some aspects—as one of the participants in one my studies (Anderson & Adams 2011) suggested—"Aren't we all a little bisexual?"

For this chapter, I draw on that research that Adi Adams and I performed concerning the perspectives of male bisexuality among 60 male soccer players from three geographically diverse US universities (Anderson & Adams 2011). The results showed that these athletes accepted bisexuality as a legitimate and non-stigmatized sexual identity. We also found that they intellectualized an understanding of bisexuality in highly complex ways. Furthermore, while only a very small minority of these men had engaged in same-sex sexual behaviors, at some level, most players recognized some degree of bisexuality in their own identities. I therefore suggest that these results are a product of increased exposure to and contact with homosexual persons, leading to decreasing cultural homohysteria, finally resulting in increasingly open discussion and complex understanding of sexual behaviors and identities that were once erased or stigmatized in men's teamsport culture.

The Recognition of Bisexuality in an Unlikely Place

As Chapter 1 showed, from early youth, and throughout early adulthood, boys and men are encouraged to participate in team sports (O'Donnell et al. 1998) as a way to provide them with opportunities to establish and display heterosexual forms of hyper-masculinity. Competitive team sports therefore traditionally existed as a microcosm of society's conservative sexual and gendered values, myths, and prejudices about the variations in men and women, while also actively constructing them to exhibit, value, and reproduce traditional notions of heterosexual masculinity.

The literature concerning men's team sports shows that this conservative culture has also limited athletes' awareness of the fluidity of sexuality. Among teamsport athletes, one same-sex sexual experience has traditionally equated with a homosexual orientation, something I have described as the one-time rule of homosexuality (see Chapter 7). However, if just one same-sex behavior is associated with a homosexual identity, then men are culturally equated into one of only two viable categories of sexuality: homosexuality or heterosexuality. This cultural conflation (of any same-sex behavior as being consistent with the sexual identity of homosexuality) effectively erases bisexuality as a viable category of sexual identification.

While this tendency to polarize sexual identities limits our sexual/ emotional range as human beings, it also serves a functional/conservative purpose. By polarizing sexual identities to straight *or* gay, Klein (1993) suggests that men are provided with a method of eliminating the threats of uncertainty and fear that the recognition of their own bisexuality triggers inside them.

Multiple gender scholars have also shown that, in periods of high homophobia, emotional and physical intimacy between men is discouraged because it too is associated with a homosexual identity (e.g., Ibson 2002). Accordingly (and contrasting with physical affection between women), when homosocial tactility or emotional intimacy occurs between men of Generation X, it is/was almost always mis/taken for sexual desire (Thompson 2006).

Klein (1993) suggests that men's avoidance of emotional and physical intimacy is perpetuated by a myth that such intimacies are inspired by sexual desire and are precursors to sexual intimacy. Indeed, sexual desire is often perceived as the traditional missing link between a friendship and a romantic relationship (Thompson 2006). Thus, to ensure the separation of sexual desire from their lives, men also avoid homosocial emotional and physical intimacy. This has traditionally left boys and men prohibited from holding hands, softly hugging, caressing, or kissing, in either public or private places (Kaplan 2006). Men's demonstrations of intimacy are, therefore, generally relegated to the hyper-masculinized spheres, such as playing sports.

I theorize that all of this derives from a culture of extreme homohysteria, which also compels men to join hyper-heterosexualized organizations (such as sport). This means that sport has been particularly resilient in reproducing a conservative form of orthodox sexuality as homophobia/biphobia has been used to maintain this culture. But then again, all of that pertains to men of Generation X—men of *i*Generation view matters differently.

Bye Bi Myths of Bisexuality

Bisexuality has, of course, faced more challenges than just its erasure among teamsport athletes. In recent times, stigmatization and discrimination have been documented as characteristic of the bisexual individual's life-experience (Herek 2002). In less polarizing subcultures, those identifying as bisexual have often been stigmatized as neurotic, unable to love, or "incapable of making up their minds." Bisexual individuals have also been subject to double discrimination, facing hostility from both heterosexuals and homosexuals (Ochs 1996).

Furthermore, bisexuals have sometimes been described as simply being in transition into pure homosexuality, or being sex crazed (Klein 1993).

Thus, the overwhelming social attitude toward bisexuality has been one of denial, erasure, and/or stigma. This is even evident in academic literature, which favors self-identification over one's sexual predisposition. In other words, men "who have sex with men" are regarded as being on the down-low, curious, or heteroflexible, rather than simply bisexual (cf., King & Hunter 2007).

These myths and misattributions may however be relegated to a particularly conservative period of American history. Attitudes of *i*Generation toward sex and sexuality are changing—and they are changing rapidly. For university students, in addition to rapidly decreasing stigma against same-sex sex, there also exists a culture where many students avoid romantic relationships (Anderson 2010b). Instead, undergraduates frequently engage in casual sex—a culture of hooking up (Bogle 2008). I argue that these trends increase the viability of alternative categories of sexuality, expand social and political landscapes for sexual minorities, and reduce the disparity between acceptable gendered behaviors; or at least create more space for the open discussion of behaviors traditionally coded as non-heteromasculine.

The driving theoretical hypothesis of this chapter is that homohysteria has been central to the production and stratification of men's sexualities as culturally valued or subjugated. Homophobia/biphobia has been used by men as a weapon to deride other men in establishing this hierarchy. Therefore, if homophobia is on the rapid decline there might be a reconstruction of the one-time rule of homosexuality (in which one act of homosexuality is equated with a homosexual, even if having many acts of heterosexuality), and the relationship between sex, masculinity, and sexual identity construction. Given this potential reconstruction, it is plausible to expect individuals to give credence to multiple subject orientations and identities. As a result, greater cultural legitimacy may be given to bisexuality as a sexual identity.

In order to examine this thesis, my colleague and I used participant observation and qualitative interviews of 60 (18–22-year-old) players from three separate university soccer teams in the United States. In order to analyze a range of university settings, we strategically selected universities in diverse geographical locations. Politically, these locations represented strong variations in attitudinal positioning.

One team was from a small Catholic college in the American Midwest (n = 20); the second represented a small liberal arts college in the American South (n = 19); the third was a large liberal university located in the Northeast (n = 21). Of the 60 men, 52 were white, six were black, and two were Latino. In accordance with standard best practices for conducting ethnographic research, we defined our samples as each and every member of three different sports teams, and thereafter sought to collect information from those defined population samples. Therefore, the sample is valid of the team's culture, as no members are excluded. Universities were chosen to include geographic variability, and a stratification of NCAA membership (from Division I to III).

Decreasing Homophobia Leads to Decreased Biphobia

As with all my research into the relationship between straight athletes and attitudes toward homosexuality, the men on these teams contrasted older descriptions of contact sports as highly homophobic organizations. The men on these teams demonstrated an inclusive form of masculinity that is not situated in intellectualizing or behaving in homophobic ways. Although two men expressed homophobic sentiment in private interviews (both from the American South), the rest of the 58 were inclusive. I found multiple stories of players knowing gay men or showing acceptance of and support for homosexuality; and no measurable intellectual homophobia among them.

Pro-gay attitudes were expressed not only in interviews (where players have anonymity) but in social situations, too. For example, we were sitting with a group of eight soccer players in a food hall, when one of the researchers asked, "Any of you have gay or bisexual friends?" "My uncle is gay," Brett responded. Jordan added, "My best friend from home is gay." Kaden said, "I got a gay friend at home, too. He's not my best friend but he's a good friend." These types of conversations occurred with men in all three teams, in a variety of social locations. In other words, athletes on these three teams were not afraid to talk about their support for gay men in front of their peers. Nor were they afraid to admit to sharing homosocial intimacy with gay men.

But does the acceptance of homosexuality necessarily indicate an acceptance of bisexuality, too? It is important to note that my research colleague and I almost always (but not exclusively) framed our questions and our discussions in terms of "sexual minorities." Or we asked, "Do you have any gay or bisexual friends?" But as the answers above indicate, men on these teams mostly erased bisexuals (and other sexual minorities) as specific sexual identities from these conversations. "Gay" became the catch-all for all sexual minorities. Either that or bisexuality was erased a step earlier, because they had gay friends, and not bi friends. Either way bisexuality was consumed to within gay.

However, in-depth interviews suggest that there nonetheless exists an extensive degree of acceptance of bisexuality among these young men. We *always* asked if the pro-gay attitudes these men expressed could also be applied to bisexual men. "Of course," they answered without exception. So while bisexuality is somewhat erased from casual public discussions, it is equally accepted with homosexuality.

Part of this bisexual acceptance may be due to social contact with gay men (Baunach et al. 2010). Contact theory—which maintains bias toward a whole group can be reduced by meeting just one member of that group—has been widely used in discussing decreased homophobia (McCann et al. 2009). What has not been researched, however, is that contact with gay men leads to acceptance of bi men as well. More significant, while some of these men report learning inclusivity through contact with a gay man, most of these men report never having been homophobic or biphobic in the first place. This, too, is consistent with research that shows today's youth are not socialized into homophobia the way previous research shows they once were (Anderson 2009). This decreasing homophobia seems to have led to more accepting understandings of bisexuality, too.

Complex Understandings of Bisexuality

Interviews with these 60 soccer players indicate that most of the men maintain complex understandings of the relationship between sexual orientation, sexual behaviors, and gendered intimacy. For example, when these men are presented with questions designed to examine for their perspectives on the one-time rule of homosexuality, all of the men dismiss this rule as overly-simplistic homophobia. When we asked James, "If a straight guy had sex with a guy once, would it make him gay?" he answered, "Only if he wasn't attracted to women." He then looked at the interviewer as if to say, "That's a stupid question." The point is: however we worded our questions about the one-time rule of homosexuality, we found it was dismissed. To these men, sex with a man can, but *does not have to*, equate with homosexuality. This was even the case with the two men who expressed some homophobia.

Unlike the way men discussed sexuality in casual conversations, most of these men recognized the complexity of sexual identity and orientation in interview. Mike said, "What does it really mean to be gay anyhow?" Mike found the notion of one same-sex sexual experience equating to homosexuality absurd: "Maybe my grandpa thought that way, but come on!" He added, "Having sex with a guy doesn't necessarily make you gay. You could be gay, but you might be bi, or you might just be a straight guy having sex with a guy."

Most of these men showed an understanding that sexuality is broken down into at least three constituents: identity, orientation, and behavior. In understanding sexuality in this more complex perspective, they reject a binary notion of sexuality. So while they did not believe that having sex with a man automatically made one gay, they did recognize that it might make one bisexual; although defining bisexuality proved difficult.

When asked to "describe bisexuality" many of these men initially offered an explanation that being bisexual means being equally sexually attracted to both men and women. As Paul stated, "It's about having equal preference for women and men." John said, "It's when you like both the same." But when asked to elaborate on their initial statements, most of these men were quick to clarify that it does not have to be equal attraction between men and women. "Of course," Tim said, "You can like guys 5 per cent of the time and girls 95 per cent of the time, or the other way around and be bisexual." When Frank was asked if liking girls 95 per cent of the time and guys 5 per cent makes one bisexual he answered, "I don't know. You could call it that, sure. Or you could say he's straight but he likes guys a bit. Either way, I don't really care, it doesn't matter who you like." And when Paul was asked if one can be 95 per cent straight and 5 per cent gay he said, "Of course. Most of us probably are."

Implicit in these discussions, of course, is the acceptance that bisexuality exists. Our interviews were largely absent of the stereotypes of bisexuals as incapable of making up their mind; being in transition to coming out as gay; or being "greedy." Most of these men did not believe these stereotypes. When Jon was told by one researcher that, "Some people think bisexuality doesn't exist, that it's just gay guys who are too afraid to say they are gay," he responded, "That's just stupid! I don't know of any bisexuals at this college but I'm sure they exist. Nobody doubts girls can be bisexual so why doubt guys can?" He added, "Statistically, they must be out there."

We found this an interesting theme: almost all of the men in this study maintained that bisexuality exists among men, and most (as we will get to later) even recognize bisexuality in themselves, but few know male friends who publicly identify as bisexual. This is probably because far fewer bisexual men come out of the closet than gay men (PEW 2013). Bisexual man can, if they choose, take advantage of a heterosexist culture and be perceived as straight because of their interest in women. In other words, most bisexual men discuss publicly their desires for women, but not men.

Mark said, "I've got gay friends on campus but I don't know of any bi guys." He added, "I've met some bi girls back home. So if girls can be bi then guys can, too." Kevin also said that while he knows bisexual girls, he does not know any guys. "Wait a minute," he said, "Surely I must know some." After a moment's reflection, and still unable to think of any, we ask why he thinks bisexual men exist, even though he doesn't know any. "I think it is a matter of homophobia," Kevin explained:

> It's cool right now for girls to be into other girls. I don't think it's bad for guys to say they are into other guys...I don't think there is much homophobia, but it's also not "cool" yet. Maybe it will be in a few years. But, right now, a guy just doesn't get the same credit with his friends for doing guys as he does for doing girls. So if you're a guy, and you like girls too, I guess it just makes sense to say you're straight.

Tim maintained that bisexuality is as common for men as it is for women: "If, whatever, two out of five girls are into other girls, well you know it's gonna be that way for guys, too." Clint, who grew up on a farm in the Midwest, agreed, saying that he believes that the difference between gay and straight is "blurry." He added, "I have gone to gay bars, I've even kissed one of my friends. Does that make me gay? Does it make me bisexual?" He continued, "This categorizing people stuff is kind of stupid, don't you think?" We expressed to Clint that while we understand that it may very well be stupid, it is nonetheless a social phenomenon; and we wonder why he chooses to describe himself as straight. Clint smiled, "You got me there. I guess it's because I've only been with girls, so far."

Others also intellectually challenged the polarization of sexual binaries, even if they do not identify as bisexual. Tom said, "I don't get it. Why do we have to be straight or gay, or whatever? Why can't we just be?" Tom's teammate Danny said, "Or why can't we be somewhere between. Can you really be a hundred per cent something?" Still, both of these men also identify as heterosexual.

Accordingly, interview data suggests that while these men are not identifying as bisexual, they (at least) intellectualize bisexuality. They demonstrate that, at an intellectual level, sexuality is positioned on a continuum. What is perhaps even more interesting, however, is that not only do they recognize that bisexuality exists, but at an intellectual level, they recognize their own bisexuality, too.

Recognizing Bisexuality in One's Self

Most of the men in this research comment that they understand bisexuality to encompass a broad spectrum of variables, while a minority predominantly categorizes bisexuality as the presence of physical attraction, and/or acting upon this attraction. For example, and representing the minority view, Justin said, "Thinking or saying a guy is good looking doesn't show bisexuality, and loving straight male friends isn't bisexual either." Justin therefore positions sexuality as being defined by sexual desire/behavior alone. However, most men complicate this perspective.

Indeed, the majority of these men recognized emotional attachment and emotional expression as components of sexuality. Perhaps this is why nearly all of the men we interviewed recognized some bisexuality in themselves. "I think we're all bisexual to some degree," Sean said. "I mean, I don't think it's purely a physical thing, I think it's an emotional thing, too." When asked to expand upon this idea of bisexuality being a universal sexuality, he said, "All I'm saying is it's more complicated than just the physical." Sean's reasoning rejects any definition of sexuality based on sexual behavior alone: and this is the shared perspective.

Corey maintains that bisexuality is human nature at its best. "Bisexuality is fascinating," he said. "Someone who can dig [be attracted to] both men and women is fascinating because they don't distinguish—they just dig humans. And there's something cool about that. It's beautiful." Corey also touched upon an area that most of the men in this study identify with—they are not afraid to express their love for their male friends. "I love Dom."

Whereas boys and men have traditionally avoided emotional intimacy (Pollack 1999), or at least the verbal recognition of that intimacy, these men are proud and verbal about their love for their mates (see Chapter 6 for more on this). This was true regardless of the team studied: these men expressed a great deal of affection. Jay said, "I love John, he's my friend, my bro. I'd do anything for him." And when asked how his love for his best friend compared to the love he has for his girlfriend (of four years) he answered, "It's close. You ever watch *Scrubs* [the TV show]?" he asked. "It's like me and John are like JD and Turk [two of the main male characters who are emotional but not physical lovers]." This type of affection was commonplace among teammates: they were not shy about calling their affection love. Clint, Sean, Jay, and multiple others postulate that there is a connection between love and sexuality. One of the players said, "I love my best friend more than my girlfriend, doesn't that make me a little gay?"

Thus, not only did we find an overt acceptance of homosexuality and bisexuality among a group of men traditionally understood to be characterized by homophobia; and not only did we find that these men rejected the one-time rule of homosexuality and complicated notions of what it means to be bisexual; but we also found that, at some level, these men recognized bisexuality in their own personal but not public identities. In one-on-one interviews, 48 out of 60 identify some bisexuality in their own lives.

When given a verbal scale of zero to ten, with zero being 100 per cent heterosexual and ten being 100 per cent homosexual, 12 of the men score themselves as a zero, 32 scored themselves as a one, 12 scored themselves as a two, and four scored themselves as a three.

We asked those who did not score themselves as a zero why this was the case. "I'd probably say I'm a two," Alex told us. "And why not a zero?" we asked. "Because I like to hug guys," Alex responded. "It's not like it is sexually pleasurable contact, but I'm really comfortable with male contact." Kaden also rated himself as a two:

> Behavior wise, I'd say a two or three, I'm down with physical contact. And I've thought about what it would be like to be gay. Not that I question my sexuality. Everyone probably has thought about it at some point, even if they don't talk about it.

Kaden also gives us his interpretation of where others might place him on the scale. "I think outsiders would put me as a five or something like that, because other people might label some of my behaviors as gay, or not what someone who was completely straight should do." He laughed, "Sometimes I just go along with it to keep people guessing. Like, I'll hug people and hold on for a bit longer than they expect."

Luke told a similar story of keeping his sexuality ambiguous:

> I was holding this friend of mine. We were both topless in my room at a party and this girl walked in. We thought we'd be smart and say we were gay to see what her reaction would be and if she would believe it or freak out or whatever. She was totally cool with it and ended up telling us she was bisexual and telling us all about it [he laughs]. I guess she trumped our story!

Two other men also told us that they had thought about what it would be like to be gay, and had also discussed their own sexuality with friends. Both concluded that they were straight and now rate themselves on the scale as a two. Others rated themselves a one or two because they have had some form of sexual contact with a man. "Well, I've kissed guys before: a couple of times, on the lips, and a million times on the cheek. Conventionally that probably doesn't make me 100 per cent straight," John said.

Correspondingly, we asked those who scored themselves as a zero why they did so. Here, almost all of these men explained their straightness in relation to an absence of same-sex behavior. "I've never done anything remotely sexual with a guy," Mike said. Jessie said, "I'm strictly attracted to women, and I'd never have intercourse with a guy." Adam also rated himself as a zero but he was clear to identify that this rating is not borne out of homophobia.

Thus, firstly we found that the majority of these men give cultural currency to bisexuality as a legitimate sexual identity. Second, they maintained inclusive attitudes toward homosexuality and bisexuality. Third, although none identified as bisexual publicly, most of these men intellectually understand some bisexuality in their lives.

It is a significant finding that these men did not defensively assert their pure heterosexuality. This adds to empirical evidence that suggests many heterosexually-identifying undergraduate men are increasingly moving away from aggressively defending their sexuality as "100 per cent straight."

Old Myths Die Hard

While the vast majority of these men offer a refreshing emotional and intellectual outlook on men who have sex with men, it is also important to note that a handful maintained dispositions about bisexuality that resemble what older research has found. For example, Klein (1993) suggested that bisexual men are oftentimes understood to be non-existent, neurotic, or hypersexual. We found some evidence of this sentiment in some of these men, too.

Steve jokingly encapsulated some of this sentiment by suggesting that, "Maybe they [bisexuals] are just horny." David positioned bisexuals as curious or experimenting, saying, "They are gay and like having sex with women also, or they're straight and they are curious." But while David described bisexuality as having two forms (you're either predominantly gay or straight), he asserted that he would call them bisexual if that's how they identified.

Three men positioned bisexuals as confused. Mike, for example, said, "I think it means to be unsure of yourself as to who you are. Unsure of what you want." Rod told us that he thinks bisexuality might be "a little bit of confusion. Most bisexual people don't know what they are, I think." "You probably fall for one or the other in the end. It might just take you a while to decide." Brett said that bisexual is what people call themselves when they are in transition between straight and gay. "I'd call them very undecided. I've always thought of bisexuality as a transition period—they haven't figured it out yet [whether they are straight or gay]."

However, these men did not appear to be entrenched in their positions. When they were questioned about them, they did not feel a strong desire to be correct about their positions. Thus, after hearing the perspectives of my research colleague and myself, they agreed that there was merit to our argument that matters are more complex than they originally thought. This indicates that although there are still some myths about bisexuality circulating among jocks of *i*Generation, those myths do not appear to be generated by biphobia.

Chapter Conclusion

In interviewing and observing three geographically distinct groups of heterosexual male teamsport athletes (a traditionally homophobic social group) the research presented in this chapter investigated young soccer-playing men's understandings of bisexuality. We explored the attitudes these heterosexually self-identified men maintained toward sexual identity categorization, and how they contextualized their own sexual identities, finding that, although a few students still deny bisexuality as a legitimate category of sexual desire/identification, the vast majority recognized bisexuality as a legitimate sexuality for men. Many even challenged the binaries of homosexuality and heterosexuality, suggesting that sexuality is best understood as a spectrum.

Still, while all but two of the informants intellectualize no homophobia or biphobia, many remained personally fearful that their peers are not as accepting and tolerant of gay and bisexual men as they are. This is known as the third party effect, and it was particularly the case in the southern school. Conversely, it was not the case in the large, liberal university from the Northeast.

On this Northeast team—the most progressive of the research—there exist explicit and implicit norms of inclusivity, and most of the teammates expressed some bisexuality in their own identities under interview. However, they still do not publicly identify as bisexual. This is even true of those who had some form of sexual activity with a male. These findings therefore raise the question of why these men do not identify as bisexual. Even after team discussions have made it very clear that none of the players on the Northeast team harbored intolerance, and even after players discussed with one another that they identified as a one or two on our scale, none publicly identified as bisexual. The answer, probably, is that it is because they don't retain a large enough percentage/ desire of same-sex attraction. Still, they are not exclusively straight.

These men took into account multiple variables in understanding sexuality, emotional preference, social preference, and self-identification even though they still privilege sexual attraction in choosing how to self-identify. In this sense, my colleague and I identified a complex appropriation of gay/bi behaviors by self-identified straight men.

Another reason for avoidance of the label bisexuality may be the term bisexual itself. It was very common for men in this study to say, "I'm a little bit gay," and to then describe the love they maintain for a friend, an increased fashion sense, or other sensibility that is culturally coded as gay. These men were clearly comfortable recognizing that sexuality is more complex than just sex, and they are willing to recognize some "gay" in themselves. But it may be that they failed to identify as bisexual because, whereas "gay" and "straight" have a sexual implication but also a sensibility that incorporates non-sexual behaviors, there is not a similar "sex and sensibility" word for bisexual. In other words, we have homosexual (gay), heterosexual (straight), and bisexual (with no other colloquial word). What is the softer, broader, less clinical term associated with bisexuality?

The term metrosexual partially fills this void, and a number of the men we spoke to identify this way. But metrosexual is too heavily laden with just one behavior—dressing well. Others described having a "bromance" but this too also describes just one characteristic (emotional connection). So, at least for now, decreasing homophobia and the loosening of heteromasculine boundaries means that while men are more willing to intellectually recognize bisexuality as a legitimate sexual identity—and even to recognize bisexuality in their own, personal identities—straight men are not claiming a bisexual "middle ground." They are, however, admitting their emotional love for one another, and proudly proclaiming their bromance (the topic of the next chapter).

Part III
21st Century Jocks and Intimacy

6
Loving Other Men

Jake is a 16-year-old heterosexual male. He lives in a somewhat impoverished neighborhood in Bristol, England, with his mother and sister. Jake, however, has a rich network of friends, both male and female. He publicly expresses his love for his best mate, Tom. They grew up in the same neighborhood, attend the same school, and play on the same soccer team. Jake, exuberantly, expresses his love for Tom. Although he also has a girlfriend, Amy, Jake talks far more about his best mate, than her. This is something which is quantifiably visible in hanging out with him but also in examining his Facebook posts, where Jake posts on Tom's wall (and vice versa) with endearing terms of love. If I did not know that Jake was straight, an examination of his posts would lead you to think he's bisexual, and more in love with Tom than Amy.

Illustrating this, Jake told me that he was preparing to go on a 13-day holiday to Spain with Tom. When I inquired as to whether he feared that they might fight being together this long, he answered, "No mate, we're too close for that." "Fair enough," I responded. "And what does Amy think of the fact that you're taking your best mate on holiday, and not her?" "She knows how close we are. She's gotta share me."

While Jake still lives in a heterosexist culture, it at least permits him to have the same level of emotional and physical intimacy with his best male friend as with his female partner. For example, Jake tells me that he has a busy weekend coming up. He's spending Friday night with Amy, including sex and cuddling, as she will be staying the night at his house (North American readers will glean that Europeans are much more liberal when it comes to sex at this age). He will then be spending Saturday night with Tom, doing all of the same activities with the exception of sex. He informs me that he and Tom sleep in the same bed, and that they cuddle, too. In fact, Jake spends as many nights in bed with Tom as he does with his girlfriend.

"Look at this message Tom sent me yesterday," [Tom had just returned from a week away] Jake tells me with pride. He hands me his mobile phone and I read the message aloud: "Love you, this week has made me realise how weak I can be without you. And I don't like not being with you :/ x."

Jake does not think that his friendship is any different than the friendships his peers share with their best male friends. For Jake, this type of emotional intimacy is commonplace. My research shows that in Britain today he is right: it is a normal experience for heterosexual boys to express their love for each other, to sleep together, cuddling in the same bed (see Chapter 9). Today's boys bond not just over talk of cars, girls, and video games, but also over disclosing secrets and building intimacy.

This type of emotionality contrasts research concerning the lack of emotional intimacy among male friends decades ago (Pleck 1981). With a nationally representative sample, Joseph Pleck (1975) showed that 58 per cent of all males questioned had not told their best male friend that they even *liked* him. This is something that grew worse in the mid-1980s, where "like" became a euphemism for love and was edged further from friendship vocabulary (Williams 1985). But it is now alien to today's male youth.

Sport and Stoicism

Research from decades ago shows that most males are not very emotionally intimate with each other (Lewis 1978; Williams 1985). For example, Olstad (1975) suggested that, although men report more same-sex friendships than women did in the 1970s, these friendships were not close or intimate. In his study of Oberlin college students (a very liberal institution) males had more male best friends than female best friends. Yet these males tended to place greater confidence in, consulted more about important decisions, and spent more time together with their best female friends than with their best male friends.

In the development of gender and sexuality politics for Generation X, sport played a central role. For Generation X, organized, competitive team sports were almost universally described as locations where heterosexual men battle for masculine dominance in Western cultures. In order to achieve the most socially valued form of masculinity, men had to repress fear, weakness, intimidation, or pain (Giulianotti 1999). This has particularly been true of sports that are intertwined with school systems (Gerdy 2002), where one's teamsport life flows into one's non-sporting social life. Here, failure to live up to the esteemed cultural construction of masculinity has traditionally resulted in males being subject to physical and discursive methods of subordination, not only on the field, but among peers in school as well (Mac an Ghaill 1994). More recently, however, more progressive attitudes are being esteemed among young men in sport.

Jake is not alone in his outright expression of love for his friend. The florid language that Jake used to describe Tom is not at all unusual among contemporary British or American youth. For example, in research on English working- and middle-class, white sixth form students, McCormack and I (2010a) show that the style of men's masculinity most esteemed among these youths approximates inclusive masculinities. We show that a decrease in homophobia simultaneously permits an expansion of heteromasculine boundaries so that boys are able to express emotional intimacy without being homosexualized by it. I find the same thing, everywhere—adolescent boys and undergraduate men expressing their love for their male friends. But it's not just love that they express; they also express vulnerability, sympathy, fear, sadness, and loneliness.

In a study of a university soccer teams in the United States using ethnographic methods discussed in the previous chapter, a senior on the team, Joe, hosts a weekly "games night." Players, girlfriends, and friends are invited. One night, we were drinking beer, eating pizza, and building a jigsaw puzzle with eight players, three girls (none were girl-friends), and one male who was not part of the soccer team. There was one giant table dominating the room, and we all scrunched around it to construct the 500-piece puzzle. As the puzzle began to take shape, Kris received a text and announced that he had to leave. There was visible tension in the room. Kris got up, said his goodbyes and then left the room. After the door closed, Dan hugged Martin, wrapping both arms around him. "Come on. Let's talk," he said. Dan directed Martin to a different room to console him.

One of the players explained to me that Kris is Martin's best friend. Lately, however, Kris was spending so much time with his new girlfriend that Martin felt abandoned. I looked to see how the men in the room would respond to this emotion of loneliness and longing. Perhaps Dan was simply removing Martin away from the others by taking him out of the room, in order to isolate him from being further emasculated? With plenty of beer in the fridge, I wondered if one of the players would take one to Martin, perhaps telling him to "suck it up," or to "forget about it."

But they did not. With three women in the room, I also wondered if the men would let them do the emotional care work. Again they did not. Instead, players intermittently got up to check on Martin, each expressing concern for his emotional state. The conversation around the table was not about what a wuss, pussy, or fag Martin was being, but about how painful it must be for him to feel that he was losing his best friend. Nobody said, "He'll be fine" (which could minimize his emotional state and help maintain his masculinity); or, "He's being a pussy" (which could build one's masculine capital at Martin's expense). This was a case of homosocial, emotional support, without fear of feminization or homosexualization. Instead of men being tough, this was a case in which men were free to express their emotions, and have them validated by their peers. When I asked Martin about his relationship with Kris the next day, he said:

> We have been friends for three years. I just wanted this last year together to be special. I know it's not right to ask him not to have a girlfriend, but because she goes to this university she just takes up all his time...I've got my friends on the team, yes. But I miss him.

I asked Martin if he had let Kris know about how he felt. "Of course," he said, "I even cried a bit in front of him."

The Social Acceptance of Jocks Crying

When I was a youth, boys did not cry. In fact, one time when I was 16, I began to lament to my friend Ken about my troubles over an emotional matter. I forget the precise topic, but vividly remember his response. My best friend did not recognize my pain or sorrow, instead he sang the lyrics to the song by The Cure, "Boys Don't Cry." I knew the subtext: he was not challenging whether I was a boy or not, he was telling me "don't cry, because if you do, we will think you're gay." Jocks might be able to cry after losing a big game, but one could certainly not cry in the face of physical or emotional pain. Even a decade later, research on British men found that they rarely cried in the presence of others, and that they could not cry over matters related to situations involving criticism from others, anger, or problems with work (Williams & Morris 1996).

On this team of American soccer players, however, matters were different. Turner said that the last time he cried was a year ago when he broke up with his girlfriend, but that he thought guys should cry more often. Martin said, "I cried with one of my best friends a few months ago. I was going to university and I was sad because I wouldn't see him until Christmas." Josh added that not only does he cry but that, "I could cry in front of anyone on the team, too." Meanwhile Clint said, "I learned not to cry when I was young. When I did my dad just beat me more. But I wish I could cry." Matters were the same among men from many of my other ethnographies, including my study of a fraternity (Anderson 2008b). These fraternity members shared anxieties and troubles, secrets and fears. So common was this form of emotional bonding that it remained acceptable for men to cry in each other's presence, something which occurred with surprising frequency. Nowhere was this more the case than the final fraternal event before senior fraternity members graduated. Here, brothers each were given an opportunity to say something about their time in the fraternity. Almost all cried in giving their speech, or in hearing of the narratives of another.

I do not claim that men have the same emotional spectrum as women to cry—research shows that women cry eight times more frequently than men (Becht et al. 2001)—but men have significantly improved upon their freedom of expression from where the literature said men were concerning emotionality in the 1980s (Askew & Ross 1988). Men in the Becht et al. (2001) study cried 6.5 times per year.

Highlighting existing limitations, Sean said, "Sometimes I feel like I want to talk about something but I don't know how...I either don't feel like I can open up about things or I don't know what to say." Frank agreed, "I don't really talk to people about emotional stuff. Maybe if you are going through something I will...so I'll tell my buddies some stuff... but not the whole story."

Thus, I found multiple levels of emotional bonding, ranging from men who have a harder time expressing themselves, to men who cry and talk emotionally with their friends. However, I found no judgment for those who related to each other in ways that the gender literature associates more with the social mechanisms through which women bond (Diamond 2002), including crying, in any of my studies. Even among men who were unable to cry, or unwilling to open up emotionally, none stigmatized, homosexualized, or in any other way look despairingly upon those who did.

Providing Emotional Care Work for Other Men

Care work is traditionally the domain of women's friendships (Cancian 1990), as men have been instead described as being more inclined to deny the need for it, and reluctant to give it. Even before the decade of homohysteria, men among the baby-boomers were socially discouraged from emoting to one another. Robert Lewis (1978: 108) wrote:

> Although males report more same-sex friendships than women do, most of these are not close, intimate, or characterized by self-disclosure. Many barriers exist to emotional intimacy between men, some stemming from the demands of traditional male roles in our society, such as pressures to compete, homophobia, and aversion to vulnerability and openness, as well as from the lack of adequate role models.

Matters have, however, drastically changed not only for the men of the college soccer team who supported their friend in missing his best friend, but in every other ethnography I conduct.

For example, in one research project on a rugby team, there existed a great deal of verbal abuse from the coach to the players (Anderson & McGuire 2010). The players did not contest their coaches out of fear of being kicked off their teams. However, athletes supported and encouraged each other to "shake off" what many called their coaches' abuse. Ollie said, "Yeah, he said those things all the time. And no, I don't like it or appreciate it. But it doesn't, you know, get to me." He added, "First, I can't be bothered to care too much about what a jerk like him thinks. So you just ignore him." Steve added, "But the other guys are there for you when the coach screams this shit at you. They give you a hug and say, 'Don't listen to him, he's a jerk.'"

Statements of support for their friends' emotional needs are abundant in my research (Anderson 2008b, 2011c; Anderson et al. 2012b). Today's jocks are emotionally available in the bad times, not just the good. McCormack (2012a) shows that this is ubiquitous for male friendships in the United Kingdom, and in my research in the United States, I find the same. For example, James is an outstanding 17-year-old runner on the team I have done ethnography on over the previous two summers in California. When I asked him how he shows compassion for his friends, he not only recounted narratives of support, but he described to me how he also symbolically supports younger runners who are not within his immediate friendship circle. For example, disappointed in not placing well enough in a race to earn a medal, James said that, "I gave my first place medal to my teammate who finished one place away from medaling." James keeps very few of his medals, saying:

> I've done this several times but I explain to them that I never got a medal my freshman year, and how I was always shy one or two spots.

I tell them that the medal is my way of showing them that I understand what it's like to be "oh so close" but not to make it. I tell them that if they medal next race, they can give me the medal back and I'll give it to someone else.

On another occasion James qualified in two races in track, and by dropping out of one it permitted the next finisher (his teammate) to attend the section finals to compete. "Honestly, I was quite scared about having only one race to qualify for the State meet as opposed to two, but I felt that it would benefit Don if he ran in my spot." The gesture was well received, and Don ended up running one of his best races of the season.

Perhaps one of the most common methods for sacrificing for the sake of a friend occurs when a friend consumes excessive amounts of alcohol. In this situation it is expected that one's friend is to sacrifice his night out in order to take care of his drunken, often vomiting friend. This was evident in our research on hazing (Anderson et al. 2012b) but equally as common this was that I saw it on multiple nights out with the teams I studied. For example, when a player was drunk on one soccer team, his friend took him home, paying an expensive taxi fair to do so.

Supporting these findings, Schrack-Walters et al.'s (2009) qualitative analysis of men's participation in athletics suggests that the development of communal and emotional affects is becoming increasingly more important between men on sports teams and finds that comments from athletes were laden with emotional intimacy. When these researchers heard men "express very high levels of affection for each other, none of the athletes qualified their statements using a heterosexual standard of acceptability" (Schrack-Walters et al. 2009: 92). Importantly, their data suggests that representing male athletes as monolithic "jock" individuals is an unfair representation of the experiences and gendered identities of all male athletes.

Thus, the emotions of love and support that young men express for each other, combined with sacrifice, are more akin to a love affair than a traditional male friendship. They are, what young men call, "bromance."

Bromance

As a consequence of fearing homosexualization or not being socially perceived as masculine, American males have been shown not to have close male friends (Komarovsky 1974; Pleck 1975). Morin & Garfinkle

(1978) suggested the fear of being labeled homosexual interferes with the development of intimacy between men: that they have not known what it means to love and care for a friend without "the shadow of some guilt and fear of peer ridicule" (Lewis 1978: 108). Men have been so alienated from each other that Jourard (1971) showed that self-disclosure, a vital component of emotional intimacy, was utterly lacking between males. Instead, young men knew that they had a friendship with another male when they did stuff together (Seiden & Bart 1975). Conversely, matters have been different for women. Women have maintained that they have a friend when they share emotions and, particularly, secrets together.

However, young men today do both. They make friends relatively easy, through doing things/stuff together (like sports, video games, drinking, exercising, shopping, or eating), but they also have the opportunity to quickly form strong, deep emotional relationships based off of emotional disclosure with one another.

This intimacy, the intimacy shown between heterosexual boys, both in the United States and the United Kingdom, is oftentimes self-labeled a bromance. One teenage athlete tells me that a bromance is "where it is like we are dating but really aren't." I suspect the "really aren't" part of his statement serves as a way of signifying that the relationship is emotionally as deep as it would be with a female, but that there is no sexual attraction. In other words, it's a love affair without the sex. Recall from the previous chapter men describing bisexuality in themselves because they maintained emotional love for their best friends. In this chapter I add further support.

Harry, 16, and who lives in the UK, explains to me that he is currently in a bromance and explains to me what it is, from his perspective:

> For me, I could say I show my love for him by hugs and saying that I love him. I can tell other friends I love them, but it's not the same sort of thing. With [names friend he's in a bromance with] it's more like in a family way; as if they were my family.

James agrees that a bromance is defined off of emotional intimacy:

> I guess since you can be more comfortable around them, you can talk about trusted things, and you know when to joke around or when not to. You know how to cheer up the person and what not. You care about them. You can hug them and what not. I'm not sure. You're just more comfortable around them.

Toan, a 16-year-old who lives in California, said that a bromance permits one to drop their gendered guard; to push boundaries:

> It offers a different more special kind of friendship. With a normal friendship, you can talk about similar things, have small conversations and have fun and what not. In a bromance, it's much more different. You can completely be yourself and be weird around them. Or at least in my case.

Alex, 18, from the UK, agrees that a bromance permits you to step outside guarded boundaries. He said that the more love you have and express for a friend, the more liberty you have to express other emotions; to push other boundaries with him. He said, "The interesting bit I think is that the more man-love you have for a friend the weirder the stuff you end up doing for laughs. Like a few years ago me and my best friend got nipple rings and had them chained together at a house party. It was funny."

Another teenage jock illustrates the similarity between a bromance and a relationship by suggesting that argumentation does not necessarily lead to break-up:

> You're allowed to be much more comfortable around them and also be mean to them and they'll understand. Like, you're able to just jump on them and they'll carry you, or you'll just cling to them, and they'll get pissed off and try to get you off. You're closer to them and are able to talk about more private things.

Others say that bromances are sometimes formed based off of shared interests and activities, but that the friendship evolves from just doing things together:

> They have similar ideas, likes, and enjoy doing things you do. You tend to be around them more because of that. I guess you could say they're your best guy friend. You can comfortably say that you love the other guy because he's so like you, and you like him so much because you guys are so similar and you get along so well. You agree with things, don't get angry much despite how you are to each other.

Corey, 19, from the United States, exemplifies what most of the men articulated, that they loved their best friends in a profound way. He said, "I love Dan. I mean I really love him. Call it a bromance if you want, but he's my boy... There's nothing I can't talk with him about."

This type of affection was commonplace among the teammates of the three American university soccer teams we performed ethnography on, but they are also common among the 15–18 year-old California boys I coach, or the California fraternity members I studied. Young men in all my studies were not shy about calling their affection love.

Not only do I see the love and intimacy of bromance in my research; not only do I hear of men telling me about their best friend(s) with terms of endearment; but I also hear from women about men's bromances. When I lecture on the topic to my students, I propose to them that homosocial bromances frequently eclipse heterosexual romances. I ask the women in my classes how many of them find that they are often the second choice compared to their boyfriend's bromance—women generally all laugh at this (perhaps a sign of genuine recognition of the esteemed place of men's friendship in their peer group) but equally important some women raise their hands. In the final review of this book, one 18-year-old undergraduate confirmed this. I asked her in front of the class, "If he had to choose you or him, who do you think he'd choose?" "Him," she said, "without a doubt." Finally, for those looking to see evidence of the bromantic nature of contemporary adolescent male friendships, all one has to do is log onto Facebook and befriend a few male youths.

Showing Love for One's Friends on Facebook

The love that young men show for one another today extends beyond their own private conversations. Social media, particularly Facebook, is bursting with florid emotions of young straight men showing their love for each other. They do this in multiple ways.

First, it is very common for young straight men to list that they are in "a relationship" with their best male friend. Ostensibly, this has the ability to publicly homosexualize one. It is not, for example, clear to those outside their immediate friendship network as to whether the "relationship status" means that one is in a homosexual or heterosexual same-sex love affair. Yet, because these young men live in a culture of inclusivity, this does not matter to them. For those who know the sexuality of the Facebook user offline, the act serves as a form of ironic heterosexual recuperation (McCormack & Anderson 2010a), but unlike heterosexual recuperation studies among men in their school settings (where their sexuality would be known to all), doing it on Facebook puts out a message to one's Facebook friends that one might not be straight. It is, at minimum, flirting with the privileging of homosociality over heterosexuality.

Another way that young men show their love is by listing their friends on Facebook as family members. Here, either they put down that their friends are "brothers" or they designate them with some other relationship label. Again, to those outside their immediate networks, nobody would necessarily know that one was not a blood relative.

Finally, and most significantly, heterosexual youth today express their love for their male friends with hearts, and touching emotional statements to each other. These messages are free for all of their hundreds of Facebook friends to see. Thus, in posting messages of love to one another on Facebook, they are not afraid to be thought gay for their expressiveness; instead, they revel in it.

Illustrating the type of love that friends show each other, I thought I'd capture some of the endearing posts that one 16-year-old American gay male has posted to his wall by his heterosexual friends. He gave me permission to scroll through his Facebook page for messages of love, and it was not hard to find them. The very first public wall posting was from a heterosexual male friend, who said to him the night before he traveled away on vacation, "Truth is...you funny as hell & you're a true friend man." The gay athlete posted to one of his heterosexual friends, "I love you [emoticon heart]." Under a photo of one of his older friends graduating, that friend has simply put a heart. Another posts a photo of him and writes, "here you go bro" adding an emoticon heart.

These sorts of postings perhaps vary to a degree. It's hard to quantify them, but I suspect that they occur more among friends in the UK than in the US, and more among university students than younger males. But the use of the word "love" is fairly libidinous on the Facebook wall posts of young men. And these are just the public proclamations; one wonders what emotional joys would be found in studying the text messages of young men?

Chapter Conclusion

Unlike young heterosexual men of Generation X, heterosexual male youth today engage in florid expressions of love between their friends. This love, both expressed in person and available to read on social networking sites, is reaffirmed when young men talk about their best friends, discussing them in the same emotionally intimate manner that they talk about their girlfriends. While males continue to bond over traditional methods (doing stuff together) they can quickly progress into more enduring friendships, and eventually into that of a bromance. Here, the emotional connection grows intense. In establishing a highly romantic but non-sexual relationship with another male the bromance makes it clear that, for this generation, love and sex can be independent constructs. One's love can be as strong or stronger for a bromance than a heterosexual romance.

It is difficult to speculate about the nature of post-university bromances. Educational settings are structured to foster them. What happens to the bromance when men enter the work world is unknown. However, I suspect that, combined with larger social forces, heterosexual men will at minimum be able to extend their relationships into their 20s. When one considers the dissolution of the institution of marriage (because of divorce, delayed entry into it, the cost of it, and the ability to achieve the same legal benefits without marriage) alongside the increased ability to achieve heterosexual sex recreationally; the increased acceptance of expressing love for a same-sex friend; and the delayed entry both into the workforce and family life, it seems likely that young heterosexual men will form sexless relationships together for longer periods than just university.

Exemplifying this, in 2006 I met two British males who openly identified as being in a bromance. They were best friends at 14, roomed together in university at 18–21, and then after graduating split up to take jobs in different cities. Shortly thereafter, however, they missed each other, so one relocated and they began living together again. At the writing of this book, in late 2013, the 23-year-old men continue to live together, not as roommates, but as best friends in a bromance. Both men pursue sex with women recreationally, and while not closed off to having girlfriends, one recently commented to me, "She would have to be a girlfriend a long time, and be very special, before I left Simon."

The narratives I speak of in this chapter therefore complicate heterosexuality. If two men share their thoughts, emotions, and lives, with each other, but are not having sex, how does that substantially vary from a husband doing this with a wife? Perhaps it only varies in the lack of loving tactility, outside of sex. Things like: kissing, cuddling, and caressing. So what then happens if heterosexual males also do this? As we will see in the following chapters—they do.

7
Kissing Other Men

In December 2007, two freshman girls from the Coaching Education Program I taught on at the University of Bath, England organized a "fun and games" session to celebrate the end of the semester. The festivities included a number of games and competitions, including one called "gay chicken." The rules were described that each pair of randomly picked, (ostensibly heterosexual) men were to motion toward a kiss, with the winner being the one who retreated last. Whereas one might expect young heterosexual boys to refuse to partake in the game, all six boys that were randomly chosen by the girls to participate agreed to play. Neither boy from the first pair "won." Instead, their lips locked in front of their peers. After this draw, the organizers determined that the next pair had to kiss for a period of five seconds. Again, no winner emerged. When the third set dramatically performed the kiss, the class cheered their originality, as one bent the other over and kissed him for half a minute. The students had no distaste for what they saw.

These events are a far cry better than the first time I had the opportunity to hear what heterosexuals thought of same-sex kissing. The year was 1997, and I was watching Kevin Kline's major motion picture *In and Out*, a romantic comedy about a gay male figuring out that he's gay. The theatre audience was willing to pay to see a gay-themed movie, but when it came to the ten second kiss that the main character shared with his new boyfriend near the end of the movie, the audience members groaned. I sat several rows behind a group of teenage boys who vocalized disparaging comments.

Since the early days of gay chicken, to British men, kissing each other has become a normal operation of undergraduate (and to a lesser extent younger) male friendships. Thus, to British undergraduates, the notion that straight men kiss other men is old news. This is fascinating when one considers that there is no historical tradition of men kissing, even on the cheek, as a form of greeting in England. Cultural anthropologist Kate Fox (2008: 191) notes that kissing for affection or greeting is only acceptable for women or gay men in England: "With the possible exception of a father and a young son, English men do not embrace or kiss one another." This is likely the same with American men. I can find no literature that describes men kissing in the United States (Reinisch 1990), but I am beginning to see the "gay chicken" era developing there.

In this chapter, I first explain the connection between sport and adolescent males kissing on the lips. I do this by examining data from 145 interviews and three ethnographic investigations of heterosexual male students in the UK, alongside short surveys of 90 heterosexual undergraduate males in Australia, and survey data of 475 men from throughout 11 American universities, as well as 75 in-depth interviews of American undergraduate men.

Results indicate that kissing occurs in all three countries, with the UK leading with 89 per cent of heterosexual male undergraduate men having at some point kissed another male friend on the lips and the United States trailing with 10 per cent of American heterosexual undergraduate males kissing.

I hypothesize that kissing behaviors are increasingly permissible in Western cultures due to rapidly decreasing levels of cultural homohysteria, and I argue that there has also been a loosening of the restricted physical and emotional boundaries of traditional heteromasculinity in these educational settings. This has gradually assisted in the erosion of prevailing heterosexual hegemony, something I describe as the one-time rule of homosexuality, which permits 37 per cent of heterosexual undergraduate men in Britain to have also made out (pulled) another male.

The One-Time Rule of Homosexuality

Heterosexuality has traditionally maintained hegemonic dominance in North American and Western European cultures, where privilege is unequally distributed according to one's perceived masculinity and sexuality (Anderson 2005a). That is, straight men with the highest degree of masculine capital tend to be rewarded, while those who break norms of heterosexual masculinity face prejudice and discrimination (Katz-Wise & Hyde 2012). In light of these harsh interpersonal consequences, heterosexual men and boys often fear being labeled as gay (Pollack 1999).

There are several ways in which men have traditionally avoided the stigma associated with being labeled as gay. Because male homosexuality is widely conflated with femininity (Johnson et al. 2007), heterosexual boys and men wishing to avoid stigma often act in distinctly non-feminine ways. For example, they generally do not work (Williams 1995) or play (Adams 2011) in feminized domains and they avoid engaging in feminine behaviors (Kimmel 1994) in order to uphold the perception that they are both heterosexual and masculine (i.e., heteromasculine). Aside from engaging in overtly heteromasculine behavior, the concealment of discrete instances of and desires for same-sex physical intimacy may also help men to avoid being labeled as gay. This is because, in North American and Western European cultures, any intimate display with a same-sex partner is conflated with a homosexual identity (Parker 2009). In line with this logic, Almaguer (1993: 253) suggested that American and Western European cultures historically carry "a blanket condemnation of all same sex behavior...because it is at odds with a rigid, compulsory heterosexual norm." Lancaster (1988: 116) similarly argued, "Even homosexual desires [in absence of behavior] stigmatize one as homosexual."

Borrowing from theories of racial hypodescent in which anyone with even a single drop of African ancestry was labeled as black (Harris 1964), I (Anderson 2008a) have referred to the total behavioral avoidance of same-sex physical intimacy as the "one-time rule of homosexuality." According to the "one-time rule," men must avoid performing even a single act of same-sex sexual intimacy, or even having any same-sex sexual desire, in order to be considered heterosexual. This widespread norm precludes men from engaging in fairly extreme forms of same-sex intimacy (e.g., recreational sex with other men), but also from more moderate forms of physical homosocial tactility (e.g., kissing on the lips or cheek), if they wish to avoid being labeled as gay.

The presence of heterosexual men kissing on the lips represents slippage, an erosion of the one-time rule. The men in my studies, regardless of whether they are located in the UK, Australia, or America, are not thought gay for their kissing. Surprisingly, this slippage to the total hegemony of what it once meant to be heterosexual began not with those who opposed the orthodox masculinity of jocks, but it emerged from the jocks themselves.

Kissing in Soccer

Steen (1995) suggests that the first same-sex kiss in British soccer occurred by Alan Birchenall of Sheffield United Football Club in 1973, indicating that it was "a joke." I have no way of knowing of the contexts or meanings behind the kiss, but it is fair to say that kissing has occurred on occasion at this level of the game before homohysteria. I suspect, but have no actual knowledge, that it likely ceased during the extreme homohysteria of the mid-1980s, as I can find no evidence of mention of players kissing in the 1980s. I strongly suspect that it did not occur because, in 1987, extreme homophobia was the reason for the outing of gay soccer referee Norman Redman. The homophobia against him was so extreme that it forced him from public life. Soon after, the Football Association moved to ban kissing among its players on the justification that it would prevent the spread of HIV/AIDS. It is unlikely that such a ban was necessary in that homophobic culture, however.

Kissing appears to have again emerged among British soccer players in the later part of the first decade of the new millennium. Still, in this masculinized field Lilleaas (2007) suggested that "two men kissing on the mouth breaks an unwritten rule," describing how in 2004 a professional player expressed his happiness during a match by kissing a teammate on the mouth. Spread across two columns, the kiss was featured in a national newspaper the following day. Journalists even began asking family members if he "had become" gay. Lilleaas highlighted that the stigma of a kiss between men did however appear to be eroding. She found that, in addition to kissing, compared to older players, younger team members were more willing to express emotions and talk openly about their sensitive sides. My research begins after Lilleaas (2007), and it adds to the historical understandings of kissing among British men.

A Kiss for Sporting Glory

My research suggests that kissing found its way into sport as part of hazing rituals in recent years (Anderson et al. 2012b). If one was willing to do something as vile as to kiss another man, in order to make it onto a sporting team, it highlighted their commitment to that team. However, the frequent use of same-sex kissing (and other homoerotic activities) as an instrument of hazing seems to have lost its lust in a rapidly decreasing zeitgeist of cultural homophobia. In our longitudinal research on sport team hazing (initiations) in the UK, we found that a same-sex kiss was simply no longer gross enough to work for hazing purposes. Essentially, in a cultural of decreasing homophobia, the stigmatized shelf-life of a same-sex kiss was limited.

The same-sex kiss then grew so commonplace in professional soccer (where it was modeled by athletes from other cultures) that it morphed from its antecedents in hazing to an expression of ultimate glory and victory on the pitch. From here, its cultural currency was made more fluid because it was symbolic of hyper-heterosexuality, as soccer players are hyper-heterosexualized by their sporting location and identities. I argue that around 2006 kissing next made its way out of sport and into youth culture, as a lark or *funny* game of chance, like gay chicken. At this stage it maintained enough homosexualizing capacity that only certain (highly masculinized) men, like jocks, could perform it—and only when drunk. From here it seems to have begun to be doled out (still judiciously) to highly esteemed mates, some of whom were not jocks, as a greeting and sign of affection, usually when drunk. By the end of the first decade of the new millennium same-sex kissing among heterosexual undergraduate men had become so acceptable that it spread to younger cohorts of men (Anderson et al. 2012a), like sixth form students, and older cohorts of men in team sports. It began to drip into virtually every corner of youth masculine culture in England. By 2010 I readily saw it occurring among non-educationally aspiring, economically disadvantaged, 16-year-old boys.

Sport does not get credit alone. Television and the internet have also spread same-sex kissing in the UK. Perhaps the British television show *Skins* carried the most cultural currency with teenagers. In 2007–2009 the show frequently portrayed straight high school boys (what the British call college) behaving in ways that would likely shock men of older generations. On one episode, the leading heterosexual character decided to give his best gay male friend a blow job. There was no justification for it, other than experimentation. Nor was his heterosexuality questioned. It was, rather, just something to do while on holiday. In another episode, he passionately kissed his best heterosexual friend (who he often shares a bed with) saying, "I love you. You are my best friend."

Studying Kissing

The boys kissing as part of classroom games was not the first time I saw "gay chicken" played at my British university. Nor was it the first time I saw two heterosexual, male university students kissing for other reasons. Throughout many of my other research projects, I had been observing, with rapidly increasing frequency, that heterosexual men were kissing their mates for other reasons during the fleeting years of the first decade of this century. I have also seen an expansion of the borders upon where the kiss is permitted. In fact, in just a few months I saw it move from a relatively "university" experience to a lower-class, harder, heterosexual youth culture. At one masculinized youth dance club I saw two men kissing one moment, and other men fighting the next.

In order to systematically determine why men were kissing, and to gain some notion of what percent of men were kissing other men in the UK, colleagues and I (Anderson et al. 2012a) decided to interview all of the players on one of the university's soccer teams, as well as to randomly select men coming out of a university library for interview, and to also look to see if it was occurring by asking younger men (aged 16) if they were doing it, too. All of those concerned considered themselves heterosexual. They were attending either one of two universities or one sixth form college (equivalent to grades 11–12 in high school). Thus their ages ranged between 16 and 25 years, with the majority of participants between 18 and 22 years.

The majority of interviews (92) were semi-structured, with in-depth interviews averaging 45 minutes (range 20–70 minutes), and using a list of topics as an interview schedule. In order to maintain conversation and facilitate the flow of the interviews, my research assistants and I did not follow questions sequentially or word them precisely the same each time. However, all of the topics were covered in each of the interviews.

Interviews began by asking the participants to self-identify as gay, straight, bisexual, or other. We then asked informants to describe their attitudes toward homosexuality. We then asked them if they had ever briefly kissed another man. Positive answers were followed up with questions relating to the nature of the kiss (how they kissed the other man, how long it lasted), and whether or not they had engaged in any form of sustained same-sex kissing. We also asked about the venue (location) in which the kiss/kissing took place and context in which it happened. Informants were then asked to describe, emotionally, what it was like to kiss another man, and what it meant to them intellectually and erotically. The interview also examined informants' perspectives of who they kiss. We asked questions about the criteria used in determining who will be the recipients of a same-sex kiss. We asked informants about their perceptions of men kissing today and why they thought it was acceptable. Also, we explored how they viewed homosexual men kissing in public. Finally, we asked questions relating to others' perceptions of men kissing (fathers, friends from home) and the role alcohol played in the initiation of kissing.

For the 53 shorter interviews, the schedule of questions was more tightly structured. For those who met criteria for inclusion in the study, in addition to demographic questions (sexual orientation, age, ethnicity, etc.), we asked questions relating to their participation in organized team sports, their attitudes toward homosexuality, and whether or not they had ever (even once) briefly kissed another man on the lips. Again, where a positive response was received, we followed up with a series of questions exploring the nature of the relationship informants had with the individual(s) they kissed, and if they had ever participated in extended kissing with another man.

British Straight Men Kissing Other Men

Eighty-nine per cent of the young heterosexual men my graduate students and I interviewed in the UK have, at least once, briefly kissed another heterosexual male friend on the lips. Our results did not include kissing one's father, kissing other men on the cheek (which also happens with great frequency today and is also culturally avowed), or kissing other men through athletic-team initiation rituals or hazing incidents (cf., Nuwer 2001). Of course, the circumstances under which these behaviors occurred, the recipients, and the meanings associated with these kisses, were multiple and varied. However, informants' kissing narratives predominantly revolved around issues of homosocial bonding and admiration for a friend.

Statistical analysis indicates that the athletes in this study engaged in significantly more kissing behaviors than non-athletes. I posit this is a result of both the fact that they maintain high degrees of heterosexual capital, and because sport promotes increased camaraderie and emotionality. Darren, a sixth form student, said, "Kissing happens all the time in football [soccer]. Loads of guys kiss on the lips after scoring a goal; you'll see it on T.V., too." Andy, who is a judo player, reported it also occurs in his sport. Will, a hockey player, commented that all athletes do it: "It's just part of sport now, isn't it?"

All of the men on the soccer team at another university said they had kissed. Grant said, "Yes. I kiss guys on the pitch. Guys I don't even know. And I'm not the only one." Grant added that he also kisses men on recreational teams, including men he is not close to. He said, "The first time it happened to me, I was 17, and I scored a goal. This guy ran over to me—some guy I didn't even know—and he just grabbed me and kissed me." When asked why kissing occurs in sport, he answered, "It's the energy of the moment. It's something that happens in moments of high emotion. It's normal in sport." These responses were mirrored by a number of athletes: the rationale, location, and meaning behind these kisses did not substantially vary between them.

Several informants suggested that same-sex social kissing occurred among men in their community-based sports clubs, too. For example, when Alex (who played cricket for a community club) was asked about kissing, he responded, "Yeah, we go out with all the older cricket lot, and they are always kissing each other." He indicated, however, that he only kisses players that are his age. "Some of the older guys kiss each other, too; but I only kiss my mates." Ryan also stated that while players on his team range from 16 to 35, kissing only occurs among those aged around 26 and under. While this does not serve as systematic evidence of kissing occurring with regular frequency in other sport settings, it suggests that research on kissing in other locales and among other demographics of men would be interesting.

Kissing Camaraderie

Our interviews showed that kissing not only occurred on the soccer pitch, but that social kissing also happened as part of a fraternal celebration off the playing field as well. This was true of both athletes and non-athletes. Thus, university men often kissed in public venues like dance clubs and house parties. Tom, a biology student, told us, "Kissing happens on nights out, yeah. It happens all the time. Just go to [names venue] tonight. You'll see it." Alex, a computer science student, agreed, "If you look for it, you'll see it; every night, in any club." Pat clarified, "It's not like if you walk in you're going to see wall-to-wall guys kissing... But, when you're with your mates, yeah, you give 'em a kiss. So I might kiss a few guys throughout the night."

Those who did not kiss suggested that it was primarily because they did not socialize in these types of gatherings. There was also a context of it being more the jocks and lads that kissed, compared to less social or popular men. Andrew said, "No. I don't do that. I don't really go out. I don't have *those* kind of friends." Matt commented, "I know everybody does it, but I just don't have many friends here. I spend most of my time with my girlfriend...but I don't have a problem with it." This sentiment was reflected among the sixth form students who did not kiss, too. As Jon said, "The athletes do that, yeah. But I'm not an athlete, and I don't go to their parties...but if I was part of that scene, I wouldn't be upset if another guy kissed me."

Of the 25 men who have not socially kissed in the British research, none were opposed to it. Ricky joked, "When I tell my mates what this interview was about, and they find out that I've not kissed a guy, you know what's going to happen? [referring to his belief that one of his friends would kiss him]...I'm not bothered by it," he said. "I'll let you know if it does, so that you can change your statistics." I received a text message from him later that night, reading, "I'm in the majority now."

Kissing Mechanics and Meaning

One factor the men in our study shared was that they did not consider their kissing a sexual act. Instead, participants likened these types of brief kisses to a strong embrace or other exuberant ways of showing affection for a close friend, at appropriate times. Tim said, "It's no more a sexual act than kissing your father," and Tom argued, "It's like shaking hands. Well, it's more than that, but it's the same attitude."

For the young men in my study, this type of kiss has been socially stripped of sexual significance. Whereas kissing a male friend on the lips would once be coded as a sexual act, the symbolic meaning of kissing has been differently interpreted by the participants. Here, kissing was consistent with a normal operation of heteromasculine intimacy. Highlighting this, when Pete was asked about which friends he kisses and which he does not, he answered, "I wouldn't kiss just anyone. I kiss my good mates." He continued, "You kiss a friend because there is no fear of being rejected; no fear of being knocked back." And when Pete was asked about how he measured who was worthy of being kissed, he said, "It's not that there is a system to who gets it or not. Instead, it's a feeling, an expression of endearment, an act that happens to show they are important to you."

A number of other men spoke of loving their friends ("mates"), too: kissing became a symbol of that platonic love. Mark said, "They [the kisses] happen because you are the guy's mate. It's an, 'I love you mate' type of kiss." Tim agreed, "Kissing others guys is a perfectly legitimate way of showing affection toward a friend." Ollie, a third year engineering student, added, "You do it sometimes when out having a laugh with your mates, yeah. But I suppose it's also a way to show how much we love each other, so we do it at home, too." When asked if these kisses were performed any different in private, he said, "Not really. No... You are more likely to pose for a camera when out and to perhaps play it up. But the meaning is the same. It means you love him."

Foreshadowing what I cover in Chapter 9, another student, Matt, highlighted how important emotional intimacy was to him, telling a story about breaking up with his girlfriend. "I was really lonely," he said. "Really depressed. So one night I asked my housemate who is one of my best friends if I could sleep in the bed with him. He looked at me, smiled, and said, 'Come on,' opening the covers to invite me in." Matt continued, "He kissed me, and then held me. It was nice... I sent him a text the next day saying, 'I've got the best friend in the world.'" Matt's story highlighted not only the intimacy he shared with his friend but that a kiss can also transcend the spatial context of partying.

Spatial Considerations

While the sixth form students in the study tended to kiss at parties or sporting events, about half of the undergraduates reported that they also kissed friends away from university parties and sport settings. Pete described his same-sex kisses as occurring "everywhere." Adding, "I don't know, maybe it's just where I grew up, but it's just no big deal." He said he was kissing men before coming to university, and listed a host of locations in which he had kissed them: a sixth form dance, the university library, and a variety of non-student dominated bars and clubs. He has never been harassed and added that his kissing has had no negative impact on his relationship with the men he kisses either. Evidence of this also comes through examination of student Facebook profiles. Here, one sees photos of men kissing mostly in pubs and clubs, but I have also seen men kissing on a train, at a beach, a music festival, and a multitude of other locations.

Harry said, "No. It's not just when we're out. It's not just because we're drunk. I probably kiss my housemates [at home] more than I do guys out on the lash [when going out and drinking alcohol]." He continued, "Like, I'll go into John's room and maybe he's lying on his bed reading. I'll bend over or lie down on top of him and kiss him; just to let him know I care about him." Similarly, Jim recalled that although his first off-the-field social kisses were performed "just for banter," lately he has been giving his friends more "endearing kisses" in non-partying locations. "It is just nice to kiss a mate," he said. Explicating this, Jim illustrated that he and a friend returned from a meaningful holiday together. "We were good friends before, but this trip just brought us together. We shared some real close emotional things and ended up great friends." He added, "So I looked at him and we just grabbed each other for a big kiss. I guess it was kind of a thank you to each other for making the summer what it was."

Contrary to heterosexual men having to physically and emotionally distance themselves from one another, our informants seemed to appreciate emotional intimacy. For those we interviewed, a same-sex kiss has been stripped of its homosexualizing significance and been re-coded as a symbol of platonic, heteromasculine affection (see McCormack & Anderson 2010a). A brief kiss, for the majority of these British men, is now a heterosexual symbol of homophilic intimacy. Real close friends, however, might do even more.

Making Out with Other Men

Many of the students said that they also engaged in *sustained* kissing with other men. Of the 145 heterosexual men interviewed, 48 said that they have (and sometimes regularly) engaged in provocative displays of same-sex kissing, which they described as being part of the repertory of jocular banter among friends. This extended kissing may be enacted for shock value, even though our data suggest that this type of intimacy between heterosexual young men is now so common that it does not seem to elicit the desired effect.

Overall, 12 (55 per cent) of the 22 sport-related students and six (24 per cent) of the 25 non sport-related students said they had engaged in a sustained kiss with other men. By way of contrast, 17 (32 per cent) of the 53 students interviewed exiting the library and one of the seven graduate students reported similarly. At the other university, 10 (63 per cent) of the 16 soccer players, and two (9 per cent) of the 22 sixth form students, said they had engaged in sustained kissing with another male.

Discussing his first extended kissing experience, Robin, a hockey player, recalled that he and his friend once tried to pull two women in a club: "We got rejected, so we just turned to each other and started going at it." Jon, a runner, recalled doing something similar: "I kissed a guy with tongues for about three or four seconds, so that some girls would do the same. You know like in the movie *American Pie 2* [where two young heterosexual college-aged men kiss to elicit a same-sex act from two college-aged women], you go, we go, you go, we go!" And, when Alex, a soccer player, was asked about this type of kissing behavior, he said, "I've kissed about three other lads that way." However, most of the men who engaged in this type of kissing did not do it in order to influence women to do the same.

One student recalled unexpectedly seeing one of his mates in a club. "I came running over to him and pulled him," he said. "Like properly." When asked what properly meant, he answered, "Like a proper pull... tongues and everything." And, when he was asked about the duration of the kissing, he answered, "Maybe ten seconds or so." Similarly, a rugby player said, "I've kissed over ten of my lad mates; and made out with some, too." Simon commented that he has one friend who gets particularly "kissy" when he is drunk. "I kiss him quite often," he laughed. And when Simon was asked if he considered this making out, he answered, "No. Not really. I mean, you can call it that if you want. I don't care. But it's not a sexual thing." Other interviews concur; they did not, personally, see this as a sexual act. Pat said, "No. It's not sexual.

You just do it for fun." Matt agreed, "Even if you're pulling another guy: it's just something you do for banter. But it's not sexual." While these men stripped the sexual significance out of prolonged kissing through homogenous banter, they nonetheless understood that *others* might view their kissing as a sexual behavior. "Of course," Simon acknowledged. "Yeah, two guys with their tongues in each other's mouths. But I guess it just doesn't matter." Matt said, "When I do it, I don't see it as making out. But I can see how others might." Conversely, Chris seemed confused about how to define it. He said that kissing a guy was, "A bit different. But apart from the stubble, it feels the same as kissing a girl." He continued, "But while it feels the same as kissing a girl, it's not the same as kissing a girl." He said whether it is in celebration, out of affection, or performed as banter, kissing other men was strictly non-sexual: "I mean it is sexual, but it's not sexy [read erotic]."

Key to this form of intimacy, and relevant to this work, these men demonstrate a shared understanding that while they were not erotically attracted to the men they kissed, they used kissing as a means of establishing intimacy, a close bond of friendship. It is this type of shared meaning that permits sustained kissing (within a semi-public sphere) to remain acceptable within a heterosexual framework, regardless of how those outside their network understood this meaning. Highlighting this, Jon said, "Did you see those two rugby players pulling in [names dance club on campus]? They were really going at it." However, when asked whether the men were gay or straight, he answered, "Dunno."

The shared understanding that kissing does not have to be erotic permitted the young men in our study to avoid being thought gay for kissing—at least within university and college culture. This was sometimes even the case when engaging in sustained kissing with *gay* men. Rory recalled kissing a gay mate, "just for fun." Mark disclosed that he engaged in prolonged kissing with two of his gay friends as well. "Just for laughs," he said. Both of these men indicated that they were drunk at the time.

Alcohol: Influence or Excuse?

Sustained kissing (making out, or pulling) is usually performed on nights out, when informants were under the influence of alcohol. This is consistent with literature that shows men frequently use alcohol in their homosocial bonding (Peralta 2007), and this is particularly true in England. Here, the age of consumption is just 18, and drinking is an integral part of social life among British university students.

Justin, a sixth form student, explained that sixth form kissing behaviors emerged at the same time as drinking. "I didn't see much kissing among my friends last year [in secondary school, where students are aged under 16] but now that we're in sixth form it happens all the time." When asked why he thought this was, he answered, "I think a lot of it has to do with drinking. You don't really drink at parties until sixth form." When asked about whether alcohol was necessary for creating a social environment conducive for men to engage in sustained banter kissing, James confirmed, "Yeah, I guess we kiss more often that way when we're drunk. But that's because we're out having a good time. Obviously, you are going to do it more when you're out having fun."

Iain, however, argued that men did not kiss *because* of alcohol. "It's not like you wake up the next day going, 'What did I do? You don't regret it or anything.'" He added, "Look on Facebook, you'll see that we don't regret it," referring to the almost ubiquitous phenomenon of heterosexual men posting photos of themselves kissing other men. Evidencing this, if you watched the full clip of the rugby team's night out that I mentioned in the introduction (YouTube account, Siwonjohn, and click on the "rugby team" video) you will note that when the rugby lads were shown their same-sex sexual exploits (including tongue to penis action) none regretted it; none chastised another as gay; instead, they all celebrated their actions.

Pete clarified the need for alcohol with humor. "I kiss guys when drunk," he said. "But I have to be *really* lashed [drunk] to work up the guts to try and pull women." Grant also indicated that when he kisses a mate, it is not because he is drunk. "Alcohol might make it easier for some guys, I guess. But I don't think that's why guys kiss." He added, "I can tell you why I kiss my friends. I kiss them because I love them."

International Variance

After publishing the data on the British men kissing, and with the help of Australian colleagues, I studied the same behaviors among heterosexual undergraduate men (using the precise same procedures) at a large Australian university. I then adapted the research into a large exploration of these behaviors among the undergraduate men at 11 different American universities.

Results from the Australian men show that 29 per cent have kissed on the lips, while just 10 per cent of those in the American sample have. However, 40 per cent of the American sample had kissed another male on the cheek, something we did not look for in the Australian or English samples.

Although the American sample reported a smaller incidence of same-sex kissing than research conducted among similar populations in the United Kingdom (89 per cent) and Australia (30 per cent), these differences should not overshadow the fact that a sizeable proportion of American heterosexual male undergraduates at the 11 universities studied have kissed or been kissed by another man on the lips (10 per cent), and that an even larger proportion have kissed or been kissed by another man on the cheek (40 per cent). Equally important, there appears to be little resistance to those who engage in such forms of homosocial intimacy. Thus, while the trend noted of undergraduate males kissing in the UK and Australia may not be as widespread in the United States, it is nonetheless present: heterosexual undergraduate men across the United States are engaging in behaviors that have traditionally been viewed as exclusively gay. This represents slippage to the one-time rule of homosexuality, and I suggest that it is the beginning of what will be a trend of increasing kissing among straight male friends.

A few years after conducting that 2011 study, I found some limited evidence (without looking too hard) of kissing's emergence from American high school students, a friend, who teaches high school in Southern California, wrote to me on Facebook:

> Alex and Jorge kiss on the lips in class. I think they got a reaction at first, but it wasn't ever anything like "ooh, gross." I think that at first kids watched them and now the kids just think that is just Alex and Jorge and maybe glance up for a second before they go back to cutting open their cats or looking in their microscopes. Sometimes Jorge sneaks a kiss from Jesus. My anatomy kids don't have problems with gay kids, so there is not really much reaction. Sometimes it is like, "Can you guys stop messing around so we can finish our lab," but never a creeped-out reaction.

And a 16-year-old high school student in the state of Washington, who emailed me after reading one of my articles online, wrote to me:

> Everyone at my school is pro-gay marriage except for the rednecks. It's normal for guys to kiss on the cheek at times, or the shoulder, or top of the head. It seems halfway between humorous and affectionate.

In theorizing the cultural lag with America, there might be a structural variance which has delayed the American kiss. Alcohol acts as a disinhibitor that escalates emotional expression, and while American undergraduates certainly consume it, it is legally restricted until age 21, whereas in the United Kingdom and Australia alcohol consumption is permitted at 18. Alcohol is widely available for consumption on British and Australian university campuses without penalty; it is even sanctioned at official university events, including university sanctioned sporting initiation rituals and university dance clubs.

Exemplifying the possible influence of alcohol on cross-cultural rates of kissing, participants in the American study who reported having kissed another man on the lips said that this behavior occurred in the context of alcohol only about 10 per cent of the time ($M = 10.29$, $SD = 28.44$). While similar effects have not been quantified in other research, alcohol consumption emerged as a dominant coded theme in British men's kissing narratives (Anderson et al. 2012a).

Chapter Conclusion

Most of the participants interviewed in the various UK settings had kissed another man on the lips. That these young men, regardless of their athletic participation, were able to kiss without being homosexualized by their actions suggests that either kissing has been stripped of its sexual significance and/or the sexual significance of two men kissing has been accepted within the terrain of heterosexual behaviors, at least within educational cultures in this part of the country.

My colleagues and I categorized and contextualized social kisses according to how they seem to have emerged. We first suggested that social kissing was determined as acceptable in sports (particularly soccer) as a celebration of athletic glory. Invasion teamsport athletes, jocks (as opposed to ice-skaters or male cheerleaders), were permitted to engage in kissing because of the heteromasculinizing nature of their competitive team sports. This is a consistent finding in sport and masculinity literature (Anderson 2005a; Pronger 1990), as it reflects the increased bravado, camaraderie, and acceptable heightened sense of emotional intimacy that comes with teamsport participation.

Kissing then merged into the social spaces university athletes mutually occupy with other students (dance clubs, classrooms, and pubs), concomitantly creating a spatial acceptance of kissing among non-athletes. Thus, jocks helped push this homosocial behavior into mainstream male youth peer culture. Here, it was widely made available to men with various degrees of heteromasculine capital. It is also made available to gay men—within these same student contexts—as the behavior seems to have removed the stigma from homosexual kissing: a same-sex kiss no longer marks one as gay in certain venues.

We also found that a large number of students have engaged in sustained kissing in these mixed student spaces. We again argue that this may be the result of a temporal-spatial shift that first began with athletes. However, unlike the simple kisses which emerged on the playing field, prolonged kissing seems to have been generated in and mostly restricted to pubs and nightclubs. Sustained kissing does not occur on playing fields or in other aspects of students' private lives.

Although many of our informants maintained that the simple kisses have been stripped of all sexual connotations, this is not always the case with sustained kissing. Although the students who engaged in this behavior maintained that they were not sexually attracted, nor did they receive sexual pleasure from this type of kissing, they were nonetheless aware that others could interpret the meanings of such behavior differently in their shared public space. Perhaps it is because of this awareness that these men played up their kissing, exaggerating it, *performing* it for heterosexualizing attention in the form of homosocial banter. Their performance can be seen as a way of using semi-arbitrary ambivalent language and behavior to produce homosocial intimacy. Thus, it follows the same principle as the mock homosexual acts that heterosexual male athletes (and men in other homosocial institutions) have engaged in for the purpose of homosocial bonding; it demonstrates that homoerotic behaviors sometimes serve as an ironic proclamation of one's heteromasculinity (McCormack & Anderson 2010a). Accordingly, heterosexual men who engage in prolonged kissing can be viewed in terms of a juxtaposition of a semi-public performance with a semi-private meaning. Because of the concurrence of public and private associations, it can be sexual, but is not always publicly coded this way because it is symbolized by homosocial joking and repartee.

There is, of course, much we cannot know about whether informants receive any sexual gratification from their kissing behaviors. Those I interview say that they do not, but this does not preclude certain individuals from taking private enjoyment. While the question of erotic pleasure was inconsequential in this research, there nonetheless exists an eroding of the one-time rule of homosexuality, and a stretching of acceptable heterosexual behaviors. This is because the behaviors of the men in this study *are* ambivalent: informants themselves were sometimes unsure whether the men they kissed were gay, bisexual, or heterosexual. Accordingly, it can be argued that there has been a subsequent slippage in the veracity of the one-time rule of homosexuality for sustained same-sex kissing as applied in this context.

Still, there are limits to the extent to which dominant ideals about heterosexuality stretch. There is no indication that the heterosexual men studied here desired to engage in or accept as heterosexual extended kissing that has the intent of deriving sexual pleasure. The current condition of heterosexual acceptability is that there is no sexual gratification from a kiss. It is therefore doubtful that, in this particular cultural context, at this particular point in time, further same-sex sexual activities would be understood as heterosexualizing. This does not mean that these men might not engage in same-sex sex; in fact, recent other research on another group of university athletes shows that 40 per cent have (Anderson 2008a). However, it suggests that further same-sex behaviors are not marked as heterosexualizing endeavors.

The findings presented in this study are consistent with my inclusive masculinity theory (Anderson 2009), which postulates a drastic reduction in cultural homohysteria among British, Australian, and American youth educational settings today. Quite simply put, young men in these geographical contexts are not as bothered by homosexuality as they once were, and this means that they are less likely to police gendered behaviors with homophobia.

It is difficult to say whether these men intend to contest orthodox notions of heteromasculinity politically, or whether they simply do so implicitly. The performance of simple kisses does not seem to reflect political intent. Instead, simple kisses reflect a mastery of their homosocial bonding in a more inclusive regional context. However, when it concerns extended kissing, respondents indicated that they knew they were actively and intentionally contesting older versions of acceptable heteromasculine behaviors. Furthermore, placing photos of both types of behaviors on Facebook enacts political agency, whether intended or not.

Claiming a same-sex kiss on Facebook is a means to extending cultural values beyond an immediate cohort of university or college friends. Most students have Facebook friends that include their teachers, parents, relatives, or others who may not understand the meanings of the portrayed kisses. Intentional or not, kissing and boasting of their kissing helps erode what has traditionally been a highly regulated culture for heterosexuals. In kissing these men—with or without understanding the potential implications of their actions—it seems these heterosexual men have also challenged heteronormativity and homophobia. Essentially, then, traditional notions of heterosexual masculinity have been betrayed by a kiss.

8
Freaking Other Men

The music blares throughout the dance hall. Youthful, intoxicated bodies hedonistically pulsate, absorbing its rhythms. The colored lights flash across the walls and reflect off the floor. John and Peter synchronize their gyrating hips to the beat. Their attractive bodies slowly succumb to the libidinal forces of the music. Their crotches join, pulsing and grinding together in synchronized form. John wraps his left arm around Peter's lower back and Peter's right hand grabs John's neck and draws him in closer. As the music and lights climax, Peter goes in for a kiss. John mirrors Peter and their lips touch.

This is not a gay club, and Peter and John are not gay. This is a British university dance club, and Peter and John are self-identifying heterosexuals who attend the university. After dancing, Peter leaves John to walk over to his girlfriend, Sarah, who is standing nearby. He takes her hand and gives her a kiss on the cheek, ostensibly, a reminder that his dance with John was no threat to the sexual attraction he feels for her.

Peter and John are not alone in the sexualized nature in which they dance. Virtually all men in this and four other university-aged clubs that my research colleagues and I conducted participant observations in saw men dancing this way. Today, young men in the UK go to clubs together, in groups or pairs, and for most of the evening dance only with each other.

It is not just men dancing together that I see. I often see two men snake through a crowded dance floor, one holding the hand of the other, so as not to lose him in the dense crowd. At the same club, men sit in a corner, one's arm draped around the other. At an inner-city, non-university club, two youths kiss. These are not one-off incidents, either. They exist as a normal operation of youth masculinities within dance club culture.

Accordingly, I suggest that what used to be subversive signs of a polarized gender and sexuality order are increasingly found in the domain of popular and normative heterosexual culture. Where at once men's bodies could never touch on the dance floor, matters have radically changed. From the fashion they wear to these clubs, to the casual kissing that occurs upon greeting or celebrating with friends, straight men today often engage with each other in ways unrecognizable to the eyes of Generation X.

Illustrating the frequency of this, I asked the 36 males of my incoming fresher class how many had freaked another male on the dance floor. All had. This occurrence, among a group of men who have come from a variety of locations throughout the United Kingdom, empirically satisfies me that the occurrence is normal for their age-group. Yet writing about dancing research is difficult.

Dancing occurs in synch to music, which is commonly understood as both reflecting and shaping contemporary culture. It's hard to put into words what dancing is, or how it feels though. Thus, in this chapter, I examine the relationship between how men dance, what music they listen to, and what political forces are at play, but I do it through my observations not interviews.

McClary & Walser (1994) emphasize how the dancing body is a significant sight worthy of academic attention, arguing that it is through the body's corporeal interpretations that the musical/historical moment is often revealed—especially when it is subversive in nature. With this in mind, I explore in this chapter not only how I see young men move together on the dance floor, but how politics affect the music they listen to, and the form of dance men use to embody that music, to celebrate it with other men.

Heteromasculinity on the Dance Floor

When I was 17, my friends and I would drive to Knott's Berry Farm, a Southern California theme park that hosted a dance club in the warm outdoor Southern California air. Here, a new style of dance was to be found. We were the first generation to be able to dance without having to learn a formalized dance. Thus, we all freely danced around the dance floor together. Well, sort of. While the boys and girls were all on the dance floor, the boys were also keenly aware that they were not to either dance together, or even too close to one other. If one were to turn to speak to a friend, one had to cease dancing immediately otherwise it might look like two men were dancing together, and as Griffin (2000) shows, when that actually happened at Disneyland in 1980, the two men were expelled from the park. The guards said, "This is a family park. We do not put up with alternative lifestyles here" (p. 126). The men were not even slow-dancing together; they were merely fast-dancing while looking at each other. In 1987, Disneyland expelled some college students for slow-dancing together, saying, "touch dancing is reserved for heterosexual couples only" (p. 126).

It was not until a decade later that men started to dance near each other, to engage with each other verbally while doing so—but then even here it was only if they were talking about which girls they found attractive, and only if they at least made pretense that at one point they would be brave enough to attempt to dance up on them.

Men of *i*Generation recognize none of this homohysteric dancing. Today, men come to dance without dates, they navigate the dance floor in their same-sex friendship groups, and they move to and press against each other's bodies. Straight men freak and grind each other, sometimes simply as a laugh, other times as part of celebration of their friendship. Their bodies are no longer repulsed by a homohysteric culture.

My observations are not limited to dance clubs in the United Kingdom, either. As part of my research on soccer teams in the US, and that of a mainstream fraternity (Anderson 2008b), I have attended multiple dance clubs. In these spaces I note that men do not dance with each other closely, they do not press their bodies to each other the way they do in the UK, but they do dance with each other in their own space. In other words, there is a cultural lag which puts distance between men. Thus, it would not surprise me should undergraduates reading this book in the US email me after its production to say that in their clubs, they dance with their bodies pressed to their male friends, too.

Dancing around Homohysteria

It's taken a number of changing social trends to positively influence heterosexual male youth to the degree that they grind their bodies into another while dancing. After all, dancing is understood to be not only a performance for others, but also a source of kinesthetic enjoyment for one's own pleasure. Thus, if two heterosexual men are willing to engage with each other's bodies this way, it must indicate a reconfiguration of how heterosexual men view their gendered identity. In my analysis, these events directly reflect the cultural level of homohysteria. In times of high homohysteria, males ask only other females to dance. In times of no homohysteria, they are free to dance with each other as they do women. In fact, because heterosexual men's dancing together is not scripted as foreplay, or sexual, men are more free to dance with each other than with women.

The apex of cultural awareness of homosexual identities existing as a static and sizeable extent of the population that occurred in the mid-1980s, the same period during which I feared dancing too close to another male while in high school, was the period our culture grew aware that anyone could be gay (sending men into homophobic performances in order to prove that they were not gay). Culturally speaking, we developed extreme antipathy toward homosexuality. Thus, in the 1980s the gay male community was hit by two substantial socio-political events. These events impacted not only gay masculinities (Levine 1998) but men's gendered understandings as a whole. The first came in the form of a cultural backlash to the gains made by gay men and feminists of the 1960s and 1970s, and the second came in the form of a virus.

Peterson (2011) writes that the development of the counter-culture in the 1960s and 1970s and the subsequent conservative backlash of the 1980s are perhaps best seen in the phenomenon of disco. Disco, he suggests, was invented by largely unacknowledged black, gay DJs who overlapped "soul and Philly (Philadelphia International) records, fazing them in and out, to form uninterrupted soundtracks for nonstop dancing" (Thomas 1995: 439). The use of black soul music, itself derived from black gospel, marks the secularization and appropriation of black church music by gay men and, thus, the reconfiguration of religious narratives into sexual ones.

Notably, disco arrived on the music scene before homohysteria. Thus, the overt flamboyance of the dance style was acceptable to young, straight men. In this same respect, disco, for gay men, became popular. It provided some of the first spaces where gay men could come together and "out" their forbidden desires to one another.

Disco came to a sudden demise, however, with the ushering in of the 1980s. The homophobic-slanted 1979 campaign of "disco sucks" set out to abolish disco and its homosexual (sexual deviancy) and feminine associations (Hughes 1994). The apex of this phenomenon was most poignantly expressed during a mass demonstration at the half-time show "Disco Demolition" at Chicago's Comiskey Park baseball stadium. DJ Steve Dahl led an over-capacity crowd of 50,000 in a ritualistic explosion of the crowd's self-sacrificed disco records; he piled them together and detonated several pounds of TNT to the crowd's chants of "Disco Sucks! Dis-co Sucks!" (Cheren et al. 2000).

Accordingly, just as disco emerged from the closet in the 1960s and 1970s, it was forced back in with the beginning of the homophobic

1980s. The flamboyancy of movement and flash of disco's attire exhibited by John Travolta in the movie *Saturday Night Fever* (1977) was no longer palatable to young heterosexual men. Disco was too gay, too soft, and too feminine. With a recession in 1979 and continuing into the 1980 election of President Ronald Reagan in the United States, alongside the 1979 election of Margaret Thatcher in Britain, cultural conservatives were determined to reclaim their respective countries from the apparently out-of-control counter-culture and New Left of the 1960s and 1970s. The excess of disco, both its material glamour and sexual freedom, could not survive such cultural changes.

This trend continued in the 1990s with the religious right's crusade to reclaim "the soul of America" (as Pat Robertson declared in 1992), which in most contexts meant to re-masculinize America. Heterosexual gender roles were to be recalibrated through organizations like the religious right's "Promise Keepers." Freud's explanation of homosexuality as the product of an absent father figure also found a renewed emphasis during this time. Mainstream culture was hell-bent on addressing and redefining the crisis of masculinity.

The political atmosphere of the mid-1980s and 1990s made its mark in dance music. Disco was phased out and replaced by the largely homophobic and "hyper-masculine" genre of rock 'n' roll. Peterson (2011) says the only surviving remnants of disco were its musical descendants, "garage" (in New York from 1977 to 1984) and "house" (in Chicago from 1984 to 1989), both derived from the original New York gay, black disco music trope. These genres, however, eventually developed into "acid house" (1988–1992), "hardcore" (1988–1992), and "industrial" (1983–1992). The new forms of club music abandoned diva narratives and instead emphasized sensory overload with pure, electronic loudness and speed, employing rigid rhythms, dark tones, and extreme frequencies.

Left in the wake of these inherently "hyper-masculine" forms, disco waned and its use was primarily transfigured into requiems for the many lost by the HIV/AIDS crisis. As Walter Hughes (1994: 156) poignantly writes, "1970s [disco] songs like 'Don't Leave Me This Way' and 'Never Can Say Good-bye' [became], in the 1980s, part of the work of mourning." Songs that once celebrated sexual excess were now being used to cope with unimaginable losses from the disease. Bodies that were once virile with heightened sexuality and donned masculinities were now stripped by the virus, poxed with Kaposi's sarcoma, and stigmatized as a contagion by ignorant and reluctant governments.

HIV/AIDS had an incalculable and unfortunately rarely acknowl-edged effect on the gender expression of men, both heterosexual and homosexual. Gay men's suspicions of other men's serostatus functioned as a form of sexual survival and fostered an environment of systematic corporeal policing among men. Such anxieties became reflexive, shaping how men developed and advertised their bodies for sexual encounters. To disassociate oneself from previous markers of gay virility, namely the hair and moustaches of the 1970s and 1980s, the sexual economy of the 1990s depended on the theory that the younger and more muscular a man was, the less likely he was to have HIV/AIDS. In the late 1980s and early 1990s, body hair became a sign of age; it meant age in particular but experience in general and thus was conflated as a prime indicator of health (Signorile 1997). This led to the ultra-masculine, hairless, shaved bodies and faces that dominated the 1990s and continue to spread throughout metropolitan heterosexual and homosexual communities to date. Men's bodies are desirable when they are depleted of hair.

Essentially, this era was more or less a corporeal pissing contest based on who looked youngest and disease-free, explicated through hairless muscularity. The hauntingly Darwinist nature of 1990s gay sexual poli-tics continued to edge the more feminine and less masculine alternative gender signs further toward the margins of gay communities.

Medical technologies of the 1980s and 1990s also added to the mas-culinization of both gay and straight cultures. Steroids were first intro-duced into gay communities as a necessity for HIV/AIDS patients, but were soon misused by many (gay and straight) men as body enhancers (Halkitis 2001). Similarly, with the proliferation of fitness industries in the 1990s (with gyms and vitamin shops becoming a cornerstone in most urban areas) men adopted new workout regimens to ensure mus-cular physiques (Pope et al. 2005).

If HIV/AIDS did anything good for the gay community, however, it comes in the fact that it brought such visibility (albeit the wrong type) to homosexuality that it solidified that homosexuals existed in great numbers. As I wrote in Chapter 2, HIV/AIDS showed "normal" society that we (gays) were lurking in every social institution.

Equally as important, it was another catalyst for gays and lesbians to talk about homosexuality from a "rights" perspective. Then, as the virus later took hold in heterosexual communities, the stigma it brought to those infected slowly began to wane. As this occurred, social attitudes began to swing back in the other direction. By 1993 homophobia, and the orthodox masculinity used to sustain it, was in retreat.

Thus, just as increasing homophobia (through the awareness of homosexuality) begat compulsory "heteromasculinity" and social distance among men in the 1980s and early 1990s, it stands to reason that a reduction in cultural homophobia would have just the opposite effect. As homophobia declines, men should be permitted—even encouraged—to come closer together, physically and emotionally. As homophobia lessens it should permit dance, with styles more akin to disco, to re-emerge—something that Peterson (2011) and Peterson and I (Peterson & Anderson 2012) argue materialized in the early 2000s.

The University Dance Floor as a Cultural Site of Shifting Masculinity

I propose that today's new cultural formations of gender and sexual categories can be best viewed in the often academically neglected landscape of the dance floor, which is a particularly good indicator of the power of the broader culture. When my male students take delight in not only dancing with each other, but also in dancing up on me (an openly gay professor) it indicates that there has been a lessening of the restricted manners in which heterosexual men move their bodies, even sexualizing themselves for gay men.

In *Dancing Desires* (2001), Jane Desmond argues that "dance provides a privileged arena for the bodily enactments of sexuality's semiotics and should be positioned at the centre, not the periphery of sexuality studies" (p. 3). This is fascinating, but difficult to prove empirically. The language used to describe dance is difficult, slippery. One struggles to organize short-lived gestures, glances, and costuming into discernible vocabularies and categories to be analyzed—vivisecting the moves of a live body and repositioning them to suit theoretical frameworks. Nonetheless, closely examining the nexus of cultural moments and movements can illuminate current gender regimes.

Besides the musical structure encased in pop music—which employs variations of tension and release with chorus/verse and density of highs/lows—the lyrics, more than any other factor, point to pop music's explicit project of uniting bodies through sexual desire. Notably, many of the hit pop songs of the early 2000s, a time in which men were beginning to shed the hegemonic baggage of orthodox masculinity, carry traces of the liberating theologies characteristic in earlier forms of disco. This was an era with the celebrated music of, for example, Destiny's Child's "Survivor" (2001) or Christina Aguilera's "Fighter" (2002). These songs uncannily recall defiant disco antecedents like Gloria Gaynor's

"I Will Survive" (1979) and Diana Ross's "I'm Coming Out" (1980) that often relied on individualism and self-reinvention. Interestingly, many of the clubs I attended around 2006–2008 mixed these songs with current pop music (along with several other disco/gay/camp songs). It is still quite common to see men dancing and singing to "It's Raining Men." One British dance club, almost exclusively inhabited by undergraduate men, makes this an anthem. When the song is played in its original version all of the men remove their shirts, swinging them around their heads. They grab each other, grinding other men close. They shout the words so loud it would be difficult to classify it as singing. Meanwhile the women vacate the dance floor, or at least move to its edges. This, a song that was originally developed and sung by women, singing about men, has been coopted in this club. It is now a song for men to sing, about themselves, in a fraternal, drunken, semi-nude, and often highly homoerotic celebration of inclusive masculinities. Indeed, McCormack (2012a) finds the sixth form (high school) students dancing in similar ways in their common room to "I'm a Barbie Girl."

Today's pop songs function as choreographic instructions to dancers. When lyrics of possession or seduction occur, the dancers on the floor have the narrative justification to approach another dancer and engage in mutual choreography, often with movements focusing on the crotch area. The familiarity with the songs' lyrics and rhythms provides dancers with a greater ability to repeat the choreographic narratives embedded in the music. It is here that codes of gender expression and interaction can be most provocatively exploited and played up-on. In British clubs today, the sex of the individual approached is secondary to enjoying the movement of the approach. The dancer thus becomes a mimetic extension of the song's story and is called upon to act it out by dancing with other bodies in the club. These bodies may have needed to be that of women a decade or so ago, but this is no longer a requirement today. In fact, young men tell me it's easier to approach a male friend to dance; there is less chance of rejection.

Heterosexual male dancers don't just dance to the music either. They lip-synch or sing along to songs they know, even mumbling the words to songs they don't know—hence further extending the music's narrative performance into what is known as a speech act that is also demonstrative of inclusive masculinities. For example, Madonna's "Music" (2000) ("Hey Mr. D.J.//Put a record on//I wanna dance with my ba-by"), and Missy Elliot's "Get Your Freak On" (2001) ("Now people gather round, now people jump around") function in similar ways. They are common and popular lyrics that inspire young men to join in—singing with gay men's divas. The lyrics not only of these songs, but of a decade's worth of songs since these, help script the act of dancing onto the dancer's body, shaping choreographic flirtations and desires and encouraging the sexual possession of other dancers' bodies. The songs can be new or old, they just need to make the male body feel good to act them out.

Exemplifying this, at another British university club, it has become tradition to play Queen's "Don't Stop me Now" (1979). Here, men again scream at the top of their lungs to Freddie Mercury's lyrics. In this club, as with many in Britain, removing one's shirt is cause for expulsion. This song, played at the end of the evening, signals to the men that it's now time to remove their shirts, as they can't be kicked out of a club that is closing. At this hour, men are dripping in sweat; sweat earned in a club hosted in a building built hundreds of years ago. There is no dehumidifier in operation, no air conditioning. Men are drenched in sweat, yet they scream, arm in arm, holding each other, thrusting an available arm into the air. Those who have not managed to pull a woman to bring home for the evening will leave the club with the same men that they came with. They spill out onto the streets proclaiming their love to each other, celebrating "having a good time, now" before returning home to sleep in each other's beds, and sometimes each other's arms (Chapter 9).

Integrating Straight and Gay Club Space

When I came out of the closet in 1993, I began (as most gays do after coming out) attending gay clubs to meet other men. Whether it be in Los Angeles, Orange County, or other major cities that I traveled to throughout the United States, these clubs were almost exclusively inhabited by gay men, and sometimes a heterosexual female friend. Straight men did not venture into "our" space. In the late 1990s my partner and I began frequenting a venue that boasted of a particularly young and good looking crowd of men. The club began at 7969 on Santa Monica Blvd. in Los Angeles, and was originally called "Tiger Beat." But after threat of a lawsuit by the teen-bop magazine of the same name, they changed it to Tigerheat.

The Thursday night event grew rapidly in popularity. As the numbers swelled it relocated to larger and larger club venues. By the time it arrived at the Hollywood Athletics club, I thought I had seen its apex. Here, in 2002, the crowd swelled with gay men, but occasionally one could find a straight male or two as well.

I remember receiving disappointed comments from my friends at the club one night. I had invited the 250 members of my sexualities class at the University of California, Irvine to attend the club with me. About 40 of them showed up, nearly half male. This might not seem like many to today's readers, but at the time 20 young straight men showing up to a gay club was remarkable. My friends, however, found it insulting: an intrusion of their gay space. Not only could they not hit on these men, but they were offended by their defensive heterosexuality, dancing and kissing the women that also came. I was asked by several of my friends at the club not to bring them back.

I moved to the UK in 2005, but in the spring of 2012, I returned to conduct ethnography on a high school running team. One of the athletes had just come out of the closet to me, so I took him back to my old stomping grounds. The club, still operating on a Thursday night, with the same DJ (Ray Rhodes), is now at the super-large Avalon, on Vine Street in Los Angeles. Of the several thousand that show up each week, around 30 per cent, perhaps more, are straight. In fact, the club has become so straight that when one reads about it on their website, hardly is the word gay mentioned. Thus inclusive perspectives on heterosexual masculinity have drawn straight men into gay clubs. Here they are able to enjoy the music more, with less fear of posturing to avoid confrontation with a heterosexual male defending his woman.

It is not just this club that has been integrated by sexual orientation. The percent of straight people attending London's biggest gay venue, GAY, has also risen sharply since I first attended it in 1998. GAY is likely 50 per cent straight on any given night. In fact, it appears to be only the smaller gay venues that remain as mostly gay clienteles; principally, those that serve primarily as a bar and only secondarily as a dance venue. Venues that exist for dance are today attracting a mix of all sexual orientations.

Yet it is not just that gay venues have become popular with heterosexuals—it is now permissible for men to hit on other men in heterosexual venues as well. In Bath, England, for example, one of the venues, Moles, gathers around 90 per cent a heterosexual crowd. Yet each week on Cheesy Tuesdays, gay men gather there as well. They kiss (pull) each other in front of the straight men, and I have pulled straight men in this and other straight clubs myself. It is this acceptability which proves to me "the proof of concept" of inclusive masculinities. When gay men can hit on straight men, in straight spaces, we know the culture has progressed.

Chapter Conclusion

Where heterosexual men were once prohibited from dancing with each other, or even dancing too close to each other (in times of high homohysteria), matters began to change in the early part of the 2000s. Dance club culture has continued to promote more inclusivity ever since. Today, in England, men dance with each other, grinding their sweating bodies (sometimes without shirts) together. They go to a dance club to dance with each other in equal measure as they go to pull or dance with women. Dancing is sexual, but the club is no longer just a venue for the expression of heterosexual desires or opposite-sex couplings. As homohysteria has declined it has even permitted disco bands to become in vogue again, and reach the masses with bands like Daft Punk.

Today's clubs serve as places to bond with other heterosexual men, perhaps to a greater degree than sport provides. In dance clubs, they explore homosocial interactions in a culture which promotes it as acceptable, enjoyable, and sometimes even important. Here, men erotically touch one another and sometimes even kiss. They dance among their gay friends too, unbothered by their pulling (kissing) in the same club space. Effectively, these students are reformulating the university's masculine peer culture, making their own inclusive world where their same-sex desires and enjoyments can find expression within a new heterosexual framework. Then, after these straight men leave the club, they rarely return home alone. Instead, they return to one of their friend's places where heterosexual men crawl into bed together, to cuddle and spoon, as they fall asleep.

9
Cuddling and Spooning Other Men

In 2013, I interviewed Stuart, a first year heterosexual undergraduate, and asked him about sleeping in the same bed with his friends. "I do it all the time," he told me. I inquired as to how often "all the time" was. "Two to three nights a week," he said. Throughout the course of the interview, Stuart told me who he cuddles in bed with, and why. I asked him about the mechanics of what happens in bed, and the meanings associated with sleeping together. It is here that Stuart told me that he even cuddles in bed with guys, immediately after "fucking a girl."

After a night of drinking and clubbing, Stuart often brings women home for sex. This is the benefit of living in a hookup culture (Bogle 2008). He has sex with these women in his bed, but does not kick them out immediately after. "You don't want to send someone out drunk alone on the streets in the early hours of the morning." But that doesn't mean that Stuart wants to sleep alongside, or cuddle with, the woman he's had sex with, either. It is at this point that he leaves her to sleep, alone, in his bed. He then goes to sleep in the same bed with one of his male housemates.

I asked Stuart if he is bisexual. He said that he is not. I asked him why he would then leave a girl in bed to be with his mate. He answered, "Just cuz I like don't wanna have to deal with them [the girls] in the morning." He added, "I would rather have time with the boys, who love me, than a girl I lusted after a few seconds ago." I confirmed the story with Stuart's housemate. "Yeah, he loves us, what can I say? We're like that. We all really love each other."

Interviews with undergraduate athletes both in the United States and the United Kingdom suggest that sleeping in the same bed with another male is normal throughout childhood, but somewhere around puberty, somewhere between 11 and certainly by 14, sleepovers generally end for the Americans. In interviewing older British male friends about sleepover practices, it also becomes apparent that males only began sleeping in beds together in the UK, out of choice, in recent years. Although it is not systematic evidence for the absence of men of Generation X sleeping together in beds in the UK when they were in university, it was not the case for the five British males in their 40s that I interviewed about it. For example, one of my heterosexual British friends, born in 1970, tells me that he stopped doing sleepovers at his friends when he was around 11, and that it was unthinkable to share a bed with a friend unless one was in a hotel on an away match. He said, "There was really no such thing as sleepovers in the UK in the 80s. There was no sleeping in the same bed after being drunk at university or out with mates in any capacity." He added, "There is the odd time when I have shared a bed with my brother on a family holiday or something and there might have be an odd occasion when it happened with a friend, but I really can't recall any." I asked him about sleeping over at other guys' places after a night of drinking. "There were occasions where a group of us have gone out, and a number of us have crashed on the floor, but not in a bed."

Another British friend, born in 1985, tells me that sleepovers were regular between ages 8–11 too, but that after that the boys started sleeping "tops and toes," one guy's head by the other's feet, as a way of symbolically indicating that they were not sexually interested in each other. This means that, for this male, as an undergraduate freshman in September 2003 through his final year of university in 2007, cuddling was not happening, at least not with him or with others that he knew of. But unlike my older friend, sleeping in the same bed was occurring— there was just no cuddling.

However, I saw my undergraduates cuddling (the opening vignette of this book) in 2006. Furthermore, in January 2007, the first episode of the British teenage drama *Skins* aired. The drama took place in Bristol, England, where I lived at the time. I suspect that the show might have been important in reflecting a behavior that was emerging among some straight young men, and while I cannot say with evidence, it seems possible that the show helped spread the behavior.

I liked *Skins* because it accurately portrayed the interactions of guys I saw both in my research and simply hanging out in my town. The accuracy of portraying teenagers closer to how they actually were (as opposed to American teenage shows like *Glee*) was perhaps a reflection of allowing youth to write the script, rather than adults. With an average writing age of 21 (according to Wikipedia) and consultancy with teenagers (including one in my studies) the physical touch between characters both reflected what teenagers did in Bristol, England at the time (see McCormack 2012a), and also made it normal for others watching the show. The critically acclaimed show regularly featured heterosexual boys sleeping in the same beds together. Any fan of the show will recall lead character Tony sleeping in bed with his mate Sid under sheets with a naked man and woman on them. Sleeping together was common practice not only with the hardened and economically deprived characters of *Skins*, but also with the upper-middle class students at the highly ranked (posh) university in which I was teaching at the time: the University of Bath. Here, sleeping in a bed with another man was not only commonplace, but oftentimes preferred. Thus, it seems that cuddling for undergraduate men likely began sometime around 2005, and was likely consolidated by the popularity of *Skins*.

Desiring to know the frequency of bed sharing, I interviewed 40 heterosexual, male students in one of my sport classes in 2010 as well as ten British sixth form (high school) students and ten American high school students in 2013. Data from the university student-athletes indicated that 39 of the 40 had slept in bed with another male. The 40th indicated that he wasn't sure if he had or had not: "I might have when pissed [drunk]," he said. In other words, sleeping in the same bed with another male was so normal, and so socially acceptable, that it would not be a highly memorable event: it is not marked by stigma. The same was the case for the ten British sixth form athletes, but it was not the case for the American high school athletes. I did, however, observe heterosexual men sleeping in the same beds in my American ethnographies of university soccer teams.

In this chapter I consider how sleeping with other men represents an act of homosocial, but not homosexual, physical and emotional intimacy between two (or more) ostensibly heterosexual males. I discuss the different type of sleeping/cuddling arrangements that exist, and even discuss how straight men cuddle with gay men. I also interview a student-athlete still in school (aged 15) in order to understand when guys begin cuddling in the UK. I finish by highlighting the difference between American and British adolescents when it comes to both sleeping and cuddling in bed with another male.

When Two Guys Share a Bed

Bed sharing that occurs between young men is sometimes "relatively" without contact, particularly before boys go to university. Guys go out drinking together, or just stay over at each other's places, and sleep in the same bed as a matter of convenience of not sleeping on a hard floor. Sleeping together is also helpful, particularly in England, where it is colder. Most British people do not run their heaters at night, living in what Americans would consider very cold houses.

It is important to remember, however, that even when two men just "sleep" together in the same bed, it doesn't mean that there is no physical contact between them. Unlike the hotel beds I shared with my American high school teammates on away trips, British beds are much smaller: what Americans call a "queen" size bed, the British call "king" sized. And most all students do not have this size bed in their rooms. The standard bed in university is called a "single." Americans will recognize this size as a bunk bed. It is just 36 inches wide (less than a meter). Beds in student's homes are not much bigger, and most students also have a single bed (36 inches wide) or, if lucky, a double (54 inches wide). Rooms are small in the UK, thus the beds are too. Accordingly, almost any bed sharing necessitates not just some, but a good degree of, physical contact from one's sleeping partner.

Despite this, sleeping together in bed is normal for undergraduates in the UK. Tom provided an example of how one might end up doing such. "One time me and all my mates went out, and I ended up walking home to my best friend's and stayed at his because I couldn't be bothered to walk the rest of the way to mine." "What did you do?" I asked, "Just knock on his door and say, 'hey wanna cuddle?'" Tom laughed, "No, we have these things called phones, so I texted him and asked if I could stay at his." Tom said that his friend said, "yes," so he walked into his friend's house (who lived at home with his parents), entered his room, took his shirt and trousers (jeans) off, and that his friend (who was sleeping when he texted) opened up the covers to invite him in. Together the two men slept in their underwear until the next morning. I asked Tom if they spooned or cuddled in bed. "I'm not sure, as I was pretty out of it," he said.

All of the 40 university athletes that I interview in the United Kingdom tell me that sharing beds is normal. "It's just what we do," one said. "There is nothing gay about it, we just love each other, and I tell him that and so why wouldn't we sleep together?"

With this knowledge I inquire about how good a friend one has to be before one is comfortable sharing a bed. Stephen indicates that they do not need to be a close friend. Accordingly, he tells me he is unable to count how many times he has done it. "Just all the time," he said. Unlike Stephen, however, Anthony has only shared a bed a few times with a guy. "Just out of convenience," he told me. Anthony is therefore more judicious about whom he shares a bed with. "Only ever close mates where we are very comfortable with each other." My interviews therefore suggest that there is variance in how often guys sleep together, and this variance has to do not only with how comfortable one is sleeping with lesser-than friends, but also, and more importantly, variables to do with drinking and homosociality.

Of all the men I interview about this, the most articulate is perhaps Oscar, a heterosexual British 15-year-old, who tell his friends that he loves them. "Yea, it happens many times. Often it's seen as just 'banter.' It kinda portrays your strong friendship for each other."

He tells me that the more popular guys at his school sleep over at each other's houses more than the less popular guys; and that those who are more confident in their heterosexuality are more likely to share a bed with another guy. When I inquire as to how one shows confidence in heterosexuality, he tells me that it relates to how much sexual experience they have with girls. In other words, having sexual relations with females bolsters one's heterosexual capital, which then permits them insurance against being thought gay for sleeping in the same bed with other males. He added:

I believe that the more a guy has done with a girl (at my age) the more confidence they have...also they become more certain with their sexuality, therefore allowing them to do the things like sleep in the same bed [with another male] or kiss each other.

But for most of the British athletes I interview, they have not thought, systematically, about the rules to who sleeps in the same bed with whom. Instead they are loose, fluid occurrences without norms or verbal articulation. Highlighting this, Jamie, a university undergraduate, tells me of a time he inadvertently shared a bed with a guy following a house party. "I don't remember all the details," he said. "But we were at a mates drinking, and I just was like 'that's it. I'm going to sleep.' So I crawled into one of the beds with some guy already in it. I knew who he was, but no, we were not friends per se." I asked Jamie if, perhaps the next morning, it felt odd sleeping in a single bed with a guy he barely knew. "No man," he answered. "It's just not a big deal."

Interviews with undergraduates make clear that there is also no limit regarding the frequency one can sleep in a bed with the same male. One might think, for example, that if two men elected to sleep in the same bed with another male every night of the entire university year, others might suspect there was more going on than just sharing a bed. This does not however appear to be the case for Tom and Pete.

Tom and Pete share a bed and a room, in their house with three other rooms and three other roommates. "We share a room to save money," Tom tells me. "But then again Pete is also my best friend. I love him. Why wouldn't I want to sleep with him?" I asked Tom if he worries people think he's gay for it. "Not at all, why would they?" he responded. "And do you cuddle?" He answered, "Yeah, like proper spoon," he said. "He's my best mate. It's a pleasure." He elaborated. "We have shared beds loads of time last year, and we thought why not save money and just share a room [bed] this year." By all accounts the arrangement has worked out well—not only have the two men saved a good deal of money on rent, but they independently indicate that they like sharing a bed, presumably for the same reason Abraham Lincoln shared a bed with James Speed for seven years (see Chapter 2)—homosocial intimacy is nice. Pete and Tom's bed sharing does, however, raise questions about how one navigates sexual desires, erections, and issues of masturbation. We begin, however, with cuddling.

Cuddling Other Men

Of the 39 heterosexual undergraduate British men interviewed who had slept in the same bed as another male, 37 say that they have also cuddled with another male. Cuddling occurs in two locations: in bed and on the couch. Cuddling on the couch tends to occur during a nap or while watching a movie with a friend. Both types of cuddling are prolific among these men, and both types of cuddling seem to increase as one ages from school, to college/sixth form, and then into university life.

There are, of course, many variations on "cuddling" so defining it is important. For the purpose of this chapter I count cuddling as anything from one guy resting his head on another guy's shoulder while watching a movie, to purposeful spooning, where two men lie next to each other, and one wraps his arms around the other and holds him tight. Both types are commonplace among undergraduates, but interviews with the university men indicate that the latter is less common for men before university. Some undergraduate men have cuddled more friends than they can remember, and others can recall each particular time. When I ask Sam, he says:

...it is very common for us to go out [late], and then the next day after class receive a text from someone saying something like "do you want to come and nap," or often we'll just be watching a movie and I'd just put my head on whoever was next to me.

Matt discussed what I would describe as a typical sleeping/cuddling arrangement. He said his best friend, Connor, is his most frequent cuddling partner:

> I feel comfortable with Connor and we spend a lot of time together. I happily rest my head on his shoulder when lying on the couch or hold him in bed. But he's not the only one. The way I see it, is that we are all very good and close mates. We have a bromance where we are very comfortable around each other and don't see anything wrong with sleeping in the same bed, or even showing that love in a club [dancing and kissing other guys] or even just at uni during the day.

When Jarrett was asked about sleeping with other males he said, "I have literally done most things with a guy." He added:

> Me and my mates are pretty close, like emotionally. We let each other know everything so we always have a big hug when we leave... when a couple mates [from back home] came to stay at uni we had to share beds too, like two per bed. We always have a quick snuggle before sleeping.

Without being prompted, Jarrett repeatedly stressed the amount of cuddling he and his mates engage in. "We're always cuddling, my lot. We're all comfortable with each other." Others highlight that cuddling occurs during the day, too. Max said:

> I probably could talk a lot about this topic, actually. Cuddling is a standard part of my uni life, really. We, very often, have hangover cuddles and naps together. I have even done it today, actually. I really enjoy it! Seriously, I do it all the time.

I inquired what a hangover nap is. The answer: after a group of friends go out clubbing together, they divide up into where they are going to sleep. Those who have "pulled" a woman have first choice of bed, and the others then sleep with their mates. But the next day, it is common to have friends over to just lie around, watching TV, playing video games, and recovering from the previous night's drinking. This is where cuddling "feels good." "If your mate has a headache you can like massage his head, or you just lie there together holding each other and laughing about how awful you feel," Max said.

Cuddling also occurs in smaller, non-drunken events. Here, guys will give each other "a cuddle" which might be an extended hug, or a smudging of heads together. Smaller gestures serve as a way to show physical affection for a mate and they are important because they occur in public as well as private. One of my heterosexual graduate students summed it up best. He said that perhaps your friend is working hard on a paper, so you "come up from behind him, maybe give him a little kiss and a cuddle just to show you care."

An example of public cuddling comes from my research where we find that the 16–18-year-old soccer players of a British academy often go to the movies together, where they lie in the bean bags in the front row (Magrath et al. 2013). They lie in them, together, like a giant game of Twister. This might be a new phenomenon and more research would be required to determine this, but at face value it seems that guys began cuddling in their rooms after drinking, which then extended to cuddling without alcohol, which then permitted other forms of cuddling (head on shoulder) in schools, the way McCormack (2012a) shows with sixth formers, and then perhaps the most recent advancement is cuddling in venues where others outside of their peer groups are present—like movie theatres.

More recently I wonder if cuddling is not being used as a way to make friends, among boys, too. Exemplifying this, I met a local sixth form boy (18) in my local gym—he became my gym buddy and friend. One day I asked him, "Have you ever slept in the same bed with another guy, holding him?" "No," he said, "And I don't think I ever will." I laughed, "Oh, you will. Trust me. You will." Months later he left for university. Two days into the first week of his undergraduate studies he texted me a pic. It was him spooning another guy in bed. I texted back, "I told you you would!" He informed me that one guy got out of bed to take the pic. In other words, he was cuddled from both sides by two guys.

It would require more research, but the scenario does make me wonder if the acceptance of cuddling might not be so common now, that cuddling is beginning to move from something you do with an established, close friend to an act of friendship-making. I can think of no other reason why the three young men, so quickly, jumped into bed together.

Spooning and Erections

While men do not always spoon when sharing a bed, it seems more frequent than not that when two undergraduates begin to sleep together there is at least a "quick cuddle" before going to sleep. This means that one guy throws an arm around another and squeezes, or maybe wraps a leg around his leg. Perhaps they let out a squirming giggle as a way to show that they are sort of mocking gay sex—something called ironic heterosexual recuperation (McCormack & Anderson 2010a).

Yet cuddling for warmth and affection, without feigning homosexuality, is also quite normal. Here, men spoon, one lying on his side, holding the next on his side: one in front (little spoon) held by one at back (big spoon). I examined with the men I interviewed to see if there was a system of who gets to be the big spoon and who the little. But there does not seem to be. "It's just whatever," Anthony told me. Others confirmed. John said, "No, you don't talk about that, there are no rules or anything. Whatever happens, happens."

Thus, it appears that because the men are ostensibly both heterosexual, there is no issue of power at play in this cuddling arrangement; unlike their spooning with girlfriends, where the men are expected to be the big spoon, one is not emasculated for being the little spoon. Stephen said, "You switch sometimes. You know, one guy rolls over so you roll over and now it's your turn to hold him."

The closeness of two bodies, regardless of sexual orientation, raises issues of sexual arousal and erection; particularly given that some males wake with erections. When I asked Sam about whether he fears getting an erection while sleeping with a mate he responded, "No. There are no worries about boners." I asked whether that meant he's not worried he will get one, or whether it meant that if he gets one it's not a big deal. "Of course you get them," he said, "every morning. It's not a problem."

Like the others, Jarrett said that he has no fear of getting an erection. "I've woken up with one before. We all have." He elaborated that if one is "fully awake" they make a joke of it: "All the boys piss themselves, maybe saying something like 'happy to see me or whatever.' We love it." He continued, "We're all close. We don't care about little things like that." I asked him if he's ever felt another guy's erection poking him. He replied, "Yeah, it's not a problem. It happens, doesn't it?"

This method of dealing with erections might best be examined through "ironic heterosexual recuperation." Here, we show that by playing up to be gay, or joking about same-sex desires, heterosexual boys, ironically, are actually proclaiming that they are straight. It is a form of banter which is mutually understood to occur because there is trust in the fact that one's friends are what they say—heterosexual.

Other men are equally direct about erections. Stephen said, "It's 2013, we don't give anyone shit anymore." In fact, he suggests that there are no limitations in cuddling as to where guys touch each other. I asked directly, "Are there limitations as to where you can touch or hold?" He answered, "Never! Sometimes you grab his cock, sort of as a joke, particularly if he's got a semi going." Here, Stephen again illustrates how ironic heterosexual recuperation works. When I asked Stephen why he grabs another guy's cock he said, "It just relieves the tension." Accordingly, grabbing another guy's erect cock serves as a way of saying, I know you have a hard-on but it's no big deal. Stephen added, "It's not like you're going to wank him." He added, "You can rest your hand on his leg, or his hand, or wherever. There are no limitations." Sam said that he does the same: "Yeah, we hold hands loads."

I asked another undergraduate, "So if you're lying on the couch, snuggling, and you are holding hands, is the hand-holding banter/a joke, or is that genuine affection?" "Banter," he first answered before saying, "Like we love each other to pieces, though. We don't have to hold hands to show each other that. We always tell each other we love each other, too." He later told me, "but you only hold his hand because you love him. Banter is how you show love." I asked if, once the banter ended, the hands remained held. "Of course," he answered. I then teased out the order of events. When one holds another male's hand, he often initiates it with banter (i.e., hey, honey I'm gonna hold your hand now). The other male returns the banter (ironic heterosexual recuperation) and then they just hold hands.

Cuddling Gay Male Friends

Cuddling is not automatically limited to heterosexual male friends, either. Both gay men and straight men tell me that cuddling is sometimes part of their friendship behaviors. James, who is gay, tells me that he cuddled with a straight male friend. "He's just a friend, not like a best friend, and it only happened once so far. But yeah, we slept in the same bed. No big deal." I asked him if he engaged in other forms of cuddling or physically tactile behaviors with straight males. "Yeah, I guess," he answered. "I sat on my friend's knee the other day, is that what you mean?" He told me that these types of behaviors are pretty common among his straight friends; "They don't treat me any different, if that's what you're asking about?"

For another gay male, Charles, these behaviors are so normal that he thinks that they are of little interest or value to me. When telling me about being held by one of his straight mates for a few minutes before falling asleep on the same couch after a party he said, "I was really drunk, and so was he. And it was a group of us in the room, so maybe my story wouldn't be so great?"

Andrew found that cuddling served as a mechanism to help his straight mates bond with him. Supporting my notion that inclusive masculinities proliferate at his university, he said:

> So I had two friends [who were also his flatmates] who I would say embraced lad culture as if it was a big joke. So sort of like anti-lads. Like they would talk about women, drink and such. However, when face to face with women they treated them with respect. It was all for show indoors. I guess that helps set their personalities a bit in perspective. They both have had girlfriends, brought girls home. When drunk I see them looking at girls. And they knew I was gay and that I thought they were attractive.

Andrew said that one night early in his freshman year one of these guys came into his room to chat. After talking about what they like, sexually, Andrew said that he likes cuddling with guys after sex. At this point, his roommate said, "I love cuddling." His friend took Andrew down to the bed, and spooned with him, while they continued to chat. This opened the door for other straight men in his flat to cuddle with him, too. In describing his two closest friends in the dorm (of eight people) he said, "So for one I was big and the other I was little spoon. Sometimes we did three-way spoons."

As with the homosocial straight men's cuddles, Andrew said, "But none of it was sexual, we literally just chatted as if it was normal, nothing out of the ordinary." He added, "But yeah, this would happen every other week for a year." He said, "One of my roommates came to my fancy dress party dressed as a spoon," assumedly a way of publicly owning his spooning with a gay male.

Finally, just as straight men told me that they, as a matter of course, gain erections while sleeping with other males, matters were obviously no different for Andrew. He told me that one time the cuddling just became too sexual for him. "With all three of us in our underwear, in a three-way spoon, me in the middle, it was really just too much. I got too turned on and just had to leave." He said that the two straight boys laughed about it, seemingly taking pride in the fact that they had turned Andrew on, and they continued to cuddle each other after he left the room.

The American Difference

When it comes to cuddling, like in every other aspect of homosocial love, American teenagers lag behind the British. For example, in 2013 I interviewed (over Facebook) ten members of a high school boys cross country team that I coach in California over the summer. They indicate that they have few sleepovers, but when they do, the friend sleeps on a couch or the floor. This greatly varies compared to ten British males of the same age that I interviewed. Garrett, who is 16 and American, said that he isn't allowed to sleep over at friends' houses, because his dad doesn't trust him. "He thinks I'd do stupid shit to get in trouble." Still, Garrett said that if he could sleep over at a friend's, and his best friend did want to sleep in the same bed, he would have no problem with that. Still, he wouldn't cuddle.

It would be hard to describe Garrett as homophobic—not only does he spend time alone with me (an openly gay coach) but he actively advocates for gay rights on his Facebook profile, and has several gay male friends. Ultimately, he doesn't really have an answer as to why he wouldn't want to cuddle with his best friend, but homophobia is not a possible reason. Nor does it stem from a lack of ability to show affection to other males. Like others on this team, Garrett is highly expressive with his emotions, letting his friends know that he loves them. His Facebook wall is full of expressions to his friends about loving them.

Joseph, 18, is an American athlete who has slept at a friend's house "a few times." Still, he has never slept in the same bed with another male on one of these sleepovers. When I asked where he sleeps he said, "I'm comfortable anywhere, so usually like on a couch or the floor or something." And when I asked him if he would sleep in the same bed if his best friend were to ask him to, he said, "I'd maybe say no. I don't know. I've never been in that situation before." Despite this fear of physical affection, Joseph is clear to state that he expresses his love for his best friends in person. When I asked him if he tells his best friend that he loves him, he responded, "All the time."

I attribute these cultural differences between what teenagers do in the States versus the UK to homohysteria. Evidencing this, Tony, 18, another runner who has been highly vocal about his pro-gay stance, said that while he's only spent the night at a friend's house "a couple of times" in his four years of high school, he has never slept with a friend in the same bed. Like the others I interview, he's highly expressive about his affection for his friends verbally, but does not sleep in the same beds or cuddle with them. When I asked why he has not slept in the same bed with a friend he answered, "I don't know. I wouldn't be comfortable with it."

So we essentially have two sets of teenagers, one British, the other American, both with highly positive attitudes toward gay males, and both of whom express their affection verbally and through digital media, like Facebook. Yet in the UK teenagers readily sleep in the same bed with their friends, and usually cuddle/spoon as part of that, and in the US the friend sleeps on the floor. This illustrates the power of homohysteria to shape cultural behaviors, even after the meanings of those behaviors have been lost.

In other words, this is a matter of cultural lag. The teenagers in America I interview don't know why they do what they do; it is an artefact of men from a previous generation who avoided sharing a bed with another male because it was a sign of homosexual desire. Or more aptly put, refusing to share a bed, or cuddle a friend, was a way of saying, "I'm not gay." Yet, three of the men I interviewed here are regular members of the Gay Straight Alliance at their school, and thus do not fear homosexual suspicion. A cultural lag of homohysteria seems the only viable explanation.

Still, my research on university American undergraduates shows that men do sleep together, perhaps not as often, and with considerably less cuddling, but they do willingly share beds. Unfortunately, I have not systematically collected data on American undergraduate athletes to assess what percent of them are cuddling. I have seen it, many times in my ethnographies, but I have not (yet) systematically surveyed or interviewed American undergraduates about the behavior. That is the stuff of future research.

Finally, one of the men I interviewed on the American cross country team was just 15, yet he (the youngest of the Americans I interviewed) does sleep over at his friend's house. Here, he tells me that he sleeps on the couch, usually with another male. Sometimes, he said, legs or arms will touch. He is gay. So perhaps the cultural lag of homohysteria I speak of is already dissipating.

Chapter Conclusion

Sharing a bed with another male is more than just a matter of convenience; it is a symbolic way of showing and receiving love for a friend. Sometimes this is out of convenience, but oftentimes it is out of desire to share intimacy with another friend. In an act perhaps unthinkable to men of Generation X, British men frequently express their affection through cuddling, whether it be on a couch or in a bed—and many times spooning. There are no written rules about bed sharing, and this permits a great deal of flexibility of what can happen in a bed. Generally, the younger one is, the less physical affection there is in bed, but by the time men have made good friends as undergraduates, they not only spoon, but sometimes grab each other's erect cocks as a form of banter, a way of expressing that it's okay they got a hard on while lying in bed with another male. They also, tenderly, hold hands while spooning.

Thus whereas men of Generation X once stopped sleeping over and sharing beds around puberty, in the UK this behavior does not end today—at least not through the university years—and there is even some evidence that in the United States teenagers are having, albeit fewer, sleepovers, too. Because they are beginning to share beds in university, I suspect that the cultural lag will quickly subside, and high school boys will readily begin sharing beds in the United States, too.

Finally, there is one interesting factor that I point out in concluding this part of the book. I have shown young men freaking, kissing, cuddling, sleeping in the same beds, and telling each other that they love each other. But what if the men have a girlfriend? Do these activities count as cheating? Also, if they give to one another all their love, their physical affection, their time, and bed space, only reserving sex for women, what does this tell us about the nature of homosocial intimacy?

Part IV
21st Century Jocks and Sex

10
Cheating on Girlfriends

Recent decades have brought an erosion of orthodox views and institutional control of sexual behaviors and relationships in North American and Western European cultures. This is made evident in the growing percentage of people who engage in pre-marital intercourse, the social and legal permission for divorce, the markedly expanded social and political landscape for gays and lesbians, and what some would suggest is a lessening of the traditional double standard for heterosexual intercourse, permitting women to have casual sex with less social stigma (Bogle 2008). For university students, there also exists a culture where many students avoid romantic relationships; instead, undergraduates frequently engage in casual sex, something called hooking up.

Although these changes may mean that students now have sex before dating, these social-sexual changes do not seem to have affected how heterosexual undergraduates value monogamy once they establish sexually romantic dyadic relationships. When it comes to undergraduates who engage in coupled relationships, there seems to be very little progress toward the acceptance of any model of relationship coupling other than monogamy. Open relationships, polyamorous relationships, or any other creative model of loving and fucking remain marginalized. There remains but one socially positive sexual script for heterosexual and gay/lesbian couples, and it is a decidedly pro-dyadic form of sexual monogamy (Anderson 2012a).

However, just because social attitudes do not condone sex outside of one's relationship does not mean that sex outside one's relationship fails to happen. Cheating is rather normal for men of iGeneration. This chapter reports on the results of 120 interviews about monogamy and cheating with undergraduate, heterosexual men, of which over half were athletes. The men come from multiple universities in both the

United States and United Kingdom and 86 per cent of the athletes have cheated in some form (from kissing to fucking), not ever, but on their current partners. This compares to 65 per cent of the non-athletes.

Thus, with this chapter, I am interested in the multiple factors that influence how these young men view monogamy, open relationships, and cheating; why they cheat in such high numbers; and how they rectify their cheating in relation to their esteem for monogamy. I analyze the results through two complementary theoretical lenses. I first utilize hegemony theory, calling monogamy's privileged social position *monogamism*. I then show that, as part of the operation of hegemony, a cultural reverence for monogamy prevents critical scrutiny concerning the *costs* inherent in monogamy.

I suggest that there exists a cultural unwillingness to adequately examine the price that monogamism has on the sexual and emotional health of (ostensibly) monogamous couples, and I show that despite monogamy's hegemonic cultural dominance, multiple forms of nonmonogamies nonetheless exist as the covert norm for many of my participants.

Instead of attributing their nonmonogamous practices to moral failings however, I suggest that cheating occurs because of the unreasonable social expectations of monogamy—particularly concerning emotional desires that conflict with strong biological desires. Thus, in this chapter, monogamy is scrutinized for negatively affecting the quality and duration of coupled relationships.

Related to jocks specifically, I show (Anderson 2012a) that young male athletes cheat more than non-athletes, likely because they have the sexual capital to do so. But I also question whether cheating is not more pervasive because whereas it used to be that in the past heterosexual men could only emotionally open up to a girlfriend, today, as I showed in Chapter 6, they also open up emotionally to, and even cuddle (Chapter 9) with, their male friends and bromances. This perhaps makes the total value of a girlfriend less.

Monogamism

Despite all of this cheating, the desire to be thought monogamous remains important for the heterosexual undergraduate men of *i*Generation. They are adamant that they value monogamy—that they support it as the ideal personal and cultural relationship model. For example, Michael describes monogamy as "the ideal," and Ryan describes it as the "Only natural way to love someone." Still, others infer allegiance to monogamy through ignorance of other relationship types, as many of the participants had never heard of an open relationship. As reflected in many interviews, after Ben was told what an open relationship was, he said, "If you're not doing monogamy, you're not really in love then, are you?"

Despite this reverence for monogamy, however, there is considerable variation in how participants understand this term. For example, Ben maintains his identity as monogamous because the only woman he fantasizes about having sex with is his new girlfriend. Others fantasize about women other than their girlfriends, but like Tom, "know better" than to tell their girlfriends this. Joe discusses his attractions to other women *with* his girlfriend, while Matt engages in role-playing with his partner, pretending she is someone else during sex. More permissive yet, Alex flirts with strippers before faithfully returning home to his girlfriend with reported heightened sexual energy. Other heterosexual men have kissed or received oral sex from other women without their partner's permission. Dozens of heterosexual men in my study of 100 (20 were gay) have engaged in extradyadic sexual intercourse—one over a dozen times. One of the couples has even had a threesome. What is of interest, however, is that despite these varied extra-relational sexual desires and practices, all of these men nonetheless consider themselves monogamous.

These varying social scripts highlight the diversity of systems governing "monogamous" relationships. The participants unanimously identify as monogamous, even though their behaviors vary widely. Thus, it seems that, to these men, it is less important as to what they *do* sexually, and more important that they *identify* as monogamous. In other words, participants who fail to live up to monogamous expectations tend to go about pretending to their partners (and to others) that they are, in fact, monogamous. This is the same type of stigma avoidance that occurs with homosexuality in a period of homohysteria. Men go through great lengths to appear to be what they are not.

However, further discussion with participants reveals some cracks in this monogamist thinking. Ben said, "It's okay to *want* to have sex with other women; it is just not okay to act on it." Ant agrees, "I want other women, sure. Sometimes I *want* four or five of them in a night (laughs), but that doesn't mean I have other women." But participants also equate monogamy as the "natural" outcome of supreme love—the ideal form of coupling—even though they simultaneously believe that their desire for recreational sex is biologically driven. Tom said, "Yeah, I want sex with other women. Of course. I'm male. But if I love my girlfriend enough I shouldn't want it."

When I pointed out that he has earlier indicated that he wanted sex with other women because he *was* male, he reconsidered his statement. "I don't know. That's weird. I do want sex with other women, but I shouldn't [want it]." Hence, Tom navigates two contrasting and heavily naturalized beliefs: (1) that the desire for monogamy results from true love; and (2) that men naturally desire recreational sex even when in love.

Tom is not alone in this dissonance. Despite expressing reverence for monogamy, many participants made it clear that monogamy does not come naturally, or even with ease to them. This is likely to be particularly true of men in college, who experience a culture that valorizes hooking up for single men.

Tony said that he struggles "all the time" with not cheating. "I get mad at her," he said. "I want sex with other women, and I know she'd never let me, so sometimes I just feel like cheating because I'm not supposed to." James, too, said that he desperately wants other women. "I can't stop thinking about other women, I'm sure I'll cheat. I mean, I don't want to. But I will." Still, James said that he's not happy about this. "It sucks. Really, it sucks. I don't want to cheat, but I really want sex [with someone other than his girlfriend]."Accordingly, most of the participants suggested that they live with the competing and contrasting social scripts of sexual desire for extradyadic sex and the emotional desire for monogamy. I call this *the monogamy gap* (Anderson 2012a).

The Monogamy Gap

Interviews suggest that this gap does not normally appear at the relationship's onset, which is generally characterized by heightened romance and elevated sexual passion. None of the participants cheated within three months of dating. Instead, cheating generally began after six or more months. Mike said, "No. I had no desire for sex with other women at first. All I could think about was her." But after these elevated levels of passion and romance decline (sometimes plummeting) matters begin to change. Dan said that although he has always fantasized about other women, he used to be content to have sex only with his girlfriend. Referring to his earlier sex life, he said, "It was hot...real hot. But in time, it just lost some of its appeal. We did things to spice it up, and we still have something of an active sex life, but I can't say that some other girl wouldn't be nice from time to time." Similarly, Jon said, "When I first started dating her I thought she was so hot I wouldn't want any other woman for the rest of my life, but that's just not the way it turned out to be."

The declining interest and frequency of monogamous sexual activity to which Dan, Jon, and Mike refer is the norm for men partnered two years or more in this study. These men expressed that, in time, their emotional desire for monogamy no longer aligns with their somatic drive for recreational sex. In other words, the longer they are partnered the more they desire recreational sex with others.

While most participants coupled only a few months are generally satisfied with the quality and duration of the sex that comes with monogamy, after two years, participants generally express contradictory feelings, wanting but not wanting recreational sex with others. This two-year variable was so common that one might call it "a two-year itch." This changing direction of their sexual desires (between two months and two years) highlights the myth that monogamous desire is a natural product of "true love."

The cognitive dissonance created by the competing desires for monogamy and recreational sex is likely made particularly salient for men in college. In addition to their heightened sexual energies, these men also experience contradictory sexual social scripts: one that suggests they should prove their masculinity through adventurous pursuits of sexual conquest (Adam 2006) and another that romanticizes the progression of dating, love, and monogamy (Thompson 2006). Furthermore, university-aged men exist in gender-integrated sex markets with women of high sexual capital, variables that may inflate the tension caused by the monogamy gap. For example, when I asked Jon if he thought it was harder to remain monogamous at the university compared to when he's at home he said, "Yeah, it's amazing [at the university]. It's like being a kid in a candy store. There are hot girls everywhere. It would be easier to resist cheating if I were at an all-boy's school or something."

Cognitive dissonance theory complements hegemony theory in analyzing these interview data. This is because, whereas cognitive dissonance theory suggests that people are likely to creatively and selectively seek information to reduce their cognitive dissonance, hegemony theory maintains that the categories we choose for critical examination are always those of the subordinated. Thus, monogamism carries serious implications for these participants because those inclined to resolve the tension of the monogamy gap seek messages that highlight the utility of monogamy and problematize nonmonogamies, reifying, naturalizing, and shoring up monogamy's dominance in the process. This leads most participants to creatively, shamefully, and secretly rectify the tension of the monogamy gap—something motivated by shame and accomplished through cheating.

Cheating

Data from this research documents that despite a reverence for monogamy, most jocks do not follow their own monogamous ideals. Most express wanting monogamy socially and emotionally, while simultaneously expressing a desire for extradyadic sex. The desire for recreational sex, both compelling and enduring, eventually influenced about 86 per cent of jocks who had a girlfriend (for more than about four months) to cheat, as defined by doing something physically sexual (not web-based) that would be considered as cheating. While some participants readily identified their actions as cheating (primarily those who told me they had vaginal sex), those who performed other forms of sex (including kissing, and in one case a heterosexual receiving oral sex from a man) normally identified their actions as "sort of like cheating" or "not really cheating."

All participants who cheated expressed a lingering anxiety that their girlfriends (or others) would find out about their transgression. This fear is particularly true for those who also feared that logistical factors could threaten to expose their secret. For example, Dan attended a party with his friend Ryan, where he met a woman from another university. The two made out in a vacant room, but not without Ryan noticing. Dan said:

> I had insane fear the next day. You know, that she would find out I wasn't where I said I was. But then I began to forget about it, you know like I didn't think about it all the time... Still, whenever my girlfriend was around me and Ryan together, I totally stressed that he would fuck up and say something about it.

Dan also said that his cheating generated a further, unintended consequence. Dan later felt himself wanting to detach from Ryan's friendship, but felt he couldn't for fear that Ryan might be more inclined to reveal his secret.

Cheating participants also fear social ramifications should friends or family members learn of their cheating. Paul said:

> The guilt sucks, but it's not like I killed someone or anything... But try telling that to her friends (laughs). My friends [presumably male] might be more understanding of it, but her friends [presumably female] would be pressuring her to break up with me.

Paul's response indicates that how individuals evaluate (judge) cheating may be gendered, but more important, it highlights the cultural pressure that cheating victims have to end their relationships. The result is that women are socially compelled to break up with their cheating boyfriends even if they do not wish to: breaking up serves as an identity protection mechanism from a monogamist culture, something taught through social norms and expectations of the media.

In addition to the fear and anxiety these men express, each cheating jock also maintained a varying degree of guilt about it. Dan said that while he maintains no guilt when masturbating to thoughts of other women, after once having vaginal sex with another woman he felt tremendous and overriding guilt—guilt which remains over a year later. "I can't forget about it," he said. Yet despite the guilt and fear of discovery, Dan has yet to tell his girlfriend—he is too afraid of the consequences. "If I tell her she will certainly break up with me."

Interestingly, despite his guilt, and because his cheating has not been discovered, Dan claims to feel little reason *not* to cheat again. "If she finds out about the first one, she's going to break up with me. So why not do it with her [the same girl] again?" This is consistent with other literature on cheating, which finds that once men (or women) do cheat, they are likely to continue cheating (Wiederman & Hurd 1999).

This data suggests a pattern concerning cheating. After entering into a sexual relationship, participants initially feel satisfied with monogamy, maintaining a sexual fulfillment that comes from early relationship bliss. At this stage, most view those who cheat as immoral, and rarely consider that they might themselves one day cheat. I suggest that this heightened early romance validates the myth that monogamy is sexually fulfilling, making it easier for men to commit to it. However, the participants' sexual fulfillment is mostly short-lived, and eventually most participants desire recreational sex with other women—even if they still enjoy sex with their partners. Stuck between both wanting monogamy *and* the type of compelling, novel stimulation that comes with recreational sex, the initial strategy most participants adopt for dealing with the monogamy gap comes through fantasizing about others, spicing up their sex lives, and the use of pornography. But once habituation causes even these strategies to grow ineffective, cheating grows increasingly tempting.

The men I studied have a harder time warding off cheating, because their athletic abilities and good looks are idealized by culture. Thus, jocks find themselves desired by women and gay/bi men. When they did cheat, their initial cheating episodes almost always occurred under the influence of alcohol. Then, after cheating, most participants attributed their "failings" as something that "just happened." Subsequent conversation, however, usually revealed some intent on cheating; they placed themselves into situations in which their agency gives way to chance of sexual activity. In Jon's case, he knew that a particular woman was interested in him, so he volunteered to walk her back to her room after a party. In reflection he said, "I know it was a stupid situation to put myself into, but I was drunk." And when asked if he would have readily volunteered to walk someone home to their dorm that was not sexually attractive to him, he answered, "No. I think I would have stayed and had another drink."

While interviews suggest that most participants primarily cheated because of the sexual monotony that comes with long-term sexual exclusivity (combined with a high sex drive), other structural variables make cheating *more likely*. As others have shown, these include separate habitation from one's partner (Paik et al. 2004) and gender-integrated living situations (Anderson 2008c). Other influences surface from participants' access to a direct sexual marketplace, like a university (Laumann 1994); and a cultural hyper-sexualizing of men's gendered masculine identities at this age (Klesse 2006), alongside their sculpted bodies.

It is also important to consider that cheating is also influenced by a rational choice in weighing the opportunity/cost in staying with a partner, compared to expressing interest in exploring nonmonogamies with them. This is supported by the fact that none of the informants maintain that they cheat or cheated in preparation to break up with, or because they no longer loved, their partners, although a few of the men (like Jon) felt that it was "no great loss" after his girlfriend found out and broke up with him.

Still, Jon was an exception to the rule. Most of the men maintained that they loved their girlfriends when/while cheating. Matt, for example, said that he cheated on his girlfriend of three years. When she found out, she broke up with him. Matt suggested that he desperately loved her, and when asked to explain to someone who doubted this how he could support such a statement, he answered: "She broke up with me two years ago, and I still, desperately, want her." Matt revealed how he still cries over her loss, and how he wants, more than anything, to be with her again. Thus, although participants did not numerically quantify their love, I argue that most participants' social scripts about how they feel/felt about their partners indicate that cheating does not (or at least does not always) represent a loss of love for their partners.

Cheating Out of Love

Although stereotypes of jocks suggest that they cheat out of misogyny, or a lack of valuing women, this was not the case with the jocks

I researched. Some expressed more love for their partners than others, but none of the men maintained that their cheating resulted from a *lack* of love or disrespect for women. Nor did they say that they cheated as a way to look for a new girlfriend. Instead, they unanimously expressed that the reason they cheated came from a compelling desire for extra-coupled recreational sex, despite their genuine romantic interest in their girlfriends.

This finding might anger some readers. Hegemonic perspectives on cheating unconditionally maintain that if someone loves their partner they would not cheat. The other side of this equation is that those who "were cheated on" are expected to be so socially damaged that they are compelled to break up with their partners. However, this is far too simple an understanding of the relationship between men, sex, and love—matters are much more complicated.

Mark said, "It's not that I don't love her. I totally love her. I just need sex with others. You know what I mean?" Joe said, "I feel that I love her, I mean I don't want to be with anyone else [emotionally] but I guess my actions don't line up with that." He then emphasized, "But really I do love her." Dan said more defiantly, "Of course I love her. I was just horny."

These social scripts suggest that these men do not cheat because they are romantically unsatisfied; instead they cheat because they are romantically satisfied but sexually unsatisfied. Thus, a subversive interpretation of monogamism is to suggest that these men cheat because they *do* love their partners—they are simply too afraid to take the chance of losing them by expressing a desire for recreational sex with other women.

Supporting this, many participants suggest that they love their partners even more after cheating: violating relationship terms brings reflection and evaluation as to how much their partners mean. Of course one can argue that these men could, or perhaps even should, constrain themselves from cheating, but that does not change the circumstances of whether (or how much) they love their partners. For example, when Mark is asked if he has ever considered telling his girlfriend that he would like to have casual sex with other women, he said, "Are you kidding me? She'd dump me in an instant." Joe sarcastically agreed, "Right, tell my girlfriend that I love her, but that I need sex with someone else. That would go down well." And Mike added, "You just can't say that. There is no good way to say that."

This is not to suggest that all men cheat because they love their partners; certainly *unloving* partners are also likely to cheat. Perhaps if I had specifically interviewed men who had broken up with their girlfriends,

I might have uncovered other data. However, this was not the case for *these* participants. Treas & Giesen (2000) inadvertently support this "cheating out of love" hypothesis, because they find that cheating is more likely to occur among men who have stronger somatic sexual interests (a higher libido), something that athletes likely do. If cheating were solely a result of failed love (i.e., it was not about sexual desire), one's libido would not be a significant variable in cheating rates. I therefore suggest that, for at least some men, cheating becomes a sensible and *rational* choice in weighing the odds of the opportunity/cost to have their growing desires for recreational sex met, while not jeopardizing their relationship status by honestly expressing this desire for extradyadic sex to their partners.

Further highlighting the utility of this framework (particularly for college students), they do not have long-standing investments in their relationships, and they are not legally or religiously bound to their partners. Cheating is also made easier for undergraduates because they exist within a rich sexual marketplace. Furthermore, none have children or are married. Thus, they are culturally, legally, and financially free to break up with their girlfriends, should their love expire.

I suggest that the construction of monogamy as the only acceptable sexual script (monogamism) is so strong that the influence occurs at the cultural, interpersonal, and psychological levels. Monogamy's hegemony is so powerful that my participants see no other viable alternatives. For example, when I discussed with Paul the potential for opening up his relationship (so that he could have extradyadic sex without cheating), he quickly answered that cheating was better than being in an open relationship because "at least with cheating there is an attempt at monogamy."

I argue that this data calls for a more complex view of cheating than monogamism offers. The cultural ascriptions of character weakness and personality disorder that many attribute to those who cheat largely fail to critique the structural power relations between social morality, natural (or naturalized) sexual desires, and sexual recreation, something that comes with a more sociological approach to the construction of sexual and gendered identities and behaviors. Therefore, instead of describing participants who cheat as lacking character, love, or morality—social scripts that hold monogamy as a test of personal character and romantic fortitude—these interviews suggests that cheating for these men emerges from a culture that offers no socially acceptable alternatives to the sexual habituation and frustration that occurs with relatively long-term monogamy for young, virile men. The dominant cultural, political, religious, and media messages that contribute to a sex-negative and monogamist culture demonize all but a select few "charmed" sexual practices and sexual identities (Rubin 1984), so that the monogamous mantra of "cheating as the product of failed love or psychological disease" constrains other possibilities from social or personal consideration.

In light of the near-total social control that monogamy has over the practice of those who choose to enter into romantic relationships in this culture, I suggest that cheating becomes the *sensible* answer to the monogamy gap. Cheating provides men with the best chance to have their desires for extradyadic sex met, while also maintaining their relationship status. Cheating permits them to manage their social identities in a way that honesty with their partners (or others) would not. Thus, covert cheating occurs for these men as a result of the infeasibility of monogamy to sustain a sexually charged and varied sexual relationship alongside the cost of monogamism. Not only do they risk hurting their partners and their relationships, but they simultaneously subject themselves to guilt, shame, anxiety, and confusion—all for the manner in which they rectify their dissonance. Monogamists therefore go about living between the oppressive layers of sexual want and emotional contentment. Those espousing the value and righteousness of monogamy not only promote their own cognitive dissonance, but they contribute to the stigma of those who are capable of outthinking social oppression.

Chapter Conclusion

In using semi-structured interviews with white, heterosexual, undergraduate men who had once maintained a girlfriend for three months or longer, this chapter highlighted the hegemonic mechanisms associated with the cultural ideal of monogamy. I described the process of subordination and stratification through the cultural stigmatization of nonmonogamies as an effect of monogamism. As with other forms of hegemonic oppression, I showed that jocks desired to be associated with the privileged paradigm (Rubin 1984) and consequently extolled the virtues of monogamy, even if they do not themselves adhere to its basic principles. And, as with other forms of hegemonic oppression, monogamism necessarily means that the institution of monogamy itself goes largely unexamined. Instead, all critical discourse regards the "immorality" of nonmonogamies. So, even though I find monogamy fails as a social institution for these men, it nonetheless retains its privileged social position as the only acceptable form of romantic coupling. None of this is new. Men of Generation X fell prey to the same monogamistic scripts.

Where matters have changed for the jocks of *i*Generation, however, is that the cultural esteem for monogamy comes into sharp contrast with other sexual social scripts. One of those competing scripts is that of being single, so that one can pursue recreational sex with a number of different women. Another variance for this generation concerns the ease upon which they can cheat. Not only do they possess highly sexualized and desirable bodies (so did jocks of Generation X) but they exist in a culture in which women are more willing to have casual sex with those bodies. Finally, men of *i*Generation can cheat in other, digital, ways on the internet. Here they can (and do) webcam with others, but they also arrange hookups for physical sex.

I postulate that jocks view cheating as a temporary solution to the stress related to the gap between the competing and incompatible desires of wanting new, exciting, and thrilling sexual stimuli, while simultaneously being socially constructed to desire monogamy, all the while fearing telling one's partner they desire otherwise (the monogamy gap). Supporting this thesis, the longer men were coupled, the more likely they were to cheat. However, this might also reflect growing strength in the relationship, which could ward off termination if their partner discovered their cheating. Furthermore, cheating seems to be only a temporary solution to the monogamy gap, so cheating frequency often increases with relationship duration.

I also found that jocks were significantly more likely to cheat than nonathletes. Of the athletes I interviewed, 82 per cent had cheated, compared to 65 per cent of the non-athletes. I suggest that this represents the fact that athletes maintain higher degrees of sexual capital. That, plus the fact that they travel a great deal for sporting competitions, means that they are perhaps given more opportunity to cheat. One could, perhaps, also argue that the sex-segregated nature of team sports means that young men learn not to value women as much, and thus cheating on women is less morally stigmatized. Still, it's possible that while valuing their girlfriends, jocks do not need them as much. They are capable of having their emotional needs for empathy, disclosure, bonding, and love met with other men (Chapter 6), something not available to the jocks of Generation X (Morin & Garfinkle 1978). A girlfriend might offer the advantage of sex, but if one's sex has been habituated, and lost its thrill, and one did not feel that losing the girlfriend would be a major emotional loss because one had their buddies and bromance(s), it provides less pain if one is broken up with because their girlfriend found out they had cheated. In short, men of Generation X needed a girlfriend for emotional support (Komarovsky 1974) and sex; men of *i*Generation need them less for both.

Given that heterosexual sex seems easy to obtain in today's university hookup culture (Bogle 2008), staying with a partner is likely to reflect legitimate emotional attachment after the excitement of early relationship sex wanes. It is for these reasons that I suggest that cheating exists as a rational choice. It is based upon an opportunity/cost analysis to provide cheaters with the recreational sex they want with the monogamy (or at least the delusion of monogamy) that they are culturally compelled to maintain. Cheating is a safer strategy for acquiring recreational sex than requesting permission from their partners, but it has an added advantage: almost all of the men I talked with said that while they (in some capacity) desire the ability to have sex with other women, few were willing to permit their girlfriends to do the same. Cheating then results not only because they fear losing their partners (should they ask for extradyadic sex), but it remains a way for men to have their cake and eat it too. Men continue to desire to restrict their partners' sexual lives, while justifying their own sexual transgressions. Accordingly, the old double standard still exists for jocks of both generations.

11
Pornography, Masturbation, and Sex with Other Men

The idea about sex between men has long repulsed and fascinated modern societies. It is the fascination of straight men having gay sex that, I suspect, will make this the most read chapter in the book. Because of this, I am going to take the opportunity to flesh this chapter out. I present the empirical data later in the chapter, first providing a historical analysis.

The analysis I perform in this chapter comes at a unique historical time. Perhaps at no historical moment has homosexuality been so polarizing. While the anti-gay forces in much of the Western world are rapidly subsiding in defeat, acts of same-sex intimacy are still punishable by death in a number of Islamic countries around the world (Frank et al. 2010). Homophobia is also rapidly rising in Russia, Uganda, Zimbabwe, and many other Middle Eastern, Eastern European, and African countries, with draconian laws and unabated violence.

The discrepancy between the lives of the young British and American jocks I discussed in previous chapters and what is occurring in other countries is related to both rates of religiosity and the degree of contact with sexual minorities. As sexual minorities have continued to come out of the closet in the West, this has accelerated the demise of homophobia. However, the increased visibility of homosexuality in the West has also begun to entrench more conservative nations in homophobia: they see American homosexuality, but do not yet see it in their own families. Thus, as homosexuality has become more visible in American media, and as more socially progressive countries introduce marriage equality, much of the rest of the world has reacted with increasing homophobia.

Western victory for homosexuality also has a far-reaching impact on the lives of heterosexuals. As a cultural awareness grows that homosexuality exists as a static and immutable sexual orientation of biological origins (LeVay 2010), it promotes a wider terrain of gendered behaviors to be adopted as socially acceptable for heterosexual men—the focus of this book. However, the benefits of a culture free of homohysteria are not just limited to gendered interactions; there is also a promotion of sexual freedom, for both gays and straights.

In this chapter I discuss the impact that jocks are having on decreasing homophobia in the West. Principally, this comes from their pushing the boundaries, and thus promoting reduction of the one-time rule of homosexuality. It is the same-sex sexual or pseudo-sexual acts that jocks engage in that this chapter is principally about. But this privilege to enjoy same-sex sex without stigma has not come easy, and we still have a way to go. So while this chapter ultimately shows that it is increasingly permissible for heterosexual men to engage in pseudo-sexual or sexual acts with other men, it has come as a result of a very long and oftentimes deadly cultural war—one that jocks used to be on the wrong side of. I would therefore be remiss for not enlightening readers about the types of same-sex activities that occur among men in sport without first laying the groundwork for how this freedom has been won.

Assertion 1: Sex Wins

When I discuss the cultural ethos of sexuality for members of Generation X or *i*, it is important to understand that I'm discussing the moralizing of sexual desires: fundamentally, there should be no generational difference in the strength, frequency, or targets of those sexual desires. This is because sex is a basic driving force of the human condition, and the internal drive for it is generally stronger than social conditioning against it. Years ago, Robert Park (1929) suggested that when sexual desire exists between two people—as long as circumstances permit enough time and opportunity—sex will occur. I do not make such an absolutist claim here, but I come close. As a general rule, regardless of social convention, sex wins out. Sex most always finds a way. I am not alone in this proposition.

In response to the increasingly sex-negative culture that came with the Industrial Revolution, Easton & Hardy (2009: 10) write: "But human nature will win out. We are horny creatures, and the more sexually repressive a culture becomes, the more outrageous its covert sexual thoughts and behaviors will become…". This "sex wins out" philosophy is likely particularly true of men world-wide whom research shows that, among other differences, have the desire for more sex partners and have higher sex drives than women (Lippa 2007).

I learned the lesson that sex wins out when I was quite young. I grew up in an incredibly homohysteric culture, and so I desired to change my sexuality. I determined that if I were to avoid thinking about guys while masturbating, I could redirect the source of my attractions. The strategy saw me struggle against my desires for years. Not only did I fail to reach orgasm while thinking of a woman (the closer I got to orgasm the more I thought of guys) but I then subjected myself to a great deal of guilt after achieving orgasm to the thoughts of guys. Yet, this guilt did not stop me from being horny again, nor did it redirect my attachments. My sexual desires were stronger than I could prevent. Sex won out.

The same is illustrated by the high degree of sex crimes in the Muslim world. I have for example a photo of two 16-year-old gay boys who were hanged in Iran for having same-sex sex. Some Islamic cultures also condemn women to death for cheating on their husbands (Betzig 1989), yet people still have gay sex, and heterosexual women still cheat. Similarly, the previous chapter made it clear that even though jocks wanted monogamy on the one hand, they were not doing it very often on the other. The point is, that despite existing within the strictest of cultures, the law and religious prohibitions maintain hegemonic power in shaping our attitudes toward sex, but they do not prevent it.

For those of you who may have watched NBC's *To Catch a Predator* several years ago, you may have made this observation yourself. If not, I recommend you watch the show on YouTube. The show chronicled police operations where adults posed online as 13- or 14-year-old girls. Adults of all ages and backgrounds (but always men) would hit on the operatives online and then chat for hours before eventually talking about sex, and their desire for sex with the "kid." These men then showed up to the front doors of the children, not knowing it was a police operation. After entering the house a young-looking actor answered the door. The production company secretly filmed the dialogue between the young actor and the "predator." After a period of time, the show's host (not an officer) would suddenly emerge with several television cameras. A journalist, he would then interview the men about their sexual desires and intentions, before the man was arrested. A persistent theme was just how many of the men said that they suspected it was a police operation before coming. Despite this, like moths to a flame, they were still compelled to take the chance. At the moment of realization, many of the men said, "I knew it." For these men, despite their misgivings, sexual desires won out.

My point is that our human drive to seek out the type of sex we desire is so strong that people will risk losing their families, careers, being imprisoned, or put to death for it. The intellectual desire, our socialized or religiously held beliefs, are unlikely to be effective in stopping it. Our sexual drives have more durability than our socialized prohibitions against them. It is this fundamental principle that makes the combination of organized religion's war against homosexuality and socio-sexuality (sex for pleasure) such a noxious combination. On the part of the church, it is also a brilliant economic move.

Assertion 2: Generation X Declared War on Gay Men

Conservative Christians love a crusade. They have led them against abortion, feminism, alcohol consumption, communism, witchcraft, single mothers and, of course, non-Christians. But it was not until the 1969 Stonewall Riots, which launched the gay rights movement in America, that they began to focus (or rather needed to focus) on homosexuality. Not just the sexual component of homosexuality, but the category as a whole, or part thereof.

When examining the relationship between religions and those they persecute, it is important to remember that, above all, organized religion is not about a belief in a higher power, or doing well for one's neighbor. That might be the motivation of individual Christians, but it is not the historical purpose of organized institutions of religion. At this level of worship, this is about business. One needs simply to look to the absurd wealth of the Catholic Church for evidence.

The religious business model is a highly effective one. It has worked for roughly two thousand years. Its principle is to scare and guilt people into parting with their money. This is the origins of "repenting," in which one literally paid the Catholic Church a penance in order to buy one's way out of hell. With this scare and built premise serving a primary tactic for wealth generation, what the church needed was to find a natural human condition, one that is so strong that, even if the church preached holy-hell against it, humans would nonetheless partake in it. The answer came through sex. Knowing that sex will win out, what better way to raise money than to stigmatize human sexuality?

The noxious connection between homosexuality, American religiosity and its wealth generation came to the media's forefront with the anti-gay politicking of a former Miss America, Anita Bryant, in 1977, but it came to full fruition in the 1980s. This was not only because of HIV/AIDS, which made homosexuality more visible, but also as a result of decreased church attendance (i.e., fewer people paying their membership dues). This was less to do with a loss of religious sentiment than it was the realities of a growing number of two-parent working families, and the convenience of watching television evangelism in one's own living room,. Thus, simultaneous to church attendance declining, the advent of cable television brought various ministries into millions of American living rooms.

A problem with televised evangelism, however, is that in order for the church to profit, they still needed patrons to offer up their money. When one physically attends church, a basket is passed around, and there thus exists collective peer pressure from the congregation sitting beside you to put money in the basket. But no such collective pressure exists on television. Television evangelists therefore capitalized on AIDS hysteria and homophobia to milk money from callers who could conveniently donate with their new inventions—the credit card and tone dial telephones. Christianity essentially became an infomercial.

Organized religion sensationalized and demonized homosexuality, warning that it would bring God's day of reckoning. These white male preachers sold to the American populace a cultural cure to homosexuality: "Donate money to us and we will fight the gay agenda." Television stars and TV evangelists, like Anita Bryant, Jerry Falwell, D. James Kennedy, Lou Sheldon, Pat Robertson and other ogres of immorality, used (and still use) the airwaves to defame gay Americans, requesting money be donated in order to stop evil homosexuals from destroying pure American heterosexual families. For this tactic to work, however, the church needed to portray homosexuality as a choice. If homosexuality were widely understood to be what it actually is, a product of biological processes (i.e., not a choice), they would have less luck at raising hatred against this minority. The decision to label homosexuality as a choice was both brilliant and devastating. It had far-reaching, awful implications.

The anti-gay war entered the American political divide in 1980. Here, the Democratic Party maintained a platform supporting gay equality. The Republicans took the opposite. With the election of homophobic Republican Ronald Reagan that same year, America quickly headed into homohysteria (see Chapter 2). For the next three decades the Republican Party aligned itself with fundamentalist Christianity, casting itself as the party of homophobia. This had devastating consequences: lack of funding for HIV/AIDS, slowing the search for a cure; the over ten thousand military members kicked out of the United States Armed Services (including important operatives decoding Al-Qaeda messages); the thousands of gay youth who committed suicide because they bought the ugliness of Christianity's myths against them; the countless bullying of sexual and gender minorities; the denial of family, rights, jobs, and social equality to those who don't fit their narrow model being human.

There weren't only consequences for sexual and gendered minorities. The homohysteria that this crusade engendered would also push acceptable notions of masculinity to the extreme. As I spoke of in Chapter 1, out of fear of being thought gay, men were compelled to align themselves with orthodox masculinity, including the violence, stoicism, risktaking, and "suck it up mentality" that it required. How many young men have died sowing their masculine seeds through reckless behavior, fighting, drinking, or joining the military in the name of being macho? Masculinity was, during the 1980s, and remained so until only recently, a public health crisis. America stunk of masculinity. Nowhere was this more exemplified than in the jock.

Although lacking the financial power of organized religion, high school, college, and professional jocks contributed to this ugly culture of hate. Jocks established their identities as not only heterosexual, but as opposed to homosexuality, femininity, or anything that did not meet their very narrow identity perspective. Those who did not fit their mold were cast out, bullied, harassed, and vilified for their "lesser" heteromasculine status. It was this era, this jock mentality which nearly drove me to suicide at 16, and it was this same ugly jock culture that a decade later influenced an American football player to brutally assault one of my athletes—falsely presuming him to be gay (see introduction).

It was only after the 2012 second-term election of Barack Obama that the Republican Party and most organized Christian religions began to change their anti-gay tactics in America. Not because they have realized the errors of their ways, but because they now realize that preaching anti-gay bias no longer provides them the same profit it once did. Increasingly, anti-gay bias is a liability, not a financial asset. This is true for both members of Generation X, those in their 40s today, and for *i*Generation.

Evidencing this, in a survey of 1,000 men, the gay-friendly, softer, and more intellectual Barack Obama was the third most admired male (30 per cent indicated they look up to him) while his predecessor, the homophobic and anti-intellectual G.W. Bush, came in 14th, with half the votes at 15 per cent. The conservative ideologues are just now beginning to realize that they have lost the three decades long cultural war against homosexuality. Increasingly, Americans reject homophobia, from both its politicians and preachers. As older, homophobic customers die off, they are replaced by a more inclusive generation that will not stand for it.

I add to this discussion one final note about those propagating the now dying cultural war against gay men. Even though this section is a bit off topic, I provide it here so that I am not portrayed as demonizing straight men only. This section therefore concerns the fact that the war against homosexuality is sometimes led not only by men in search of financial or political profit, but also by gay men victimized by cultural homohysteria. Homophobia oftentimes appears as an attempt to cover up their same-sex desires, something Freud discussed as reaction-formation.

Empirically testing this theory, researchers at the University of Georgia (H. Adams et al. 1996) surveyed heterosexual men for their attitudes toward homosexuality. They next strategically selected men who represented either extremely homophobic or extremely gay-friendly attitudes (leaving out those in the middle) and attached erection meters (a plethysmograph) to their penises (when a penis grows erect in the jar it pushes air out, moving a dial up).

The participants were then shown gay male pornography. The men who identified as highly homophobic demonstrated significantly more sexual arousal than the gay-friendly group. Interestingly, when the highly homophobic group was asked about their level of arousal, their ratings of erection and arousal to homosexual stimuli were not significantly different from the gay-friendly men, suggesting that they consciously or unconsciously denied their arousal.

I could list here pages worth of politicians and religious leaders who have been caught having sex with another man, despite building their careers off of homophobia, but one simply needs to go to www.ranker.com/list/top-10-anti-gay-activists-caught-being-gay/joanne to see a selection of them. These are just a few who have acted out against gays in order to deny their own homosexuality. This is not just an American phenomenon. In 2013 the leading Catholic in Scotland, Cardinal Keith O'Brien, was revealed for not only having an affair with another priest, but for groping men as well. He was notoriously homophobic.

These situations occur as a result of extreme homohysteria. When gay citizens live within a culture that not only demonizes homosexuality but also understands that a sizeable portion of the population is gay, it is tempting to ward off gay suspicion by projecting homophobia. In cultural moments of homohysteria, gay men become homophobic for the same reasons that straight men do, to cast off homosexual suspicion. And because it is impossible to definitively prove that one is not gay, one must prove and reprove and reprove this status. It is reasonable to suspect that if one is capable of saving oneself from homophobic cultural treatment, one would attempt such. Thus, as hypocritical as these homophobic men are, there is logic in their promotion of homophobia.

Assertion 3: Generation X Lost the Cultural War

Since the early 1990s, both qualitative and quantitative studies have shown a significant decrease in cultural and institutional homophobia within North American society. There are numerous, long-term, academic investigations and popular polls showing the rapid pace at which cultural attitudes are changing. Attitudes toward homosexuality are improving so fast that I hesitate to give percentages—which are certain to be out-of-date by publication. Thus, I provide just one here, the American Broadcasting Channel (ABC) news poll.

I use the ABC poll because it has traditionally shown slightly higher rates of approval to gay marriage than other polls, thus buying me some lag time between the writing of this chapter and the publication of the book. In 2013, ABC's survey extended evidence of a remarkable transformation in public attitudes. Support for gay marriage has gone from 47 per cent in 2010 to 58 per cent in 2013. Most significant to my research, gay marriage was found to be supported by 81 per cent of adults younger than 30, compared with just 44 per cent of seniors. Still, that is up by more than 10 points in both groups just since March 2011. In a sentence, we are witnessing the death of acceptable homophobia (McCormack 2012a).

It is reasonable to suspect these changing cultural trends have implications for the reduction of stigma for those enjoying same-sex sexual activity, or for pseudo-sexual activity (like masturbating together). It is also evident that what counts as gay sex is rapidly changing. As we saw in Chapter 7, what used to disqualify a male from the terrain of heterosexuality, a same-sex kiss, is now so common in the UK that it doesn't even count as an act of sex.

There is very little actual data on what percent of heterosexuals would engage in same-sex sex, however. A 2013 poll by the magazine *Time Out, London* concluded that 42 per cent of the city's population would engage in it (this is a very liberal readership base). They showed a large gender gap, with 60 per cent of women suggesting such, but only 23 per cent of men. There is no further information about the poll, so I must use extreme caution in even discussing the poll in an academic book. What fascinates me about the poll however is that after it was released it did not raise further questions, investigations, or backlash. Thus, whether it accurately reports the percent of those living in London who are willing to engage in same-sex sex (I doubt it does) it is nonetheless significant to note that cultural conditions have changed so much that it failed to spark outrage—not even from the religious right.

This discussion is not independent of sport. Competitive, organized team sports—particularly those requiring brute strength and physical contact—became part of the homophobia project of the 1980s. For decades academics and non-academics highlighted that sport was a highly homophobic enterprise. In fact, in 2006, I gave a talk titled, "Hoist the Anchor: How Sports Stymie Social Progress." My premise was that attitudes regarding homosexuality in sport lagged ten years behind the dominant cultural attitude; that sport served as an institution which aimed to thwart the progress of sexual and gender minorities. But it was also during this time that the social attitude toward sexual and gender minorities was rapidly shifting. In light of this, I suggested that if sport did not readjust to this liberalizing, it would be judged as a vestige of an outmoded time, and begin to decline. For sport to survive, it must, I argued, adhere to changing cultural perspectives on sexuality.

This book is evidence that sport has met the challenge. My research makes clear that teamsport athletes are no more likely to be homophobic than non-athletes. Today, jocks emerge in a generation which does not accept homophobia, and their sporting participation does not give them a pass in this. In fact, while jocks may have resisted declining homophobia, they simultaneously pushed for broader heteromasculine boundaries (Ripley et al. 2011, 2012). When they began to embrace homosexuality, they helped push back the barricades of homohysteria. This is what happens when youth grow up with a free sharing of knowledge, alongside contact with sexual minorities. This is what happens when youth grow up free of religious or political persecution in the digital age.

Assertion 4: The Primary Tool used to Win the War was the Internet

Until recently, sex between men has been a highly stigmatized form of human pleasure. Homosexuality, however, has moved from what Oscar Wilde called "the love that dare not speak its name" to become an increasingly accepted, and sometimes glorified, form of human sexual interaction for members of *i*Generation.

As sex has become less stigmatized, mainstream media texts and other cultural practices using pornographic styles, gestures, and aesthetics have become more prominent in all aspects of commercial culture—and this leads to a further erosion of sex as stigmatized. This process, which Brian McNair (2002) describes as a "pornographication of the mainstream," has developed alongside an expansion of the cultural realm of pornography, which has become more accessible to a much wider variety of audiences through the internet. This is much different than how boys used to consume pornography (Attwood 2010).

Whereas teenage boys once traded baseball cards, today they trade digital pornography clips obtained free from websites. Where once they snuck a peek of their father's *Playboy*, today they have access to pornography on their cell phones. Instead of flipping through pages of still shots of normally nude individuals posing, the world of interactive and dynamic pornography has come to fruition. The internet provides anyone the ability to instantly access a display of sexual variety—of any type of sexual variety in all manners.

Here a whole range of bodies fuck in all combinations, styles, mixtures, manners, and video quality. But bodies also fuck with all forms of once highly taboo sexual object choices. Any sexual fetish can be located in the cyber world, and a few hours of exploration might subject one to images they previously had no idea they would be aroused by. Whatever you desire to see—people being urinated on, toe sucking, self-sucking, bondage and sadomasochism, chubby people, older people, group sex, animal sex, scat, objects of all sorts being inserted into anuses and vaginas, public sex, oral sex, facials, incest, and even child pornography—can be found on the internet.

In a study of over 1,000 teenagers in Norway, Træen & Štulhofer (2013) reported that 96 per cent of gay and heterosexual men, 92 per cent of lesbians, and 84 per cent of heterosexual women had viewed internet pornography. Furthermore, for the first time in history, rather than simply looking at an erotic drawing, reading an erotic text, or salivating over an erotic photo, today it is possible to interact with the subjects of our sexual desire. We can sex text from our phones, masturbate to the text and/or webcam images of a friend, or find a plethora of people to have sexual chat and/or webcam with that we don't know, found in any number of sex-related chat rooms. If you want you can pay to watch professionals online, too. We can upload our own pornography to amateur websites and take delight at knowing that others are fantasizing about us.

There are no age controls for these websites, and no need to register a credit card. Accordingly, Dines (2010) suggests that kids today access pornography on average at age 11. And while she uses this fact as part of a moral panic argument about porn, pornography is undoubtedly popular with a large swath of the population; after all, *sex* remains the most popular word typed into search engines. Thus, whereas governments used to control porn in a misguided attempt to prevent it from unduly influencing its citizens into sexual deviance, today's governments cannot control it even when they try to. The internet has ended such prohibition—and efforts to the contrary are futile. I am not critiquing the panoply of sex and sexual variety on the internet. I think it wonderful. It provides what some feminists concerned with pornography have been calling for all along: not an abolition of pornography but an explosion of the subjectivities of differing kinds of people in pornography (Ellis et al. 1990). This explosion of pornography has reshaped and greatly expanded our cultural/sexual pallet of opportunities: gone is the expectation of heterosexual missionary sex. The internet has sparked a revolution of sexual practice, but it has also sparked a revolution in the liberation from oppressive norms.

For example, the internet has been useful in reducing cultural homophobia through making homosexuality (and gay sex) visible. Today's Porntube.com generation see, early and often, sexual images that arouse or entertain them: whether accidentally or intentionally, my students tell me that they view video clips of gays, lesbians, and others once stigmatized by the Victorian cult of heterosexual boredom. Often a heterosexual cannot find his preferred images of heterosexual intercourse without filtering through the images of the acts once so socially tabooed. Curiosity of the other, or perhaps a desire to simply see what others enjoy, tempts the heterosexual-minded young male into clicking on the link, watching what their fathers despised so much. In viewing gay sex they grow desensitized to it. In fact, as I find with my heterosexual male students after showing them gay pornography in my sociology of sexualities class, some of them are even aroused by it. Thus, I propose the internet has been instrumental in exposing the forbidden fruit of homosexual sex, commoditizing and normalizing it in the process (Træen & Štulhofer 2013).

Also highlighting how the internet has been useful in democratizing sexual desire, it has provided lesbian, gay, bisexual, transgender, and other forums to organize for political action; forums to share life narratives; and forums for heterosexuals to ask sexual minorities "anything" about their sexual lives. Clearly, the internet has been beneficial in making visible these lives to the "normal" heterosexual world. The internet has taken away the fear for us to ask about one's sexual orientation, too. For example, Facebook asks whether one is interested in men, women or both. This part of the basic information package one can publicly present to the world. This has severely reduced the notion that homosexuality (particularly) is a "private" affair, thus it has helped reduce heterosexism. It is increasingly less acceptable to assume that one is straight.

The commoditization of extreme pornography makes yesterday's stigmatized bedroom activities normal, perhaps mundane. The study of Norway's adolescents showed that seeing novel sex on the internet inspired adolescents to try it in reality (Træen & Štulhofer 2013). Thus, the range of sexual behaviors we can partake in and discuss with our friends is greatly expanded and this gives us more opportunities to expand our boundaries of what is gay/straight, degrading/invigorating, dangerous or boring. The internet has, in my estimation, been useful in rescuing human sexuality from the hand of moralists; particularly those who use a misguided belief in religious doctrine to shame us into platonic bodies. The internet has both helped shape and been shaped by a more inclusive, sexualized, and wider-gendered generation. Today's youth are nothing like those of my youth. They are not Generation X, they are instead a generation of sex, love, and inclusion. They are hippies without the flowers. *i*Generation use their *i*Phones and *i*Pads to spread inclusion, because they are concerned with their feelings and not what old men think. They use their agency to construct a new pro-gay, pro-sex society; one in which men freely love other men. The ground under their beds is shaking with sexual and gendered diversity and inclusivity.

Pseudo-Sexual Activities in Sport Hazing

While hazing initiations have various purposes and meanings for team-sport players, it is commonly hypothesized that they occur because they mirror—in one event—the sacrifice and subordination that existing team members expect of new members or "recruits." Hazing initiations are believed to serve as a test not only of recruits' masculinity, but also of their readiness to concede their agency to the power structures of team leadership (Kirby & Wintrup 2002). Hazing is thought to be a ritualistic enshrining of leadership positions, where team leaders are granted considerable power while recruits are positioned as docile. However, hazing is also thought to serve multiple other social control purposes.

Donnelly & Young (1988) demonstrate that initiations act as a socialization process that shapes the identities of recruits into a form that suits the team's subculture by bonding team members around a common experience. Kirby & Wintrup (2002) develop this analysis by suggesting that the main purpose of hazing is to "grow the team" with those that are like-minded, recruiting players who are willing to share team norms, values, attitudes, and behaviors.

Others have theorized that the process of initiation rituals presents the opportunity for recruits to prove their commitment to the team, and for veteran members to gauge how successfully recruits have been socialized into adopting the team's subculture (Bryshun 1997). Accordingly, the extent to which athletes are accepted on a team is often determined by their adoption of the team's ethic. This means that if recruits are able to demonstrate appropriate roles and behaviors, they are more likely to be accepted and welcomed as a worthy member of the team (Donnelly & Young 1988).

A recruit refusing to be initiated often results in veteran members punishing the recruit through social exclusion or even physical abuse. This humiliation and isolation is usually more intense and its effects more enduring than the experience of the initiation itself (Johnson & Holman 2004). Thus, hazing is frequently regarded as the lesser of two evils, creating the perception that recruits freely choose to be initiated. Hazing initiations therefore become an avenue through which this power structure is maintained and perennially reproduced: recruits who have been hazed are less likely to challenge the power structure because they have previously undergone this initiation ritual (Allan & DeAngelis 2004).

Examining why athletes themselves engage in initiations, the most common rationale is that they are a key means of creating team cohesion (Bryshun 1997). Recruits often describe the experience of hazing initiations as a positive bonding experience between friends (Feist et al. 2004). Furthermore, athletes assume that the more extreme a hazing initiation is, the greater the level of commitment and interdependency will be produced. However, recent research suggests that despite these athletes' perspectives, initiations fail to promote group unity (Allan 2009); and others question whether team cohesion positively impacts on performance. Thus, the perseverance of the myth of team cohesion resulting from initiations speaks to the importance of these rituals in young men's lives.

In order to make sense of the behaviors that commonly occur in hazing activities, and to enable theoretical examination of hazing's intersection with masculinity, two of my colleagues and I (Anderson et al. 2012b) conceptualized four forms of hazing activity that emerged from a review of hazing literature: (1) physical acts of violence; (2) anti-social behavior; (3) excessive alcohol consumption; (4) and of concern to this chapter, same-sex sexual activities.

Same-sex sexual activities serve the purpose of feminizing and homosexualizing recruits to establish and reaffirm their position at the bottom of the team's heteromasculine hierarchy (Anderson 2005a). At the most extreme, several episodes of anal rape (usually with objects) have been reported in hazing episodes. However, the most frequent types of sexually-related hazing practices come through mock sexual behaviors: same-sex kissing, nakedness, and consuming alcohol off of other men's bodies (McGlone 2010). Nowhere is this more evident than in the sport of rugby.

In a seven-year study on rugby and men's hockey initiation rituals, my colleagues and I (Anderson et al. 2012b) documented a good deal of pseudo-sexual activities. For example, Rob described how he forced recruits to drink beer poured through the butt cheeks of another player, and Jack said, "One fresher had to put one of the older guys' dick in his mouth because he spilt his pint over him. It was pretty hilarious for everyone." Tim said, "We made one guy kiss another guy's ass, because he was getting a bit lippy."

In another hazing event, recruits were told to wrestle each other in togas. However, because of the high levels of drunkenness, the togas regularly fell off, and players were wrestling (with little skill) in just their underwear. The other players shouted comments like, "Don't get fucked" and "Take that pussy down" in ways that homosexualized the activity and marginalized the loser of each bout. Here, the sexualized wrestling bouts were taken as a literal demonstration of superiority: the winners are praised for their strength and power while the loser is homosexualized.

In another incident, recruits were made to drink a mixture of milk and water and a thickening agent (designed to look like ejaculate) out of a condom. Players were told that it was the ejaculate of veteran players. This did not seem to be taken seriously by players, who were just relieved that it did not contain more alcohol. One player exclaimed, "Thank fuck it's not more vodka!" In an interview afterward, the event organizer said, "That didn't work too well. They were just happy we laid off the drink." Interestingly, even though the organizers attempted to degrade recruits with symbolic forms of same-sex sexual activity, it maintained little traction in this instance. Other hazing stories include men being made to jerk/wank each other or drinking another guy's urine.

Our seven-year study of hazing practice also found something of interest. While early years saw lots of men kissing, once kissing became common practice among university students, as shown in the university studies, the player "upped" the homosexual activity to include the above-mentioned acts. However, in the last two years of the study, these acts disappeared.

I therefore argue that in a period of intense homohysteria, same-sex sexual activities are valuable in hazing because of the stigma attached to homosexuality. Performing same-sex sexual acts homosexualizes recruits, which relegates them in the masculine hierarchy and proves the recruits' devotion to the team and their willingness to comply with the requests of the senior team members. Accordingly, I also suggest that same-sex sexual activities will maintain little salience for hazing in cultures where homosexuality is not highly stigmatized. This is because veterans are unlikely to subordinate recruits because recruits no longer have a fear of being homosexualized. Instead, in a gay-friendly culture, men are more likely to partake in acts of mock heterosexual sex, as a homosocial bonding mechanism.

Mock Gay Sex

When I was in high school my friends and I never pretended to engage in gay sex. Furthermore, I can find no research showing a high prevalence of jocks pretending to fuck or suck each other (even if fully clothed). However, interviews and observations with players from virtually every sport team I have researched show a great deal of mock homosexual sex today. For example, one player bends another forward and grinds against him from behind. Others might shout "take it" as both men laugh. At one large-scale athletic contest, I watched as one men's team after another lined up to take a team portrait with a professional photographer. The teammates had to squeeze together tight for the photos. This proximity promoted the men to joke with one another, almost always pretending to fuck one another and bantering about their mock homosexual behavior. This is standard behavior for straight male athletes today. This type of mock sexual activity does not occur among women, or between gay men and their female friends. It is almost exclusively reserved for heterosexual men, among themselves; and it seems to mostly occur among jocks.

I interviewed Jonathan, an 18-year-old semiprofessional soccer team player in the United Kingdom, about these activities. "Oh yes. All the time," he said. "Guys will be under the covers pretending to masturbate together, making noise and all." He then went on to tell me that he assumes they are not actually masturbating, but that nobody pulls the covers off to find out. Instead, his teammates make comments, cheering the men on and encouraging them to do more pseudo-sexual things. "Sometimes two guys will kiss each other and then slip under the covers to pretend they are doing more," he said. They will "be lying on top of each other under there, and the bed is rocking as one guy is pretending to fuck another."

I have seen, multiple times, one jock lying atop another pretending to fuck him on the bed. In one example I can think of, both boys wore nothing but nylon shorts. Here, one thrust his hips into the other, and all the while they both screamed in imaginary ecstasy. For my part, I laughed alongside them. After all, there actually is something funny about these types of masculine, jocular behaviors. But if one steps back a minute and asks questions about "why" men seem to universally partake in these behaviors, it opens up some interesting ideas.

For example, another time one boy was sucking the finger of another, who had placed his finger out of the front flap in his underwear. The other guy placed himself on his knees in the position one would when giving a guy oral sex. He grabbed the guy's waist, pulling him into his mouth. How is this much different than real oral sex? Obviously one is sucking a friend's finger and not his cock, but apart from that, it's fairly realistic. Or, what does it feel like for one straight boy to be shirtless, wearing thin, silky running shorts, to be lying atop another boy, feeling their shirtless bodies rub together, feeling their groins rubbing? This is a profoundly intimate act that, although done in the name of banter/horseplay, still has sexual or at least pseudo-sexual properties to it.

One can theorize these situations in several ways: (1) the acts represent real sexual attractions that are culturally repressed; (2) they represent experimentation with same-sex sex; (3) they represent horseplay only, and even though skin is rubbing, there is no sexual feeling whatsoever. However one desires to read these situations, they are hard to get at academically. Men are always defensive in talking about them. They insist that these situations represent nothing more than just guys joking around. From a gay male perspective, it seems that there *must* be some physical enjoyment in the act. Even if not sexual, there must me some neurological pleasure in feeling your groin rub against another body. It is for this reason that I call these types of activities mock sex, or pseudo-sexual activities.

I do not have an answer but am nonetheless fascinated by why it is that only young men do this. Why do women not? Why do gay men not pretend to mock fuck their female friends? Would this not be the same scenario? I do not want to suggest that these events are indicative of homosexuality or bisexuality, but I do suggest that they show that perhaps there is something erotic about homosocial males together.

However one interprets these events, men do them in other homosocial institutions (like the military or boarding schools) as well. They engage in it not only to bond with one another, but to ironically show that they are heterosexual too. Thus, key to this form of intimacy—and relevant to this work—is that the men I interview, and teams I observe, express a shared understanding that they are not erotically attracted to the men they pretend to fuck or masturbate with, but that they are emotionally close to them. Because men did not do this a few decades ago, it suggests that today's jocks are freer to associate with once stigmatized behaviors. This extends to masturbation as well.

Masturbation

The stigma against masturbation, that was so prolific during the homohysteric 1980s, has vanished. Whereas when I was 18 none of my friends would ever have admitted to masturbating, for the young men reading this book, an anti-masturbation culture does not resonate. Young men today do not have to "admit" to masturbating; instead it is assumed that all young men (and increasingly women) just do masturbate. Highlighting how matters have changed, only six years after Laumann (1994) studied this (finding 63 per cent of men admitting to masturbating once in the previous year), Gerressu et al. used data from a 1999–2001 survey (published in 2008) to show that 95 per cent of men reported having masturbated at some point in their lives and that 73 per cent reported masturbating in the four weeks before their interview, with 51.7 per cent saying they had done so in the previous week.

More recent research highlights even higher rates of masturbation. For example, research conducted in 2008 on 886 boys in seven middle-schools of British nationals found that boys began masturbating at about 12 years old, and by the time they were 19 years old 93 per cent were admitting to masturbating (Unni 2010). Meston & Ahrold (2010) show that 97 per cent of white undergraduate men say that they have masturbated. These high rates of reported masturbation (compared to previous studies) are illuminating of the changing social attitude toward masturbating, not only because they are higher than previous research but also because they are derived from Texas, a conservative and religious state.

In an unpublished classroom exercise, Professor Michael Bailey at Northwestern found that of the 276 undergraduate men he surveyed, the average male student masturbated 17.6 times per month. The largest group however were those masturbating more than 30 times a month. In a very real sense, masturbation has gloriously come out of the closet. Highlighting this, Kontula (2010: 375) writes:

> Over the last decades, the rate of Finnish people who masturbate has truly exploded. The proportion of male respondents jumped

from 74 to 97 percent... The figures for the youngest respondents are actually somewhat higher. In 1971, only approximately 60 percent of middle-aged men had occasionally experimented with masturbation. Thereafter the experimentation and practice of masturbation has progressed rapidly from one generation to the next... Masturbation frequency increased substantially with each survey. For example, the proportion of respondents in the youngest age group who had masturbated during the preceding month grew between 1971 and 2007 from 36 to 85 percent for young men... Of those who had masturbated in the last 24-hour period, the proportion of young men had jumped from 4 to 29 percent.

The message I take from my undergraduates in Britain (as well as from the men I researched in America) is that young men are more worried about whether they masturbate enough to be considered normal, as opposed to fearing they are the only one to indulge in such wondrous pleasures.

Not only do today's youth masturbate more often but they also talk publicly about it. They share conversations with others about how often they jerk off; some even talk about what techniques they use. For example, last semester one student asked (in front of the sociology of sexualities class) why it was that his wanking was better while rubbing his nipple. Similarly, when I was describing that anal sex feels good for men because the prostate is rubbed from the inside (pushing the ejaculate out harder), one young heterosexual man asked if that was why it felt better when he fingered himself while masturbating. These types of conversations were also commonplace with the American men I studied in my ethnographies of the soccer teams. There was much talk about masturbation techniques. There was no shame in saying, for example, "Right guys, I'm going home to rub one out." When I queried them about their sexuality, asking if they ever thought of guys when jerking off, few said they had; but none protested that they did not jerk off.

This social discourse around masturbation is found on the internet, too. Those looking to hone their masturbation skills might check out www.advancedmasturbation.com, www.letsmasturbate.com, jackinworld.com, male-masturbation-techniques.com, a2zmasturbation.com, askmen.com, the-penis.com, aboutmasturbation.com, ivillage.com, advancedmasturbationtechniques.com, onanibcs.com, mymasturbation.com, secretsofmasturbation.com, masturbation-passion.com, masturbationpage.com, knowhowmasturbate.com, mysecrethealth.com, mymalesexuality.com, holisticwisdom.com, greatmasturbationtips.com, allsexguide.com, jackintech.com, and hardysmasturbation.com.

These are, of course, only a partial listing of the webpages devoted to masturbation that end in .com. We can also list the websites devoted to masturbation in the domain name that ends with .net, or for the more conventional, simply click on Wikipedia—there are even masturbation techniques discussed there. Desire a visual? Just YouTube "masturbation."

To highlight how normal masturbation is today, on one site there are around 20,000 videos that guys have posted of themselves sucking their own cocks (and what percent of guys can do that?). If that many have posted videos of this, how many have posted videos of generic masturbation? On one page alone I found 30,000 videos of guys masturbating. It is unlikely that these are only gay men posting their videos. Instead, I have read commentary under a number of them in which the male is asked if he minds gay men masturbating to them; the response conveys the sentiment of one poster who said, "It's there for everyone to enjoy."

Athletes have, I suggest, played a role in facilitating a masturbation-friendly culture. This is because they are heterosexualized by their sporting participation, and this buys them some heterosexual insurance to push boundaries of acceptability. It is therefore ironic that the very men who were charged with retaining orthodox notions of masculinity may have also been responsible for their undoing. For it's not just that jocks felt comfortable pretending to fuck each other, and discussing masturbation, but my research also shows a fair amount of mutual masturbation.

Mutual Masturbation

Throughout the first decade of the new millennium, the only time I heard stories of mutual masturbation occurring among athletes concerned when young, closeted gay male athletes sensed that another athlete might also be gay. The athlete generally tried to arrange so that they could share a bed with the other on an overnight trip. These occurrences then involved one player making very slow advancement on another. Normally, pretending to be asleep, he would ever so slightly touch his heel to the other guy's leg, or a hand to his side. Either way, the gay athlete hoped the other player would respond by moving it closer. For the other guy's part, he normally waited a minute after the first touch, so that if the first touch was not intentional, it didn't seem he was too willing. Thus, after the first touch was returned, the second advancement was made. Slowly, in the course of time, the two bodies merged together, oftentimes concluding in quietly jerking his bedmate off so that the two guys in the other bed could not hear. These types of stories are abundant among gay athletes, as they are among gay male youth in general, but there are not as many stories of heterosexual men masturbating together. Well, until recently that is. Since around 2010, however, there seems to have been an increase in the percent of young men that have masturbated with another friend. These masturbation sessions do not represent organized circle jerks, or even drunken events. Instead, they represent what can occur when one lives in a culture of decreased homohysteria, with the technology to have webcam sex in the presence of a sexualized female. What normally occurs is two men (or more) spending the night in a friend's room and surfing the internet, to talk to women on webcam. The boys do not set out to masturbate together, but just as one gay boy made a slow and progressive movement on another, the female slowly beckons the boys to do more. The boys look at each other smile a bit, make a joke, and then remove their hard cocks to show the girl on the other end. They essentially bargain with her to do more, to take more off. The exchange oftentimes ends with both boys masturbating together, sat aside each other, so they can both see her on the monitor.

Sometimes events go further. Young women, using their erotic capital, beckon the boys to kiss, or oftentimes to wank each other off. Again, with the desire to see more of the nude female, and to please her, they often (not always) comply. The boys look to each other, kiss each other, and then immediately return their eyes to the monitor. Other times, they cross arms and jerk each other off for a while. How do I know this occurs? I see it all the time.

I have not systematically examined for this behavior in the men I interview, so I cannot say with what frequency this type of behavior occurs. I know of the behavior because I see it regularly on the porn sites I visit. Apparently, there is more than one porn-sting operation in existence. Companies hire a female to bate young men into the above scenarios, selling the video to others. Either that or women post these videos of their own free will. However they emerge on the internet, there is no shortage of them! The videos are fascinating to watch, as the young men find themselves in a situation not all together unlike that of the locker room. Just as nobody sits them down and explains to them locker room culture, what you can and cannot do, it's the same when they find themselves jerking off together. How long are you permitted to look at the other guy's cock? How long do you have to jerk him off for when an attractive female asks you to?

Whatever one's interpretation of events, there exists decreasing stigma around males masturbating together. Whereas it used to be that one act, or pseudo-act, of same-sex sexual activity disqualified one from socially perceived heterosexual status, there has been a slippage to this rule in recent years. As homosexuality grows less stigmatized, so do acts of it. What seems to be important in order to draw men into physically, sexually or pseudo-sexually engaging with each other is the presence of a female—even if only on a screen. Whereas guys sometimes jerked off together while watching porn, the presence of a "live" person on the other end of the computer screen makes jerking off together much more acceptable, much less gay. And if this is the case with a woman pictured in digital pixels only, how much power might a woman have to draw men to engage with each other sexually, in person?

Sex with Other Men

In this section, I use ethnography to examine the relationship between masculinity and same-sex sexual behaviors among heterosexual men in a feminized terrain. I show that the one-time rule of homosexuality is no longer at play among these young men, at least not if the same-sex experience occurs in pursuit of heterosexual desires.

The objective of this project was to analyze how informants' homophobia and notions of masculinity may be changing in response to decreasing cultural homophobia. The participants are 68 self-identified heterosexual men who all used to play American high school football but became collegiate cheerleaders because they were unable to make their university football teams. While a self-selection process cannot be ruled out (i.e., it is possible that men most affected by the masculinization process of football do not become cheerleaders), most of the informants reported that upon entering cheerleading they often times held orthodox notions of masculinity, including sexist views and overt homophobia. The men, between 18 and 23 years of age, came from diverse regions from throughout the United States but 80 per cent are white, middle-class men, so generalizations are limited accordingly.

The observation (on competitions) occurred with dozens of teams throughout the United States. However, the participant observations were conducted on one team each from the South, the Midwest, the West, and the Northwest. Two of these teams belonged to the "orthodox cheerleading association" and two belonged to the "inclusive cheerleading association." The total number of heterosexual men from these four teams numbered 47, of which 13 participated in the formal interviews. All informants knew the nature of my study.

Cheerleading as a Transitional Heteromasculine Space

Cheerleading squads traditionally support other athletic teams with sideline cheering, but today's cheerleaders also compete in complex dancing and stunting routines where a number of judged criteria determine success. Despite this evolution, men who cheer remain stigmatized as gay, so few try out for collegiate cheerleading without persuasion (Anderson 2005b). To recruit men, existing cheerleaders use a variety of tactics, including the sexualizing of female cheerleaders and the heterosexualizing and masculinizing of male cheerleaders. One university's cheerleading recruitment poster highlights all of these methods. Featuring an illustration of a bikini-clad woman sliding into a pool of water it reads, "Want strong muscles? Want to toss girls? Our Cheer Team needs stunt men!! No experience needed." Ex-football players are somewhat receptive to these recruitment efforts. After failing to make their university's American football teams, all of my informants clarified that they missed being associated with an athletic identity and/or being part of a team, and they judged cheerleading as an acceptable final effort to return to team sports (Anderson 2005b).

While these men still embody many of the cultural symbols of heterosexual masculinity—their new sport has not decreased their muscular strength or aesthetic sexual appeal—they nonetheless believe those outside cheerleading view their masculine capital as diminished and their heterosexuality as suspect because cheerleading is a culturally feminized sport. In their research on collegiate cheerleading Grindstaff & West (2006: 515) note, "Cheerleading is a key site for the production of emphasized femininity," and men who cheer are commonly perceived as homosexual because of this. They add, "*Everyone* we encountered in this study spoke of the gay stereotype for male cheerleaders" (ibid.: 511). My research concurs. One of my informants said, "As a football player, all the girls wanted me. I was very popular. Now, nobody knows who I am, and if they do, they think I'm gay because I cheer." Scott agreed, "Yeah, lots, most, of the people think we're gay because we cheer."

Whereas these men once occupied a dominant position at the top of the heteromasculine stratification as American football players, they now view their current sporting location as subordinating their masculinity and subjecting their heterosexuality to scrutiny. Where they were once masculinized and heterosexualized because of their association with American football, their transgression from it now homosexualizes and feminizes them. Reactions to their homosexualization and feminization range from apathy to hostility. Ryan aggressively defended his sport when I asked about the stereotype of male cheerleaders as gay. "It's absolutely not true!" he yelled. "I hate that stereotype. All it does is scare away worthy men who might want to cheer" [meaning orthodox acting men]. Conversely, when I asked Eugene how he felt about people thinking he was gay he said, "It bothered me a little at first, but now I don't care. Not in the slightest...".

Whereas my previous research (Anderson 2005b) on these groups of men examined the institutional and organizational attitudes that influenced their perception of masculinity (orthodox or inclusive) and their changing attitudes toward women and their athleticism (Anderson 2008c), in this chapter I show that the liminality of this space leads these men to revise heteromasculinity as well. I find that each of these groups (inclusive and orthodox) views differently heteromasculinity as a combined category of hegemonic gender and sexuality dominance.

Heteromasculinity among Orthodox Cheerleaders

When Tim introduced me to his teammate, Jeff, he said, "Jeff is the homophobic one on the team." I shook Jeff's hand and asked why that was. "I have no problems with gay men," he said. "I just don't understand why some have to prance around like little girls. Being masculine isn't about who you sleep with; it's about how you act. Your verbal inflection doesn't got to be a flamer." Jeff said his coach and one of his teammates are gay (both male), "But, you don't see them acting like that."

Jeff used the term "straight-acting" to describe how gay men "should" act, saying homosexuality is not problematic but acting feminine is. As I have shown elsewhere (Anderson 2005b) Jeff's position is influenced by norms coding men's expression of femininity as "unprofessional" within the orthodox cheerleading association. Men who don't meet "professional" expectations are stigmatized for "giving us all a bad name," and contributing to the homosexualizing and feminizing culture surrounding men who cheer.

Jeff expressed anger over one particular cheerleader, Carson, who is known for both the quality of his stunting (he holds two individual national championship titles) *and* his flamboyancy. However, the following evening we ran into Carson at an intra-squad cheerleading party. After a few drinks Jeff asked, "Who wants to take a body shot off me?" Flamboyantly jumping up and down Carson shouted, "I do! I do!"

The room erupted with laughter as the individual with the least hetero-masculine capital volunteered to perform a sexually charged drinking game on the man with the most. Jeff smiled, motioning Carson to come closer. "Go for it," he said as he removed his shirt and lay down on a hotel room bed. Carson poured alcohol into Jeff's naval, pinned his hips to the bed, and erotically licked it up, running his tongue considerably lower than Jeff's naval—all to the cheers of onlookers.

The way Jeff allowed Carson to perform a sexually charged drinking game on his body may be surprising, particularly concerning his view that gay men should "act masculine." I wondered, *was allowing another man to lick his body also consistent with masculinity?* When I later asked about this Jeff answered, "I bet there are lots of things about me that would surprise you." He continued, "One time, me and [teammate] Trevor had a threesome with a girl. Yeah, well, I actually had a three-some with [teammate] Drew, too." Jeff said that he also "made out" with his teammate, Ian, and once, "jacked him off a bit." I followed up with open-ended probes to confirm these assertions and found there has been a regular sexual combination of two men and one woman among five of his nine heterosexual male teammates.

Although Jeff indicated that these behaviors were not simply a matter of two men separately engaging in heterosexual sex with the same woman, he also considered himself heterosexual. "I'm not attracted to them [men]. It's just that there has to be something worth it. Like, this one girl said she'd fuck us if we both made out. So the ends justified the means. We call it a good cause. There has to be a good cause." Similarly, when I asked Jeff's teammate Patrick if he had sexual experience with men, he replied, "No. Not yet. But I will. It's just that there has got to be a reward. If I have to kiss another guy in order to fuck a chick, then yeah it's worth it. It's a good cause."

Illustrating the malleability of the good cause scenario, Jeff, Patrick, three other heterosexual teammates, and I went to a gay club, where Patrick met a woman, who agreed to take him back to her apartment for sex. In the dance club's restroom Patrick told me, "Maybe I'll see if they [Jeff and the woman] want to have a threesome." Thus, Patrick, who earlier stated there must be a "good cause" in order to have a threesome and had already secured heterosexual sex for the night, overlooked this good cause antecedent and propositioned her for a threesome (to which she agreed). When I asked Patrick what specific interaction would take place with Jeff he said, "Well, for the most part it would be about getting it on with her, but like we might do some stuff together, too." Patrick said he would also allow himself to receive oral sex but was not sure if he would give oral sex to Jeff. He then smiled and said, "It depends on what she wants." Some readers might be surprised that women are active in their desire for threesomes with men. But Hughes et al. (2004) showed us that while 78 per cent of heterosexual undergraduate men were interested in threesomes, also 32 per cent of undergraduate women were. Thompson & Byers (2013) found among their undergraduate population sample of 240 that 8 per cent of heterosexual undergraduate women had a threesome, while 24 per cent of the men did. These figures would seem to indicate that (because three times as many men are having threesomes) there must be a lot of two men, one woman threesomes. This research also found low peer group negativity toward threesomes.

The good cause scenario underscores that it is the subjectivity of desire for another man which is problematized not the sex itself, something I argue reproduces heterosexual privilege. The good cause scenario retains the subjectivity of heterosexual desire and the need for a woman's sexual presence (and her request for their same-sex sexual behaviors). This seems to help Jeff and his teammates negate suspicion of homosexuality so the good cause scenario therefore becomes the mantra for acceptable same-sex practices, even if the guidelines are not followed. Jeff and Patrick report being *so* heterosexual they are capable of engaging in same-sex sex without threatening their social identities as heterosexual, similar to how boys with high masculine capital are given more permission to associate with femininity compared to boys lacking masculine capital. Accordingly, Jeff and his teammates are therefore able to manage their same-sex sexual behaviors within a heterosexual framework, avoiding discussion of a gay or bisexual identity. They can partake in limited forms of same-sex sex as long as it takes place in pursuit of or in the presence of heterosexual desires: the good cause scenario.

Stuart said, "I've done that," when discussing this type of sex with informants of another orthodox team. "Yeah, switches and trains," Kevin confirmed. When I asked what switches and trains were Kevin answered, "Switching is when each guy is fucking a girl and then they switch and fuck the other girl. Trains are when a line of guys wait to tag-team a girl." Stuart elaborated, "You just sort of stand around waiting to fuck her. Hell, I even got my leg shot [ejaculated] on once!" When I asked Stuart if this bothered him he laughed, "No. It was kind of an assumed risk." And when I asked why he liked threesomes he responded, "Hell, if you're gon'na hit up a chick, it's cool to have another guy there to talk about it."

Stuart's phrase, "Hell, I even got my leg shot on," made me question, *how could he get ejaculate on himself if he was waiting behind another guy for his turn at the "switches and trains?"* He answered, "Well, my friend was fucking her and I was making out with him while he was doing it." Similarly, when I asked Stuart's teammate, Tim, if he had done anything sexual with men he answered, "Yeah, sure. Why not? I made out with a guy once and I would let a guy blow me. I'm not gay but I think all guys wonder what it would be like. And I bet guys do it better anyhow."

Heteromasculinity among Inclusive Cheerleaders

Not all my informants viewed the expression of femininity among men as unprofessional or undesirable. The men I describe as representing inclusive masculinity (about half the men in collegiate cheerleading at the time, but I suspect far more than this are today) did not feel compelled to act in orthodox masculine ways. Among the heterosexual men I classified as exhibiting inclusive masculinity, I found nine of the 15 asked said that they have slept in the same bed with a gay men, I found none to be uncomfortable hugging another man, and all of the 11 men I went dancing with danced with other men too. All of these men danced flamboyantly during cheerleading competitions and the men from one team even wore women's competitive apparel, because it was better fitting than what the manufacturer offered in the men's version.

I found this inclusive perspective influenced the permissivity of heterosexual men's same-sex sex differently than the orthodox men in several ways. First, I was struck by the comparative ease with which many of these men discussed their same-sex sexual practices. Upon learning that I was gay, four men immediately informed me that they once had sex with a man. Second, a woman's presence was not required for these men to engage in same-sex sex. Pete said that he, Sam, and another (now graduated) heterosexual teammate once shared a room with Aaron (an openly gay cheerleader). "We let Aaron give the three of us a blow job," he told me without hesitation, and then added, "And we're not the only ones who've done stuff with guys." He then listed the names of others who engaged in same-sex sex.

When I asked Sam's teammate, Tom, if a woman's presence was neces-sary for same-sex sex he said it might be a "bonus" but it was *not* required. His friend, Joe, added, "Hey, getten some is getten some." And when I asked if they were afraid others might think they were gay because of their same-sex sex Tom clarified, "Just because one has gay sex, doesn't mean one is gay." This disclosure also confirms what gay male cheerlead-ers frequently tell me about engaging in sexual practices with straight male cheerleaders. Carson (half-jokingly) said, "Honey, I've sucked more straight dick than gay. It's almost to the point that when a guy tells me he is straight, I just wan'na say, 'yeah, you're straight—straight to bed.'" The difference between these accounts and other accounts of straight athletes who have sex with men is that my informants are more willing to engage in these behaviors without anonymity, something I attribute to a lessening of traditional sexual mores and the decreasing levels of cultural homophobia found among men of this cohort (Anderson 2005a).

Informants of the other inclusive cheerleading team I conducted participant observation with also viewed same-sex sex as compatible with heterosexuality. Mike expressed several times kissing and receiving oral sex from men. Still, he said, "I don't perceive myself as gay. I like women far too much for that." When I asked Mike if he identifies as bisexual he said, "Not really. I mean, you can call me that if you want. I'm not into labels and I don't think anybody is one-hundred percent anything, but I consider myself straight. I'm just not a homophobe." His teammate, Rob, added, "Yeah, I let a guy give me a blow job once and I don't think that makes me gay."

None of these men discussed "good cause" scenarios or "switches and trains" as men from the orthodox association did. In fact, several outwardly questioned the polarization of sexual identity categories altogether. When I asked Jonathan if he thought gay men could be masculine he said, "Of course. Masculinity has nothing to do with sexuality. I have really flamboyant friends who are straight too." And when I asked if he thought men who have sex with men are gay he said, "Not really, no. They can be, but don't have to be. And gay men can have sex with women too. It doesn't mean they're straight."

Chapter Conclusion

Athletic culture has come a very long way since the highly homophobic and highly homohysteric 1980s. Where once even admitting to masturbation was proof of one's homosexuality, the sexual pallet available to young heterosexual men today has rapidly widened. *i*Generation has removed stigma from all types of sexual activities: masturbation, oral sex, anal sex, hooking up, group sex, and gay sex. We live in a culture in which the slut–stud dichotomy is decreasing; one in which women have more sexual agency; and one that supports gay marriage. The only strong sexual stigma to remain is that of cheating on one's partner, but despite that stigma cheating is nonetheless well more than the norm among youth.

I attribute these changes to two dominant influences. The first is that *i*Generation is increasingly losing its religiosity, and even for those who maintain a belief in God, they are unwilling to accept homophobia as part of that theology. *i*Generation has essentially achieved the goals of the hippies, without overt politicking. They are not political in the respect that they hold marches or demonstrations, but *i*Generation shows their political affiliation through "likes" on Facebook. This form of media, of politics, should not be discounted: it is highly effective in changing public opinions.

In this chapter I highlighted the importance of this cultural shift, not only for freeing up attitudes toward sexual and gender minorities, but also in reducing the one-time rule of homosexuality for straight men as well. I showed that while my research found some sex occurring between gay and straight men, rarely did it occur between straight men: circle jerk and soggy biscuit exist mostly as locker room lore. Nor did I hear enough stories of straight men masturbating together to heterosexual porn to suggest that it happens with any real frequency. However, matters began to change when the subject of heterosexual desires appears on screens or in person. Once men have the opportunity to get off in the presence of a woman, the one-time rule of homosexuality goes out the window.

I first described a great deal of men engaging in mutual masturbation on the internet to the presence of other women on webcam. Despite the internet being literally loaded-full with these scenes, I cannot say how frequently it occurs among teamsport athletes, because (sadly) I have not systematically investigated for it. Even if I did investigate for it, I'm not convinced that participants would be all-too honest with me. This is for two reasons. First, in the moment, sex wins out. Men are compelled into sexual acts by states of horniness that, the minute they achieve orgasm, they think differently about. This makes it hard to recount these activities to a gay male researcher, who they inherently know will be turned-on by the very recounting. Second, I do not think that young straight men are as versed in talking about their same-sex sexual or pseudo-sexual activities as they are capable of partaking in them. Like the locker room, there is uncertainty in how to communicate about the activities that occur there. No better evidence of this emerges than from men who pretend to fuck each other in bouts of "mock sex." The men unanimously describe these events to me as "just banter" in the UK, or "just joking around" in the US. But there are lots of way men can joke around—there must be a reason mock sex is the predominant way.

What this tells us is that men are likely better in the doing than they are in the explaining. And this makes it difficult to research activities that require a good deal of explanation. It makes it even harder when one's participants may not want to disclose the information in the first place.

It is for this reason that co-ed collegiate cheerleading seemed a prime location to examine for same-sex sexual activity among heterosexual men. This is because cheerleading offers a team culture with a large number of gay and straight men. This fosters an environment where there is more open discussion of what it means to be gay, straight or bisexual, and there is more opportunity for the exploration of same-sex behaviors, because one has willing gay teammates to try it with.

I had hoped that cheerleading would provide me with such a cultural milieu going into the research. I suspected that the athletic culture would be different, not only because there were gay men in the sport, but because they also competed alongside women. However, I feared that detractors might suggest that all cheerleaders were just gay men in the first place. Thus, I strategically selected my participants for interview, only taking those who had previously played high school football. This association buys the men a good deal of heterosexual capital, and makes it harder to dismiss their same-sex activities as simply closeted gay men.

Then, in researching self-identified heterosexual men who transgressed from the heteromasculinizing sport of high school American football to the feminizing and heterosexualizing sport of collegiate cheerleading, I first described this transition as triggering a reconstruction of social identities in order to retain some of the privilege of their lost hetero-masculinity. I showed that they did this by subscribing to one of two dominant and competing forms of normative masculinity within cheer-leading culture: orthodox or inclusive masculinity (Anderson 2005b).

The men I describe as exhibiting orthodox masculinity slightly alter a traditional, sexist version of masculinity by welcoming gay men to participate in their anti-feminine attitudes. For men in this group, homosexuality *is* acceptable but the expression of femininity *is not*. Gay men who refuse this conditioned acceptance remain stigmatized—perhaps the reason Jeff spoke disdainfully about Carson or other men who openly do femininity. Accordingly, masculinity for men in this group remains mostly conceptualized within well-established feminist findings: in order to be a "real man" one must not be "like a woman" (Chodorow 1978) although, importantly, one can now be gay. While violating certain aspects of the sexuality order is accepted, these men are not yet able to, or willing to admit to, having sexual *desire* for another man: they can however have sex with him. Perhaps this is why none of their threesomes occurred with gay men.

Conversely, men who I described as subscribing to inclusive masculinity co-created a culture that made masculinity available to gay men—and femininity available to straight men. These informants even celebrated the expression of femininity among men and stigmatized men who acted in orthodox masculine ways. To these men, Carson was a source of pride. Thus, men exhibiting inclusive masculinities not only separated the hegemonic powers of sexuality and masculinity from heteromasculinity, but they contested the privileging of orthodox masculinity over inclusive masculinity and (to a lesser extent) the privileging of men over women.

In addition to finding homosexuality compatible with masculinity, I also found that the cheerleaders negated (or at least lessened) the one-time rule of homosexuality, reconstructing it to be compatible with certain forms of same-sex sexual activity.

In total, 40 per cent of the 49 self-identified heterosexual men I asked said they once engaged in or continue to engage in some form of same-sex sex. However, informants framed differently the conditions in which this same-sex sex was thought compatible with heterosexuality. Those subscribing to orthodox masculinity saw their limited forms of same-sex sex acceptable only if performed in pursuit of heterosexual desires (a "good cause" antecedent that did not always turn out to be compulsory), while those subscribing to inclusive masculinity did not require the presence of women or explicit heterosexual desires.

For men of the first group, same-sex sex was largely seen as a way of sharing "conquests" with "brothers," mutually reassuring each other of their heterosexual desirability. It was also a way to get and give pleasure from men, although the subjective desire for men remained stigmatized. For men of the second group, same-sex sex was largely viewed as an acceptable form of sexual recreation without threat to one's heterosexual identity, as long as their interactions are also limited to kissing, oral sex, and mutual masturbation.

Despite these differences, the frequencies of informants who have sexual experience with other men are equal between those I grouped as orthodox and those I grouped as inclusive. Nine men from the two orthodox teams confirmed participating in same-sex sex, while ten men from the two inclusive teams confirmed participating in kissing, oral sex, and "jerking another guy off." Interestingly, I found no variance in how heterosexual teammates who had not, or not yet, had—or did not admit to having—similar sexual experience viewed their teammates' same-sex sexual behaviors. Most said, "It's not for me," or "I don't care what people do," but (importantly) none of the 49 overtly stigmatized their teammates for their same-sex sex.

Collectively, interviews with jocks, both American and British athletes, tell me that they no longer subscribe to the one-time rule of homosexuality; they recognize that sexuality is more fluid; and do not stigmatize gay sex. Instead, they engage in it through exuberant mock sex with their peers, kissing other men, sometimes wanking with them, or having threesomes. This highlights a vast attitudinal difference compared to men of Generation X, who highly stigmatized same-sex sexual interactions.

Conclusions

The first mission statement for undoing conservative notions of masculinity may have been the Men's Center Manifesto, from the University of Berkeley (Berkeley Men's Center 1974). In their declaration of men's liberation they wrote:

> We, as men, want to take back our full humanity... We want to relate to both women and men in more human ways—with warmth, sensitivity, emotion, and honesty. We want to share our feelings with one another to break down the walls and grow closer. We want to be equal with women and end destructive, competitive relationships between men... We are oppressed by this dependence on women for support, nurturing, love, and warm feelings. We want to love, nurture, and support ourselves and other men, as well as women... We want men to share their lives and experiences with each other in order to understand who we are, how we got this way, and what we must do to be free.

In this book, I have argued that university men, including jocks, today have achieved the aims of this declaration—and more.

This achievement has not been easy. Western culture policed men's behaviors more strictly in the decade following this proclamation. Thus, in the 1980s, athletic capital and homophobic discourse stratified adolescent men in a king-of-the-hill style competition for the upper rungs of a masculine hierarchy. Much like the childhood game, where the most dominant male occupies the top of the hill and physically pushes weaker boys down it, the contestation for masculine stratification was played out on flat sporting fields.

In this type of jock-ocratic culture, boys who scored the most touchdowns, goals, or baskets symbolically occupied the top of the hierarchy, where they often naturalized their status by marginalizing other males with homophobic language. Those who were softer, weaker, less athletic, or more feminine were regarded as homosexual and were normally relegated to the bottom of the stratification. Boys who rode atop the masculine hierarchy were required to maintain their social location through the continuous monitoring of masculine behaviors, in order to assure complicity with masculine expectations of the time. Thus, a continuous process of homosocial patrolling occurred, both by self and others, as boys who deviated were routinely chastised for their aberrant behavior.

In this manner, homophobia hurt both gay men and straight men. Homophobia prohibited all men from partaking in culturally feminized activities, lest they were homosexualized for it. The fear of being thought gay, in a period of intensely high homophobia, was enough to steer most all but a brave few young men away from activities, behaviors, symbols, or other associations with femininity. In doing this, the notion of what it meant to be feminine expanded, leaving less space for men to navigate. This was a culture that I describe as homohysteric.

The jock-ocracy, however, existed as a historically situated system of organizing and valuing masculinities because during the 1980s (when the jock ruled supreme) there was a convergence of multiple social trends. First, the AIDS crisis of the 1980s made homosexuality visible and popular wisdom maintained that one in ten were exclusively gay. Yet the extreme homophobia of the era—a vehemence toward same-sex sex, love, or identity, or even sympathy from heterosexuals toward homosexuals—meant that most gay men, particularly in sport, kept their homosexuality secret. The lack of visibility of gay men in sport and on high school and university campuses permitted homophobia to flourish, mostly uncontested, both inside and outside of sport. Anti-gay antipathy was promoted by conservative politicians, and shouted from mountain-tops by virtually every pastor, preacher, pope, deacon, and any other religious leader(s) of the time (with exceedingly few exceptions). For those straight men who thought differently, questioning homophobia would lead to accusations that that person was gay themselves (why else would they contest it?).

However, the homophobic 20th century jock was also "so straight" that it permitted a (specific and limited) place where boys and men were actually permitted to touch each other and bond emotionally (Pronger 1990). The sporting exception was not so because team sports were locations friendly to homosexuality; quite the opposite: sport was suffused with such high degrees of homophobia that it built heterosexual insurance for the jocks that played it. Accordingly, the only reason the guys in a football huddle could wrap their arms around each other was because they operated under the belief that homophobia had excised all gay players and even homosexual desire from sport. Thus, the performing of gender-transgressing acts was both a symbol of a fag (for one group) and the symbol of a heterosexual jock (for another).

Since 1993, homophobia has been on a rapid decline, replaced by more inclusive attitudes, particularly among youth. The men I speak of in this book—adolescent and young male athletes from both the US and the UK—no longer live in a homophobic culture. And because they do not hate homosexuals, there is less reason to fear being thought one. When one is less concerned about being thought homosexual, one is free to do things that are socially coded as belonging to the terrain of homosexuals. Then, as more heterosexual men started to do these behaviors, they stripped the homosexual connotation away from them. This has created a virtuous circle of expanding, acceptable, behaviors for young men to engage in, without homosexual suspicion.

Whereas sport used to define a particular, conservative type of "hegemonic" masculinity, jocks can no longer be stereotyped. To assume athletes are homophobic, stoic, or emotionally or physically alienated from other men would be to pre-judge them: it would be an act of prejudice. In fact, in many ways the 21st century jock is ahead of his non-athletic peers. In my studies I find that jocks express love to one another as much as non-athletes do, but that they engage in *more* kissing and cuddling with other men than non-jocks. Thus, it is the heterosexual capital that jocks used to defy their own rigidly imposed masculinity culture which ultimately betrayed that code and permitted more expressiveness and tactility. Once homophobia began decreasing, jocks exhibited a wider range of behaviors, pushing into terrains that were homosexualized/feminized. In other words, they continued to use their heterosexual capital to make these spaces acceptable for men to occupy. This next meant that less masculinized men could follow suit. In many ways jocks made it okay to love and touch other men.

Being a jock still brings an allure of heterosexuality, and that—just as it did in the 1980s—permits young heterosexual male jocks to exhibit an even greater terrain of expanded behaviors. The multiple investigations of jock culture in this book make it fairly clear: it is gay-friendly jocks who have the credibility to step into homosexual gendered terrain which makes it safe for others to follow, de-stigmatizing homosexuality in the process and opening a gate for men to identify as mostly heterosexual instead of exclusively heterosexual. Whereas old-school masculinity theorists once described teamsport athletes as extremely homophobic and gender conservative, this is not the case today.

In the introduction I listed characteristics attributed to the 20th century jock as stuck-up and self-centered, aggressive, rude and arrogant, handsome, muscular, and athletic, unintelligent, abusing alcohol and drugs, generally popular with girls, and having sex earlier and more casual forms of it. Many of these stereotypes might still hold true. Teamsport athletes are still violent in sport, and they certainly abuse alcohol, and are popular with girls. But unlike the 20th century jock, the 21st century jock is not a bully against people who are "uncool" or less popular than they are; they are not highly homophobic, reluctant to cry, afraid to hug or hold a friend too long; nor are they unwilling to show weakness or fear.

Not all will like my analysis of the 21st century jock. Some will argue that homophobia has not decreased, but that it has merely changed forms. To this there is the undoubted truth that homophobia has become so unpopular that where it manifests, it mostly does so in covert ways. But this is evidence of the change in itself. Social movements take time, and antipathy toward the minority group dissipates slowly, unevenly, and generally moves from overt, to covert, to implicit, and then (hopefully) non-existent. I would much rather someone quietly mutter that I am a fag than physically beat me. Evidencing the shift, Mark McCormack (2012a) notes that youth today call homophobia what older men call heteronormativity.

Still, some will say that the kissing, hugging, cuddling, and loving is not a genuine act of homosocial love between two straight men, but that instead it is somehow designed to mock gay men. There may, of course, have been some mocking of gay men in early kisses, but this is not the case today. The men I interview tell me that such a perspective is insulting to them. Thus, for those aligned to this thinking, I ask my readers (and fellow academics) the following: what does a straight male have to do in order to prove to you that he is not homophobic?

Others may argue that I am "cherry-picking" my data; that I take limited evidence and generalize it to the whole. These detractors will likely be wedded to a victimization framework of homosexuality. They will then look for one example to counter my thesis. They will take one example and generalize it to the whole. They will take one example, instead of systematic, peer-reviewed research, to make their claim because there is no systematic evidence showing that jocks today are as awful as they were in the 1980s. No research shows this. I say with confidence that the students reading this book will identify with it.

Depending on their geographical location and age, they may relate more to some parts and not to others. But all male students reading this book will recognize that they engage in at least some of the inclusive and loving behaviors I discuss here. Heterosexual adolescents are not that awful anymore.

I do, however, concede that I do not have answers to all of the pressing questions about what it means to be a jock today. While I have thoroughly explored the relationship between homosexuality and inclusive masculinities among teamsport athletes, I have not investigated enough as to whether these athletes remain highly sexist or not.

What Does this Mean for Women?

Gender scholars often claim that gender is relational—that what men do as part of their masculinity is causally related with what women do as part of their femininity. This is often held to mean that all masculinity practices are thought to have an impact on all of women's practices; and so a lack of change in relations with women is evidence of a lack of change among men. While it is undoubtedly true that the behaviors of men and discourses of masculinity influence those of women and femininity (and vice versa), this perspective misses out important components of gender theorizing. In addition to the lack of an intersectional approach with sexuality, race, and class, it also erases the facts that there are gendered behaviors that men and women share, and that there are behaviors that are not gendered. It fails to see gender as fluctuating in response to homohysteria.

It is, of course, vital to understand how men's practices can subordinate women. Men still maintain strong patriarchal privilege in Western cultures, and this advantage shows no signs of abating in the near future. It is for this reason that many of those who founded the field of critical men's studies did so: to help explain and alleviate the marginalization of women. But men are victimized under orthodox notions of masculinity, too. And while the social organization of masculinity might theoretically contribute to patriarchy, patriarchal relations are far more complex than just how men construct their masculinity (see the work of Sylvia Walby for more on this, e.g., Walby 2011).

My research therefore mostly, but not exclusively, focuses on men's interactions with each other. Men might be inclusive of other types of men, and still remain sexist. Or, their inclusivity toward other types of men might also make them more inclusive of women (Anderson 2008c, 2012b, 2012c): the two are not mutually exclusive. Still, in my studies of the 21st century jock, I suggest that more egalitarian behaviors among men are likely to have *some* positive impact on their social attitudes toward women. While individuals will vary, I personally doubt that the 21st century jock is more sexist than the 20th century jock. My research has documented an important trend in inclusive masculinities among male youth; but we need to look at how this affects patriarchy, race and class relations, and a whole other set of social dynamics, too.

Men's Heterosexuality and Masculinity in the Future

As a sociologist, it is my job to examine what exists, how it varies, and how this relates to the historical past. In doing such it has become obvious that cultural views toward homosexuality and masculinity are intricately related. Thus, I predict that future iterations of acceptable/ esteemed masculinity will continue to be dictated by cultural views toward male homosexuality. And because homosexuality is a minority population, its freedom, acceptance, or level of persecution is always dependent on the majority. This is the tyranny of normalcy.

Attitudes toward homosexuality can, for a number of reasons, reverse. Homosexuality was, for example, in vogue in early 20th century Berlin, before the Nazi Party came into power and unleashed its now infamous treatment on gay men (of all races and nationalities). Similarly, George W. Bush used hysteria against gay marriage to help win election for his second term, and GSS data shows it was the only "blip" in an otherwise decreasing degree of cultural homophobia in the 21st century. In "Thinking Sex" Gayle Rubin (1984) powerfully makes the point that moral panics about sexualities are often constructed in times of great social stress, as a way to distract from other social anxieties. Thus, as a minority group, sexual minorities can be victimized for the purposes of political nationalism (as in Russia contemporaneously), economic disparity, revivalist religious fundamentalism, another viral genocide, or any number of yet unpredictable events.

If I am right, it is thus somewhat ironic that heterosexual males— those with the most cultural power—have their masculinity practices held hostage by their own perceptions of homosexuality. This is why I argue that decreasing homophobia is of relevance to all; homophobia hurts all of us.

Barring unforeseen tides that turn against homosexuality in the West, however, I suspect there are a number of trends that will continue. Primarily, we will continue to see the erosion of sexual and gender binaries in Western cultures. With this will come increased physical and emotional intimacy between heterosexual men, and a diminishment of homophobia among pockets of resistance toward inclusivity. I suspect that we will see faster progress in the United States than in the United Kingdom, because essentially the US is catching up. I also suspect that a wider terrain of homosexual sex will be made available to heterosexual men without threat to their perceived heterosexuality. I suspect that, in time, men will be able to even get fucked by other men while maintaining their public persona of heterosexuality. I predict there will be a large increase in men describing themselves as "mostly heterosexual" as opposed to "exclusively heterosexual." I say this because, once homophobia dies, once homosexuality is viewed on par with heterosexuality, the behaviors that one engages in will not be important. There will be no reason to doubt the label that one identifies with. The closet will slowly disappear.

There are also three trends related to sport that will likely manifest. The first concerns the slow inclusion of transgendered athletes, and a contestation of the sexual division of sport as a basic assumption for athletic play. The benefits to gender-integrating sport are many (Anderson 2010a). I also suspect there will be a serious slippage to the cultural value we place on competitive team sports. As masculinity grows softer, there is less need for men to use violence to their bodies in order to prove their heterosexuality, or masculinity. Finally, as we learn more and more about the damages of chronic traumatic encephalopathy, fear of litigation will remove the use of the head as a weapon in sport. That journey has already begun with the National Football League paying out 750 million to former players in order to settle their suit about the effects of concussions on their mental health (Anderson & Kian 2012).

Closing Words

Around the turn of the 20th century, sport presented itself to youth as a way to masculinize and heterosexualize them. It found further use in training young boys to serve in the armed forces or industrial (and dangerous) occupations. But we no longer need industrial workers to the same extent; nor do we need to train the male masses for eventual soldiering as we did decades ago. Furthermore, without homophobia, there is less need to use sport to raise one's masculine capital and prove oneself heterosexual to peers. Thus the cultural milieu that created the 20th century jock has changed. The 21st century jock already looks less like that of his forefathers, and is increasingly distancing himself from the image.

With the air of heterosexuality around jocks, they have used the power, in recent years, to greatly expand their gendered boundaries; and this has removed stigma from homosexuality. As McCormack (2012a) argues, we are now in a virtuous circle: as acceptable gendered terrain for heterosexual men pushes into what was once considered feminine terrain, homophobia is reduced. As homophobia reduces, it permits men to push further into feminized terrain. That is, as homophobia reduces, men are able to engage in more forms of physical and emotional intimacy with each other; and as homophobia reduces, heterosexual men are capable of engaging in more sexual activity with each other, too. The more they do so, the less policing power the concept of being thought gay or straight maintains. We are therefore ebbing toward new understandings of masculinity, heterosexuality, family, friendship, and sex. It is, however, a mostly silent social movement, hardly noticed by sociologists or politicians alike. Hopefully this book will bring some attention to the wonderment that is *i*Generation.

References

Adam, Barry D. "Relationship Innovation in Male Couples." *Sexualities* 9.1 (2006): 5–26.

Adams, Adi. "'Josh Wears Pink Cleats': Inclusive Masculinity on the Soccer Field." *Journal of Homosexuality* 58.5 (2011): 579–596.

Adams, Adi, & Eric Anderson. "Exploring the Relationship Between Homosexuality and Sport Among the Teammates of a Small, Midwestern Catholic College Soccer Team." *Sport, Education and Society* 17.3 (2012): 347–363.

Adams, Adi, Eric Anderson, & Mark McCormack. "Establishing and Challenging Masculinity: The Influence of Gendered Discourses in Organized Sport." *Journal of Language and Social Psychology* 29.3 (2010): 278–300.

Adams, Henry E., Lester W. Wright, & Bethany A. Lohr. "Is Homophobia Associated With Homosexual Arousal?" *Journal of Abnormal Psychology* 105.3 (1996): 440.

Allan, Elizabeth J. *Hazing in View: College Students at Risk: Initial Findings from the National Study of Student Hazing*. DIANE Publishing, 2009.

Allan, Elizabeth J., & Gennaro DeAngelis. "Hazing, Masculinity, and Collision Sports: (Un)becoming Heroes." In Jay Johnson & Marjery Jean Holman (eds), *Making the Team: Inside the World of Sport Initiations and Hazing*. Canadian Scholars Press, 2004: 61–82.

Almaguer, Tomás. "Chicano Men: A Cartography of Homosexual Identity and Behavior." In Henry Abelove, Michele Aina Barale, & David M. Halperin (eds), *The Lesbian and Gay Studies Reader*. Routledge, 1993: 255–273.

Anderson, Eric. *Trailblazing: The True Story of America's First Openly Gay Track Coach*. Alyson Books, 2000.

Anderson, Eric. "Openly Gay Athletes Contesting Hegemonic Masculinity in a Homophobic Environment." *Gender & Society* 16.6 (2002): 860–877.

Anderson, Eric. *In the Game: Gay Athletes and the Cult of Masculinity*. SUNY Press, 2005a.

Anderson, Eric. "Orthodox and Inclusive Masculinity: Competing Masculinities Among Heterosexual Men in a Feminized Terrain." *Sociological Perspectives* 48.3 (2005b): 337–355.

Anderson, Eric. "'Being Masculine is Not About Who You Sleep With...': Heterosexual Athletes Contesting Masculinity and the One-Time Rule of Homosexuality." *Sex Roles* 58.1–2 (2008a): 104–115.

Anderson, Eric. "Inclusive Masculinity in a Fraternal Setting." *Men and Masculinities* 10.5 (2008b): 604–620.

Anderson, Eric. "'I Used to Think Women were Weak': Orthodox Masculinity, Gender Segregation, and Sport." *Sociological Forum* 23.2 (2008c): 257–280.

Anderson, Eric. *Inclusive Masculinity: The Changing Nature of Masculinities*. Routledge, 2009.

Anderson, Eric. *Sport, Theory and Social Problems: A Critical Introduction*. Routledge, 2010a.

Anderson, Eric. "'At Least with Cheating There is an Attempt at Monogamy': Cheating and Monogamism Among Undergraduate Heterosexual Men." *Journal of Social and Personal Relationships* 27.7 (2010b): 851–872.

Anderson, Eric. "Masculinities and Sexualities in Sport and Physical Cultures: Three Decades of Evolving Research." *Journal of Homosexuality* 58.5 (2011a): 565–578.

Anderson, Eric. "Updating the Outcome: Gay Athletes, Straight Teams, and Coming Out in Educationally Based Sport Teams." *Gender & Society* 25.2 (2011b): 250–268.

Anderson, Eric. "Inclusive Masculinities of University Soccer Players in the American Midwest." *Gender and Education* 23.6 (2011c): 729–744.

Anderson, Eric. "The Rise and Fall of Western Homohysteria." *Journal of Feminist Scholarship* 1.1 (2011d): 80–94.

Anderson, Eric. *The Monogamy Gap: Men, Love, and the Reality of Cheating.* Oxford University Press, 2012a.

Anderson, Eric. "Shifting Masculinities in Anglo American Countries." *Masculinities & Social Change* 1.1 (2012b): 40–60.

Anderson, Eric. "Inclusive Masculinity in a Physical Education Setting." *Thymos: Journal of Boyhood Studies* 6.2 (2012c): 151–165.

Anderson, Eric. "Adolescent Masculinity in an Age of Decreased Homohysteria." *Thymos: Journal of Boyhood Studies* 7.1 (2013): 79–93.

Anderson, Eric, & Adi Adams. "'Aren't We All a Little Bisexual?': The Recognition of Bisexuality in an Unlikely Place." *Journal of Bisexuality* 11.1 (2011): 3–22.

Anderson, Eric, & Rachael Bullingham. "Openly Lesbian Team Sport Athletes in an Era of Decreasing Homohysteria." *International Review for the Sociology of Sport*, Online First (2013).

Anderson, Eric, & Edward M. Kian. "Examining Media Contestation of Masculinity and Head Trauma in the National Football League." *Men and Masculinities* 15.2 (2012): 152–173.

Anderson, Eric, & Mark McCormack. "Intersectionality, Critical Race Theory, and American Sporting Oppression: Examining Black and Gay Male Athletes." *Journal of Homosexuality* 57.8 (2010a): 949–967.

Anderson, Eric, & Mark McCormack. "Comparing the Black and Gay Male Athlete: Patterns in American Oppression." *The Journal of Men's Studies* 18.2 (2010b): 145–158.

Anderson, Eric, & Rhidian McGuire. "Inclusive Masculinity Theory and the Gendered Politics of Men's Rugby." *Journal of Gender Studies* 19.3 (2010): 249–261.

Anderson, Eric, Adi Adams, & Ian Rivers. "'I Kiss Them Because I Love Them': The Emergence of Heterosexual Men Kissing in British Institutes of Education." *Archives of Sexual Behavior* 41.2 (2012a): 421–430.

Anderson, Eric, Mark McCormack, & Harry Lee. "Male Team Sport Hazing Initiations in a Culture of Decreasing Homohysteria." *Journal of Adolescent Research* 27.4 (2012b): 427–448.

Askew, Sue, & Carol S. Ross. *Boys Don't Cry: Boys and Sexism in Education.* Open University Press, 1988.

Attwood, Feona (ed.). *Porn.com: Making Sense of Online Pornography.* Vol. 48. Peter Lang, 2010.

Bancroft, Jessie Hubbell. *Games for the Playground, Home, School and Gymnasium.* Macmillan, 1909.

Bailey, J. Michael. *The Man Who Would Be Queen: The Psychology of Gender-Bending and Transsexualism.* Joseph Henry Press, 2003.

Baunach, Dawn Michelle. "Changing Same-Sex Marriage Attitudes in America from 1988 Through 2010." *Public Opinion Quarterly* 76.2 (2012): 364–378.

Baunach, Dawn M., Elisabeth O. Burgess, & S. Courtney Muse. "Southern (Dis) comfort: Sexual Prejudice and Contact with Gay Men and Lesbians in the South." *Sociological Spectrum* 30.1 (2009): 30–64.

Becht, Marleen C., Ype H. Poortinga, & Ad J.J.M. Vingerhoets. "Crying Across Countries." In Ad J.J.M. Vingerhoets & Randolph R. Cornelius (eds), *Adult Crying: A Biopsychosocial Approach.* Routledge, 2001: 135–158.

Berkeley Men's Center. "Berkeley Men's Center Manifesto." In J.H. Pleck & J. Sawyer (eds), *Men and Masculinity.* Prentice-Hall, 1974.

Betzig, Laura. "Causes of Conjugal Dissolution: A Cross-Cultural Study." *Current Anthropology* 30.5 (1989): 654–676.

Bogle, Kathleen A. *Hooking Up: Sex, Dating, and Relationships on Campus.* NYU Press, 2008.

Bourdieu, Pierre. *Masculine Domination.* Stanford University Press, 2001.

Bridges, Tristan. "A Very 'Gay' Straight? Hybrid Masculinities, Sexual Aesthetics, and the Changing Relationship Between Masculinity and Homophobia." *Gender & Society*, Online First (2013).

Brontsema, Robin. "A Queer Revolution: Reconceptualizing the Debate over Linguistic Reclamation." *Colorado Research in Linguistics* 17.1 (2004): 1–17.

Bryshun, Jamie. *Hazing in Sport: An Exploratory Study of Veteran/Rookie Relations.* University of Calgary, 1997.

Bush, Anthony, Eric Anderson, & Sam Carr. "The Declining Existence of Men's Homophobia in British Sport." *Journal for the Study of Sports and Athletes in Education* 6.1 (2012): 107–120.

Cancian, Francesca M. "The Feminization of Love." *Signs* 11.4 (1986): 692–709.

Cancian, Francesca M. *Love in America: Gender and Self-Development.* Cambridge University Press, 1990.

Carlson, D., L. Scott, M. Planty, & J. Thompson. *What is the Status of High School Athletes 8 Years After Graduation?* Report released by the National Center for Educational Statistics, United States Department of Education, 2005.

Cashmore, Ellis, & Jamie Cleland. "Glasswing Butterflies: Gay Professional Football Players and Their Culture." *Journal of Sport & Social Issues* 35.4 (2011): 420–436.

Cashmore, Ellis, & Jamie Cleland. "Fans, Homophobia and Masculinities in Association Football: Evidence of a More Inclusive Environment." *British Journal of Sociology* 63.2 (2012): 370–387.

Cheren, Mel, Gabriel Rotello, & Brent Nicolson Earle. *Keep on Dancin': My Life and the Paradise Garage.* 24 Hours for Life, 2000.

Chodorow, Nancy. *The Reproduction of Mothering.* University of California Press, 1978.

Clarke, Gill. "Queering the Pitch and Coming Out to Play: Lesbians in Physical Education and Sport." *Sport, Education and Society* 3.2 (1998): 145–160.

Connell, R.W. *Masculinities.* University of California Press, 1995.

Connell, Robert W., & James W. Messerschmidt. "Hegemonic Masculinity: Rethinking the Concept." *Gender & Society* 19.6 (2005): 829–859.

Cushion, Christopher, & Robyn L. Jones. "Power, Discourse, and Symbolic Violence in Professional Youth Soccer: The Case of Albion Football Club." *Sociology of Sport Journal* 23.2 (2006): 142.

Dashper, Katherine. "Dressage is Full of Queens: Masculinity, Sexuality and Equestrian Sport." *Sociology*, iFirst (2012): 1–17.

Dean, James. "Heterosexual Masculinities, Anti-Homophobias, and Shifts in Hegemonic Masculinity: The Identity Practices of Black and White Heterosexual Men." *The Sociological Quarterly* 54 (2013): 534–560.

Demetriou, Demetrakis Z. "Connell's Concept of Hegemonic Masculinity: A Critique." *Theory and Society* 30.3 (2001): 337–361.

Desmond, Jane (ed.). *Dancing Desires*. Vol. 18. University of Wisconsin Press, 2001.

Diamond, Lisa M. "'Having a Girlfriend Without Knowing It': Intimate Friendships Among Adolescent Sexual-Minority Women." *Journal of Lesbian Studies* 6.1 (2002): 5–16.

Dines, Gail. *Pornland: How Porn has Hijacked our Sexuality*. Beacon Press, 2010.

Donnelly, Peter, & Kevin Young. "The Construction and Confirmation of Identity in Sport Subcultures." *Sociology of Sport Journal* 5.3 (1988): 223–240.

Dunning, Eric. *Sport Matters: Sociological Studies of Sport, Violence and Civilisation*. Routledge, 2002.

Easton, Dossie, & Janet W. Hardy. *The Ethical Slut: A Practical Guide to Polyamory, Open Relationships, & Other Adventures*. Celestial Arts, 2009.

Eccles, Jacquelynne S., & Bonnie L. Barber. "Student Council, Volunteering, Basketball, or Marching Band: What Kind of Extracurricular Involvement Matters?" *Journal of Adolescent Research* 14.1 (1999): 10–43.

Eitzen, D. Stanley (ed.). *Sport in Contemporary Society: An Anthology*. Macmillan, 2000.

Ellis, Kate, Barbara O'Dair, & Abby Tallmer. "Feminism and Pornography." *Feminist Review* 36 (1990): 15–18.

Epstein, Debbie, Mary Kehily, Maírtin Mac An Ghaill, & Peter Redman. "Boys and Girls Come Out to Play: Making Masculinities and Femininities in School Playgrounds." *Men and Masculinities* 4.2 (2001): 158–172.

Feist, D., B. Shenton, & T. de Souza. *Induction Ceremonies in University Sport in the UK*. Unpublished communication to Athletic Union presidents, British Universities Sports Association, London, 2004.

Field, Tiffany. "American Adolescents Touch Each Other Less and are More Aggressive Toward Their Peers as Compared With French Adolescents." *Adolescence* 34.136 (1999): 753–758.

Filene, Peter G. *Him/Her/Self: Sex Roles in Modern America*. Johns Hopkins University Press, 1974.

Foucault, Michel. *The History of Sexuality, Volume 1: An Introduction*. Translation by Robert Hurley. Vintage, 1984.

Fox, Kate. *Watching the English: The Hidden Rules of English Behaviour*. Nicholas Brealey Publishing, 2008.

Frank, David John, Bayliss J. Camp, & Steven A. Boutcher. "Worldwide Trends in the Criminal Regulation of Sex, 1945 to 2005." *American Sociological Review* 75.6 (2010): 867–893.

Freud, Sigmund. *Three Essays on the Theory of Sexuality*. No. 57. Basic Books, 1975.

Gerdy, John. *Sports: The All American Addiction*. University Press of Mississippi, 2002.

Gerressu, Makeda, Catherine H. Mercer, Cynthia A. Graham, Kaye Wellings, & Anne M. Johnson. "Prevalence of Masturbation and Associated Factors in a British National Probability Survey." *Archives of Sexual Behavior* 37.2 (2008): 266–278.

Giulianotti, Richard. *Football*. Blackwell Publishing Ltd, 1999.

Gottzén, Lucas, & Tamar Kremer-Sadlik. "Fatherhood and Youth Sports: A Balancing Act Between Care and Expectations." *Gender & Society* 26.4 (2012): 639–664.

Griffin, Sean. *Tinker Belles and Evil Queens: The Walt Disney Company from the Inside Out*. New York University Press, 2000.

Grindstaff, Laura, & Emily West. "Cheerleading and the Gendered Politics of Sport." *Social Problems* 53.4 (2006): 500–518.

Grundlingh, Albert. "Playing for Power? Rugby, Afrikaner Nationalism and Masculinity in South Africa, c. 1900–70." *The International Journal of the History of Sport* 11.3 (1994): 408–430.

Halkitis, Perry N. "An Exploration of Perceptions of Masculinity Among Gay Men Living with HIV." *The Journal of Men's Studies* 9.3 (2001): 413–429.

Hargreaves, Jennifer. *Sporting Females: Critical Issues in the History and Sociology of Women's Sport*. Psychology Press, 2002.

Harris, John, & Ben Clayton. "The First Metrosexual Rugby Star: Rugby Union, Masculinity, and Celebrity in Contemporary Wales." *Sociology of Sport Journal* 24.2 (2007): 145–164.

Harris, Marvin. *Patterns of Race in the Americas*. Greenwood Press, 1964.

Hekma, Gert. "'As Long as They Don't Make an Issue of It...': Gay Men and Lesbians in Organized Sports in the Netherlands." *Journal of Homosexuality* 35.1 (1998): 1–23.

Herek, Gregory M. "Heterosexuals' Attitudes Toward Bisexual Men and Women in the United States." *Journal of Sex Research* 39.4 (2002): 264–274.

Hughes, Robert, Jay Coakley, A. Yiannakis, & M. Melnick. "Positive Deviance Among Athletes: The Implications of Overconformity to the Sport Ethic." *Contemporary Issues in Sociology of Sport* (2001): 361–392.

Hughes, Susan M., Marissa A. Harrison, & Gordon G. Gallup. "Sex Differences in Mating Strategies: Mate Guarding, Infidelity and Multiple Concurrent Sex Partners." *Sexualities, Evolution & Gender* 6.1 (2004): 3–13.

Hughes, Walter. "In the Empire of the Beat: Discipline and Disco." *Microphone Fiends: Youth Music and Youth Culture* (1994): 147–157.

Ibson, John. *Picturing Men: A Century of Male Relationships in Everyday American Photography*. University of Chicago Press, 2002.

Jansen, Sue Curry, & Don Sabo. "The Sport/War Metaphor: Hegemonic Masculinity, the Persian Gulf War, and the New World Order." *Sociology of Sport Journal* 11.1 (1994): 1–17.

Johnson, Jay, & Margery Jean Holman (eds). *Making the Team: Inside the World of Sport Initiations and Hazing*. Canadian Scholars Press, 2004.

Johnson, Kerri L., Simone Gill, Victoria Reichman, & Louis G. Tassinary. "Swagger, Sway, and Sexuality: Judging Sexual Orientation from Body Motion and Morphology." *Journal of Personality and Social Psychology* 93.3 (2007): 321.

Jourard, S. *The Transparent Self*. D. Van Nostrand, 1971.

JWT. www.slideshare.net/jwtintelligence/the-state-of-men, 2013.

Kaplan, Robert D. *Imperial Grunts: On the Ground With the American Military, From Mongolia to the Philippines to Iraq and Beyond*. Random House Digital, Inc., 2006.

Katz-Wise, Sabra L., & Janet S. Hyde. "Victimization Experiences of Lesbian, Gay, and Bisexual Individuals: A Meta-Analysis." *Journal of Sex Research* 49.2–3 (2012): 142–167.

Keleher, Alison, & Eric Smith. "Growing Support for Gay and Lesbian Equality Since 1990." *Journal of Homosexuality* 59.9 (2012): 1307–1326.

Kian, Edward M., & Eric Anderson. "John Amaechi: Changing the Way Sport Reporters Examine Gay Athletes." *Journal of Homosexuality* 56.7 (2009): 799–818.

Kimmel, Michael S. "Masculinity as Homophobia: Fear, Shame, and Silence in the Construction of Gender Identity." In Paula S. Rothenberg (ed.), *Race, Class, and Gender in the United States: An Integrated Study*. Worth, 1994: 81–93.

Kimmel, Michael S. *Manhood in America*. Free Press, 1996.

King, James L., & Karen Hunter. *On the Down Low: A Journey into the Lives of Straight Black Men Who Sleep With Men*. Random House Digital, Inc., 2007.

Kinsey, Alfred Charles, Wardell Baxter Pomeroy, & Clyde Eugene Martin. *Sexual Behavior in the Human Male*. W.B. Saunders Co., 1948.

Kirby, Sandra L., & Glen Wintrup. "Running the Gauntlet: An Examination of Initiation/Hazing and Sexual Abuse in Sport." *Journal of Sexual Aggression* 8.2 (2002): 49–68.

Klein, Fred. *The Bisexual Option*. Haworth Press, 1993.

Klesse, Christian. "Polyamory and Its 'Others': Contesting the Terms of Non-Monogamy." *Sexualities* 9.5 (2006): 565–583.

Komarovsky, Mirra. "Patterns of Self-Disclosure of Male Undergraduates." *Journal of Marriage and the Family* (1974): 677–686.

Kong, Travis S.K., D. Mahoney, & K. Plummer. "Queering the Interview." In J.F. Gubrium & J.A. Holstein (eds), *Handbook of Interview Research: Context & Method*. Sage, 2002: 239–258.

Kontula, Osmo. "The Evolution of Sex Education and Students' Sexual Knowledge in Finland in the 2000s." *Sex Education* 10.4 (2010): 373–386.

Lalor, Therese, & Johanna Rendle-Short. "'That's So Gay': A Contemporary Use of Gay in Australian English." *Australian Journal of Linguistics* 27.2 (2007): 147–173.

Lancaster, Roger N. "Subject Honor and Object Shame: The Construction of Male Homosexuality and Stigma in Nicaragua." *Ethnology* 27.2 (1988): 111–125.

Langer, G. *ABC/Washington Post Poll: Gay Marriage: Poll Tracks Dramatic Rise in Support for Gay Marriage*. Langer Research Associates, 2013.

Laumann, Edward O. (ed.). *The Social Organization of Sexuality: Sexual Practices in the United States*. University of Chicago Press, 1994.

LeVay, Simon. *Gay, Straight, and the Reason Why: The Science of Sexual Orientation*. Oxford University Press, 2010.

Levine, Martin P. *Gay Macho: The Life and Death of the Homosexual Clone*. NYU Press, 1998.

Lewis, Robert A. "Emotional Intimacy Among Men." *Journal of Social Research* 34.1 (1978): 108–121.

Lilleaas, Ulla-Britt. "Masculinities, Sport, and Emotions." *Men and Masculinities* 10.1 (2007): 39–53.

Lippa, Richard A. "The Preferred Traits of Mates in a Cross-National Study of Heterosexual and Homosexual Men and Women: An Examination of Biological and Cultural Influences." *Archives of Sexual Behavior* 36.2 (2007): 193–208.

Loftus, Jeni. "America's Liberalization in Attitudes Toward Homosexuality, 1973 to 1998." *American Sociological Review* (2001): 762–782.

Mac an Ghaill, Mairtin. *The Making of Men.* Open University Press, 1994.

Magrath, Rory, Eric Anderson, & Steven Roberts. "On the Door-Step of Equality: Attitudes Toward Gay Athletes Among Academy Level Footballers." *International Review for the Sociology of Sport,* Online First (2013): 1–18.

Mathisen, James A. "Reviving 'Muscular Christianity': Gil Dodds and the Institutionalization of Sport Evangelism." *Sociological Focus* 23.3 (1990): 233–249.

McCann, Pól Dominic, Victor Minichiello, & David Plummer. "Is Homophobia Inevitable? Evidence That Explores the Constructed Nature of Homophobia, and the Techniques Through Which Men Unlearn It." *Journal of Sociology* 45.2 (2009): 201–220.

McClary, Susan, & Robert Walser. "Theorizing the Body in African-American Music." *Black Music Research Journal* 14.1 (1994): 75–84.

McCormack, Mark. "Hierarchy Without Hegemony: Locating Boys in an Inclusive School Setting." *Sociological Perspectives* 54.1 (2011a): 83–101.

McCormack, Mark. "The Declining Significance of Homohysteria for Male Students in Three Sixth Forms in the South of England." *British Educational Research Journal* 37.2 (2011b): 337–353.

McCormack, M. "Mapping the Terrain of Homosexually-Themed Language." *Journal of Homosexuality* 58.5 (2011c): 664–679.

McCormack, Mark. *The Declining Significance of Homophobia: How Teenage Boys are Redefining Masculinity and Heterosexuality.* Oxford University Press, 2012a.

McCormack, Mark. "The Positive Experiences of Openly Gay, Lesbian, Bisexual and Transgendered Students in a Christian Sixth Form College." *Sociological Research Online* 17.3 (2012b): 5.

McCormack, Mark. "The Intersection of Class, Youth Masculinities and Decreasing Homophobia: An Ethnography." *British Journal of Sociology,* forthcoming.

McCormack, Mark, & Eric Anderson. "'It's Just Not Acceptable Any More': The Erosion of Homophobia and the Softening of Masculinity at an English Sixth Form." *Sociology* 44.5 (2010a): 843–859.

McCormack, Mark, & Eric Anderson. "The Re-Production of Homosexually-Themed Discourse in Educationally-Based Organised Sport." *Culture, Health & Sexuality* 12.8 (2010b): 913–927.

McCormack, Mark, & Eric Anderson. "The Influence of Declining Homophobia on Men's Gender in the United States: An Argument for the Study of Homohysteria." *Sex Roles,* forthcoming.

McGlone, Colleen A. "Hazy Viewpoints: Administrators' Perceptions of Hazing." *International Journal of Sport Management and Marketing* 7.1 (2010): 119–131.

McNair, Brian. *Striptease Culture: Sex, Media and the Democratization of Desire.* Psychology Press, 2002.

Meston, Cindy M., & Tierney Ahrold. "Ethnic, Gender, and Acculturation Influences on Sexual Behaviors." *Archives of Sexual Behavior* 39.1 (2010): 179–189.

Michael, B. "'Just Don't Hit on Me and I'm Fine': Mapping High School Wrestlers' Relationship to Inclusive Masculinity and Heterosexual Recuperation." *International Review for the Sociology of Sport,* Online First.

Michener, James Albert. *Sports in America*. Vol. 9000. Random House, 1976.

Miller, Kathleen E., Merrill J. Melnick, Grace M. Barnes, Michael P. Farrell, & Don Sabo. "Untangling the Links Among Athletic Involvement, Gender, Race, and Adolescent Academic Outcomes." *Sociology of Sport Journal* 22.2 (2005): 178.

Miracle, Andrew, & Roger Rees. *Lessons of the Locker Room: The Myth of School Sports*. Prometheus Books, 1994.

Miller Lite. *Miller Lite Report on American Attitudes Toward Sports*. Miller Brewing Company, 1983.

Morin, S., & E.M. Garfinkle. "Male Homophobia." *Journal of Social Issues* 34.1 (1978): 29–47.

Mrozek, Donald J. *Sport and American Mentality 1880–1910*. University of Tennessee Press, 1983.

Nauright, John, & Timothy J.L. Chandler (eds). *Making Men: Rugby and Masculine Identity*. Psychology Press, 1996.

Nelson, Mariah Burton, & Catherine Rowe. *The Stronger Women Get, the More Men Love Football: Sexism and the American Culture of Sports*. Harcourt Brace, 1994.

Nuwer, Hank. *Wrongs of Passage: Fraternities, Sororities, Hazing and Binge Drinking*. Indiana University Press, 2001.

Oakley, Ann. *Gender on Planet Earth*. Polity Press, 2002.

Ochs, Robyn. "Biphobia: It Goes More Than Two Ways." In Beth A. Firestein (ed.), *Bisexuality: The Psychology and Politics of an Invisible Minority*. Sage, 1996: 217–239.

O'Donnell, K.A., A.S. Walters, & D.L. Wardlow. "Gender and Team Sports: The Arena Where Agency Meets Communion." In E. Fischer (ed.), *Proceedings of the Association for Consumer Research* (1998): 159–177.

Ogawa, Scott. "100 Missing Men: Participation, Selection, and Silence of Gay Athletes." In Jennifer Hargreaves & Eric Anderson (eds), *The Routledge Handbook of Sport, Gender and Sexualities*. Routledge, 2014, forthcoming.

Ogburn, William Fielding. *Cultural Lag as Theory*. Bobbs-Merrill, 1957.

Olstad, Keith. "Brave New Men: A Basis for Discussion." In J. Petras (ed.), *Sex/Male—Gender/Masculine*. Port Washington, NY: Alfred, 1975.

Paik, Anthony, Edward O. Laumann, & Martha Van Haitsma. "Commitment, Jealousy, and the Quality of Life." In Edward O. Laumann, Stephen Ellingson, Jenna Mahay, Anthony Paik, & Yoosik Youm (eds), *The Sexual Organization of the City*. University of Chicago Press, 2004: 194–225.

Park, Robert E. "The City as a Social Laboratory." *Chicago: An Experiment in Social Science Research* (1929): 1–19.

Parker, Richard Guy. *Bodies, Pleasures, and Passions: Sexual Culture in Contemporary Brazil*. Vanderbilt University Press, 2009.

Pascoe, Cheri Jo. "'Dude, You're a Fag': Adolescent Masculinity and the Fag Discourse." *Sexualities* 8.3 (2005): 329–346.

Peralta, Robert L. "College Alcohol Use and the Embodiment of Hegemonic Masculinity Among European American Men." *Sex Roles* 56.11–12 (2007): 741–756.

Peterson, Grant Tyler. "Clubbing Masculinities: Gender Shifts in Gay Men's Dance Floor Choreographies." *Journal of Homosexuality* 58.5 (2011): 608–625.

Peterson, Grant Tyler, & Eric Anderson. "The Performance of Softer Masculinities on the University Dance Floor." *The Journal of Men's Studies* 20.1 (2012): 3–15.

Pettigrew, Thomas F. "Intergroup Contact Theory." *Annual Review of Psychology* 49.1 (1998): 65–85.

PEW. *Growing Support for Gay Marriage: Changed Minds and Changing Demographics.* PEW Research Center, 2013.

Pleck, Joseph. "Issues for the Men's Movement: Summer, 1975." *Changing Men: A Newsletter for Men Against Sexism* (1975): 21–23.

Pleck, Joseph H. *The Myth of Masculinity.* MIT Press, 1981.

Plummer, David. *One of the Boys: Masculinity, Homophobia, and Modern Manhood.* Psychology Press, 1999.

Plummer, K. "Generational Sexualities, Subterranean Traditions, and the Hauntings of the Sexual World." *Symbolic Interaction* 33.2 (2010): 163–190.

Pollack, William. *Real Boys: Rescuing Our Sons From the Myths of Boyhood.* Macmillan, 1999.

Pope, Courtney G., Harrison G. Pope, William Menard, Christina Fay, Roberto Olivardia, & Katharine A. Phillips. "Clinical Features of Muscle Dysmorphia Among Males With Body Dysmorphic Disorder." *Body Image* 2.4 (2005): 395–400.

Pronger, Brian. *The Arena of Masculinity: Sports, Homosexuality, and the Meaning of Sex.* St. Martin's Press, 1990.

Pryor, J., L. DeAngelo, L.P. Blake, S. Hurtado, & S. Tran. *The American Freshman: National Norms Fall 2011.* Higher Education Research Institute, UCLA, 2011.

Rasmussen, Mary Lou. "'That's So Gay!': A Study of the Deployment of Signifiers of Sexual and Gender Identity in Secondary School Settings in Australia and the United States." *Social Semiotics* 14.3 (2004): 289–308.

Reinisch, June M. *The Kinsey Institute New Report on Sex.* Macmillan, 1990.

Rigauer, Bero. *Sport and Work.* Columbia University Press, 1981.

Riley, Bettina H. "GLB Adolescent's 'Coming Out'." *Journal of Child and Adolescent Psychiatric Nursing* 23.1 (2010): 3–10.

Ripley, Matthew, Eric Anderson, Mark McCormack, Adrian Adams, & Robin Pitts. "The Decreasing Significance of Stigma in the Lives of Bisexual Men: Keynote Address, Bisexual Research Convention, London." *Journal of Bisexuality* 11.2–3 (2011): 195–206.

Ripley, Matthew, Eric Anderson, Mark McCormack, & Ben Rockett. "Heteronormativity in the University Classroom: Novelty Attachment and Content Substitution Among Gay-Friendly Students." *Sociology of Education* 85.2 (2012): 121–130.

Roberts, Steve. "Boys Will Be Boys, Won't They? Change and Continuities in Contemporary Young Working-Class Masculinities." *Sociology*, iFirst (2012).

Rofes, Eric. "Bound and Gagged: Sexual Silences, Gender Conformity and the Gay Male Teacher." *Sexualities* 3.4 (2000): 439–462.

Rotundo, E. Anthony. *American Manhood: Transformation in Masculinity from the Revolution to the Modern Era.* Basic Books (AZ), 1993.

Rubin, Gayle. "Thinking Sex." In Carole Vance (ed.), *Pleasure and Danger: Exploring Female Sexuality.* Routledge & Kegan Paul Books, 1984.

Russell, David. "Associating with Football: Social Identity in England, 1863–1998." In Gary Armstrong & Richard Giulianotti (eds), *Football Cultures and Identities.* Macmillan Press, 1999: 15–28.

Sabo, Donald F., & Ross Runfola. *Jock: Sports and Male Identity.* Prentice-Hall, 1980.

Savin-Williams, Ritch C. *The New Gay Teenager*. Harvard University Press, 2005.

Schrack-Walters, Andrew, Kathleen A. O'Donnell, & Daniel L. Wardlow. "Deconstructing the Myth of the Monolithic Male Athlete: A Qualitative Study of Men's Participation in Athletics." *Sex Roles* 60.1–2 (2009): 81–99.

Seiden, A., & P. Bart. "Woman to Woman: Is Sisterhood Powerful?" In N. Galzer-Malbin (ed.), *Old Family/New Family? Interpersonal Relationships*. D. Van Nostrand, 1975: 189–228.

Signorile, Michelangelo. *Life Outside: The Signorile Report on Gay Men, Sex, Drugs, Muscles, and the Passages of Life*. HarperCollins Publishers, 1997.

Silva, Jennifer. "Constructing Adulthood in an Age of Uncertainty." *American Sociological Review* 77.4 (2013): 505–522.

Smith-Rosenberg, Carroll. "The Abortion Movement and the AMA, 1850–1880." In *Disorderly Conduct: Visions of Gender in Victorian America*. Oxford University Press, 1985: 217–244.

Southall, Richard M., Mark S. Nagel, Eric Anderson, Fritz G. Polite, & Crystal Southall. "An Investigation of Male College Athletes' Attitudes Toward Sexual-Orientation." *Journal of Issues in Intercollegiate Athletics* (2009): 62–77.

Southall, Richard M., Eric D. Anderson, Mark S. Nagel, Fritz G. Polite, & Crystal Southall. "An Investigation of Ethnicity as a Variable Related to US Male College Athletes' Sexual-Orientation Behaviours and Attitudes." *Ethnic and Racial Studies* 34.2 (2011): 293–313.

Spencer, Colin. *Homosexuality in History*. Fourth Estate, 1995.

Steen, Rob. *The Mavericks: English Football When Flair Wore Flares*. Mainstream Publishers, 1995.

Thomas, Downing A. *Music and the Origins of Language: Theories from the French Enlightenment*. Vol. 2. Cambridge University Press, 1995.

Thompson, A., & E.S. Byers. "Lucky Number Three: Predicting Young Adult's Attitudes Toward Mixed-Gender Threesomes." Poster Presentation, International Association of Sex Researchers, 2013.

Thompson, Ross A. "The Development of the Person: Social Understanding, Relationships, Conscience, Self." In William Damon & Richard M. Lerner (eds), *Handbook of Child Psychology*. Wiley, 2006: 24–98.

Thurlow, Crispin. "Naming the 'Outsider Within': Homophobic Pejoratives and the Verbal Abuse of Lesbian, Gay and Bisexual High-School Pupils." *Journal of Adolescence* 24.1 (2001): 25–38.

Træen, B., & A. Štulhofer. "The Consumption of Sexually Explicit Media (SEM) Among Young Adults in Norway." Poster Presentation, The International Association of Sex Researchers, 2013.

Treas, Judith, & Deirdre Giesen. "Sexual Infidelity Among Married and Cohabiting Americans." *Journal of Marriage and Family* 62.1 (2000): 48–60.

Unni, Jeeson C. "Adolescent Attitudes and Relevance to Family Life Education Programs." *Indian Pediatrics* 47.2 (2010): 176–179.

Walby, Sylvia. *The Future of Feminism*. Polity, 2011.

Weeks, Jeffrey. *The World We Have Won: The Remaking of Erotic and Intimate Life*. Routledge, 2007.

Weinberg, George H. *Society and the Healthy Homosexual*. Macmillan, 1972.

Wetherell, Margaret, & Nigel Edley. "Negotiating Hegemonic Masculinity: Imaginary Positions and Psycho-Discursive Practices." *Feminism & Psychology* 9.3 (1999): 335–356.

Wiederman, Michael W., & Catherine Hurd. "Extradyadic Involvement During Dating." *Journal of Social and Personal Relationships* 16.2 (1999): 265–274.

Williams, Christine L. *Still a Man's World: Men Who Do "Women's Work"*. Vol. 1. University of California Press, 1995.

Williams, Dorie Giles. "Gender, Masculinity-Femininity, and Emotional Intimacy in Same-Sex Friendship." *Sex Roles* 12.5–6 (1985): 587–600.

Williams, D. Gareth, & Gabrielle H. Morris. "Crying, Weeping or Tearfulness in British and Israeli Adults." *British Journal of Psychology* 87.3 (1996): 479–505.

Wright, Paul J., & Ashley K. Randall. "Pornography Consumption, Education, and Support for Same-Sex Marriage Among Adult US Males." *Communication Research*, Online First (2013).

Index

CPSIA information can be obtained
at www.ICGtesting.com
Printed in the USA
FFOW02n1344020316
22028FF